THE SOCIOLOGIST
AS
CONSULTANT

THE SOCIOLOGIST AS CONSULTANT

EDITED BY
Joyce Miller Iutcovich
AND
Mark Iutcovich

PRAEGER

New York
Westport, Connecticut
London

Library of Congress Cataloging-in-Publication Data

The Sociologist as consultant.

Includes index.
1. Sociologists.   2. Consultants.   3. Vocational
guidance.   I. Iutcovich, Joyce Miller.
II. Iutcovich, Mark.
HM73.S63   1987   301'.023   86-25252
ISBN 0-275-92615-X (alk. paper)

Library of Congress Catalog Card Number: 86-25252
ISBN: 0-275-92615-X

First published in 1987

Praeger Publishers, 521 Fifth Avenue, New York, NY 10175
A division of Greenwood Press, Inc.

Printed in the United States of America

The paper used in this book complies with the Permanent
Paper Standard issued by the National Information Standards
Organization (Z39.48-1984).

10 9 8 7 6 5 4 3 2 1

To our parents
Charles and Carolyn Miller
and Joseph and Matilda Iutcovich

Contents

Figures and Tables

Preface

Just what is a consultant? Over the years "consulting" has been a loosely used term and often the subject of much ridicule. Robert Townsend (1970) indicated that a consultant is someone who borrows your watch to tell you what time it is. Or, alternatively, Herman Holtz (1983) facetiously indicated that a consultant is anyone who is out of work but has a briefcase. Perhaps some of this ridicule is justified given the practice of some consultants "out in the field." On the other hand, it must be recognized that the consultant role has become increasingly necessary in our technological society.

Jobs within organizations have become more and more specialized and it is often impossible or too costly for organizations to employ persons on a full-time basis for services that may be needed either sporadically or temporarily. Thus consultants provide these needed specialized services on a temporary basis for some fixed fee or rate or on a contractual basis. Consultants are professionals who have the specialized knowledge, skills, and experience that are needed for advice giving or problem solving.

Consulting activities and the settings in which consultation occurs are quite diverse. Professionals from a variety of fields (sociology, psychology, economics, social work, education, nursing, religion, just to name a few) now consider consultation as a legitimate aspect of their professional role, whether on a full-time or part-time basis. Furthermore, consultation takes place within many types of settings, such as hospitals, health agencies, schools, government agencies, industrial and business settings, and social agencies. This list is by no means exhaustive, but it does provide a picture of how diverse consultation activities can be.

The consulting activities of sociologists, however, have not been extensively explored. Little has been written about the consulting role of sociologists, other than the fact that it does exist. This is not to say that sociologists do very little consulting. It probably is fair to say that it has only been in the past few years that this type of professional activity has gained quasi legitimacy within the discipline. For years there has been bias within the field regarding any type of sociological work that takes place outside of academia. Consulting is viewed as "work for hire" and as such it interferes with the freedom of sociologists as scientists to pursue knowledge for "knowledge's sake." This bias is slowly falling by the wayside and sociology is beginning to rediscover its applied side.

This renewed emphasis on applied sociology has been attributed to the recent troubles facing the discipline. Included in this list of woes: students enrollments are down; sociological work is not valued and respected on the broader scene; many sociologists no longer identify themselves as such, although they may be doing sociological work; other social sciences and professions are invading our "space"; and to top all this, there are few job opportunities for sociology graduates in academia.

Applied sociology has thus offered a promising avenue for many sociologists as well as a "hope" for the survival of the discipline. In recent years there has been a considerable increase in the "applied" literature. But we know very little about the consulting activities of sociologists, which is just one of the professional roles of the applied sociologist.

The purpose of this book is to help fill that gap in literature, to explore the consulting role of sociologists, and to shed some light on both the problems and prospects associated with the consulting activities of sociologists.

This book is intended for several kinds of readers. Professional sociologists, both inside and outside academia, as well as undergraduate and graduate students of sociology, can utilize this book to explore the opportunities for consulting activities, to examine the potential for the application of sociological knowledge and methods to "real-life" settings, and to gain an understanding of the educational preparation needed for pursuing the consultant role. Additionally, nonsociologists, particularly those in organizations and settings that could potentially use sociological expertise, can use this book to gain a fuller understanding of the variety of knowledge and skills that sociologists have to offer. Ultimately, the hope is that this book will show how sociology can be useful and relevant.

The book is divided into five parts. Part I, "Application of Sociological Knowledge and Methods," examines the debate regarding the viability of sociology as an "applied" discipline. Part II, "Consulting Activities for Sociologists," describes a variety of consulting activities for which sociologists have expertise. Chapters in this part further exemplify how sociological insight can be utilized in the real world to help solve problems and/or provide specialized services. Part III, "Training Professionals for Consulting Practice," looks at the educational preparation that would be most appropriate for those contemplating a consultant role. Part IV, "Establishing a Consulting Practice," explores not only the "nitty-gritty" of setting up a private consulting practice, but also highlights some of the difficulties that can arise in any consultant-client relationship. Finally, Part V, "Sociologists in Practice," provides some concrete examples of the consulting activities of sociologists and the diverse settings of their work.

This book is not intended to be a definitive explanation of the consulting role of sociologists. It is merely a beginning and we hope it will be used as a springboard for further discussion regarding the possibilities and ways to improve and enhance the consulting activities of sociologists.

Joyce Miller Iutcovich
Mark Iutcovich

REFERENCES

Holtz, Herman. 1983. *How to Succeed as an Independent Consultant.* New York: John Wiley.
Townsend, Robert. 1970. *Up the Organization.* New York: Alfred A. Knopf.

PART I

Application of Sociological Knowledge and Methods

The increasing emphasis on applied sociology during the past few years has created a continuing debate among professionals within the field. On the one hand, there are the traditionalists within the discipline who argue that sociology should remain in its pure form—it is an intellectual activity whose purpose is to develop knowledge about the workings of society and its constituent elements. In addition to this, there are those who would argue that sociology, as a young discipline, lacks sufficient research, has technical and methodological deficiencies, and has not produced knowledge that has demonstrated relevance to the solution of society's problems. As such, sociology has not yet created the solid base from which its knowledge and methodologies can be applied.

On the other hand, there are a growing number of sociologists who argue for the development of sociology's applied side. For many, the development of applied sociology is seen as critical to the survival of the discipline. Indeed, the path to this development is not seen without its obstacles. There are problems that must be faced and overcome if the real potential of applied sociology is to be realized. In the words of Street and Wenstein (1975, 66), "With all its impurities, sociological knowledge is too important to be monopolized by professors."

Regardless of this on-going debate, there are those who have forged ahead and taken on the consulting role as an applied sociologist. Part I of this book deals with the problems, prospects, and potential opportunities for sociologists to apply their knowledge and methodological expertise in a consulting role.

In Chapter 1, Richard O'Toole, J. Patrick Turbett, and Anita W. O'Toole discuss the use of sociological theory, methodology, and substantive knowledge in consultation. A basic question they try to answer in this chapter is "What types of services do sociologists have to sell, *that some agency will buy,* in the consulting market?" In answering this question, they use the negotiated order approach to help solve sociologists' problems in establishing, maintaining, and expanding consulting relationships with practitioners. First, they identify a number of sociological consulting roles and analyze their impact on agencies. They also draw upon their own consulting experiences to show the utility of the negotiations' paradigm in consulting. Furthermore, particular problems in practitioner-consultant relationships are examined: practitioner expectations of the consultant, the consultants' knowledge of a human service area, and practitioners' problems in assessing sociological work. Finally, they discuss major issues and strategies the sociologist should consider in negotiations to secure and maintain work as a consultant.

In contrast to the positive view of O'Toole et al., Jeffrey Lange (Chapter 2) identifies and discusses many of the sociological and societal conditions and constraints that severely limit the prospects for anyone who would carve out a career as a consulting sociologist. In assessing the potential demand for sociological consultants, Lange considers these factors: (1) basic-science objectives, styles of inquiry, and the academic status that circumscribe sociology's applicability to "practical matters"; and (2) conceptions or misconceptions of the field of sociology held by prospective clients, customers, or employers of sociologists in nonacademic settings. Furthermore, Lange examines three potential consulting roles and the degree to which they are genuinely sociological and consultive work roles: the consulting sociologist, the sociologist-who-consults, and the sociologist-in-reserve.

REFERENCE

.Street, David P., and Eugene A. Wenstein. 1975. "Problems and Prospects of Applied Sociology." *The American Sociologist* 10 (May).

1

Applying Sociology in the Consulting Role

RICHARD O'TOOLE, J. PATRICK TURBETT, AND ANITA W. O'TOOLE

In this chapter we discuss the use of sociological theory, methodology, and substantive knowledge in consultation. We are concerned not only with the traditional problem of using sociological knowledge to help solve practitioners' problems, but in application of knowledge to the sociologist consultant's problems. For example, we discuss difficulties in securing and maintaining consulting relationships, and the day-to-day problems of dealing with practitioners.

We use a "negotiated order" (Strauss 1978) supplemented by other theoretical notions as a basic background for the analysis. It has been helpful to use Freidson's (1970) analysis of the development of medicine as a consulting profession to understand some of the problems of applied sociology (R. O'Toole 1982). Sociology has become fairly secure as a *learned* profession but has a different set of problems to establish itself as a *consulting* profession. We must ask, "What types of service do sociologists have to sell in the consulting market?" Academically oriented sociologists have often answered this question naively by pointing out the value of sociology to society. It would appear, since we have so many answers to social problems, that all sorts of agencies and organizations would be asking for our advice. Our experience has been that with few exceptions most practitioners, administrators, or board members of human service organizations are not really aware of what sociology has to offer.

Perhaps the more basic question is "What types of services do sociologists have to sell, *that some agency will buy,* in the consulting market?" What, for example, is there in the usual Introduction to Sociology class that would lead an administrator to call a sociologist and pay for their work on a problem? Currently, sociology is not a visible source of help the way that physicians are consulted for diseases, and, to a lesser extent, psychologists for emotional problems. Then there is the question of competition in the consulting market. Here the question becomes "What does sociology have to offer that is better than the 'barber' psychologists or those 'snake oil' social work peddlers?" Can we use entrepreneurial and negotiations skills to secure and maintain consulting work?

We have drawn upon our consulting experiences to help provide some answers to these questions. First we review the roles we have played as consulting sociologists and analyze their impact on the agency. Next, two cases from our consulting experience are presented to show the utility of the negotiations' paradigm both in solving practitioners' problems and in solving consultants' problems. For good measure, one of our failures is included. We then discuss problems that can cause severe troubles for the sociologist consultant and consider how to negotiate their solution.

Strauss's (1978) negotiation paradigm, supplemented by other relevant sources, is used to analyze the consultant-client relationship. Analysis of consultant processes using a negotiation paradigm provides insight into the dynamics of social interaction and social order. Many of the substantive areas analyzed in this book are those in which sociological work is most welcomed. Examples include negotiating cooperative structures, negotiating compromises, negotiations in bureaucracies, and negotiating working relations in organizations.

CONSULTANT ROLES FOR SOCIOLOGISTS

In our experience we have identified the following roles that the sociologist can perform in a human service organization: research, program planning and design, administration, liaison with other organizations, record keeping, communication, education and training, general information (Trela and O'Toole 1974). This list is not meant to be exhaustive either for sociologists in general or for individuals, who because of their training and experience may be able to offer a number of other skills to an agency, such as individual patient/client consultation. Sociologists with skills in marketing or accounting could provide consultation in these areas. We will discuss these roles according to the general outline provided in Figure 1.1. Following a brief description of each role we will then discuss their value according to areas of impact for the agency.

Figure 1.1
Consultant Roles and Areas of Impact

Organizational Operations

Roles	Areas of Impact
Research	Program evaluation
Program planning and design	Program development
Administration	Staff effectiveness
Record Keeping	Organizational development
Communication	Problem solving and decision making
Education and Training	Client records and program
Information	accounting

Interorganizational Relations

Liaison	Support and resources from other
Program planning and design	organizations
Record Keeping	Accountability and visibility
Communication	

Contributions to the Professional Field

Research	Linkage of theory, research, and
Communication	practice
Education and training	Contributions to knowledge
Liaison	

Source: Compiled by the authors.

Role Description

Research: This role involves conducting all phases of a research operation including problem formulation, selection or design of instruments, data collection and processing, analysis, and preparation of reports and publications of research results. Applied research generally involves more collaboration, for example, with administrators and practitioners, than scientifically oriented research.

Program Planning and Design: This involves designing or redesigning programs, often in consultation with agency practitioners, administrators, and representatives of agencies that fund programs through, for example, purchasing services for clients or as research and demonstration projects (Johnson 1983). Program budgeting is a major aspect of this role, particularly when the program is funded totally by sources outside the agency. This role is often intimately related to the research role in evaluative research.

Administration: Our experience has demonstrated the need for administrative skills because, as the sociologist's work expands for the agency, this role is often required. Duties include supervision of research workers, and perhaps other consultants, and administrative evaluation of service programs. Evaluative research involves continual coordination of research with agency administrators, service personnel, and funding organizations.

Liaison with Other Organizations: This role is largely concerned with problems of managing interorganizational relations for the agency. Our experience shows that each of the researcher's roles we describe has the potential for involving the sociologist consultant in the agency's interorganizational systems. Therefore, it may be expedient to recognize this role as distinct. The duties consist of initiating and maintaining relationships with other agencies and organizations, and, for example, responding to external requests for data on the agency. In relation to program planning or evaluation research, the consultant may be directly involved in negotiating cooperative agreements, program coordination, or some other form of interorganizational relationship.

Record Keeping: This role is related to the sociologist's skills in the collection and processing of data. It may involve consulting on the design or functioning of routine client records, departmental program records, or evaluative research data. Record-keeping consultation "becomes the basis both for administrative decision-making and for reporting agency activities to funding, accrediting, coordinating, and planning organizations at the local, state, and national levels" (Trela and O'Toole 1974).

Communication: It is useful in this role for the consultant to view the agency as a reference point in communication networks. The consultant can help to improve both the agency's position in these networks as well as specific information that is received and transmitted by the agency. Informal as well as formal channels must be considered in the development and performance of this role.

Education and Training: Included here are programs and services that the sociologist can perform as a consultant: (1) in-service training of staff, (2) educational programs for community leaders and volunteers, and (3) the informal and formal instruction of agency staff in such activities as evaluative research.

Information: A great deal of the sociological consultant's activities can be lumped together under the general category of providing information. This role ranges from such activities as giving the consultee advice on how to deal with his own organization to using sociological knowledge to help practitioners understand their clients when their behavior and values are very different from their own. Staff often request information about further university training. A good deal of advice is concerned with sociologists' knowledge of different customs and values. For example, the practitioner may ask, "Should I be worried about this or is it part of their culture?" Judgments of individual pathology or responsibility require such interpretations.

Impact of Consulting Roles for the Agency

The areas of impact for each of the consultant roles are analyzed in terms of the agency's organizational operations, interorganizational relations, and contributions to the professional field(s) represented in the agency. Areas of impact are particularly crucial to negotiations to secure, maintain, and expand consulting work with an agency. A question that deserves our attention is: "What do sociological consultants have to offer that provides better outcomes for the agency in comparison to competing consultants from other disciplines?"

Research

Areas of impact or potential goals for the consultant in the research area include improvement in program evaluation and client follow-up, implementation of programs, staff development, new initiatives in program or service development, and internal record keeping for administrative decision making. Research can be "scientifically oriented" but most is in the form of applied research, particularly evaluative research, which is described below. Some types of organizations may be interested in supporting "scientifically oriented" research in which the goals are the generation or testing of sociological theories, but this is fairly rare in our experience because of lack of funds or research funding priorities that call for immediate impact on practice. Sociologists interested in conducting "pure" research might consider using their relationships with an agency to apply through that organization for an extramural research project. In this way, the agency can enhance its research reputation. Also, its staff and trainees can benefit from the intellectual stimulation afforded by the research program. As noted, this procedure is probably best employed when the consultant has an established relationship with an agency and can then negotiate the necessary position to conduct a research program.

Program Evaluation

The consultant's greatest potential impact on the agency's internal operations, programs, and services is through evaluative research and the use of its findings to suggest organizational change. In brief, research findings can be used to study and then design programs that provide better and more cost-effective services to clients through improved use of agency personnel and other resources. In our society, evaluative research has become known as the real proof of effectiveness and agency accountability. Its results have therefore become an effective argument for continuing a program or for reducing its funds. Research data are often required by public or private funders of programs and services. However, there is still a good deal of resistance to evaluative research by agency personnel, and too much of this research falls short of meeting its potential for the agency.

These can be major issues for the sociologist to consider in negotiating a consulting relationship. Yet the market is fairly competitive for evaluative research since there are a number of professions and organizations that offer these services. From our profession's point of view we must ask: "Why should an agency retain a sociologist to conduct its evaluations? What can the sociologist contribute that is better than the others? In providing some answers to these questions we focus here on research and later turn to the issue of the use of research results by administrators and practitioners in program development. The two issues are closely related because uses of evaluative data must be one of the major considerations in research design and data collection methods. For example, data that focuses singularly on the "before" and "after" psychological characteristics of the client may tell the agency nothing about how organizational factors or practitioner-client relationships influenced program outcomes. *The sociologist brings a larger number of levels of analysis to bear on a human service program problem than other professionals.*

Sociologists have the following advantages over competing consultants. First, the sociologist brings a greater repertoire of research skills to the research program. Second, the sociologist is equipped to contribute both formal and substantive sociological theory to the formulation of the research, its conduct, and consultations on program changes *during* and *after* the evaluation. Third, as a result of both sociological knowledge and our experiences, particularly in qualitative research, we know the value of "fitting in" in the field. We know the importance of familiarizing ourselves with the culture—for example, style of work and language of the staff. Thus we can be less obtrusive as researchers and less threatening to staff. Fourth, the sociologist is more equipped, by both methodological skills and theory, to add a "formative" design to a summative evaluation that provides almost immediate and on-going results on *how* the program affects clients and the *social processes* and *social organizational* factors that are involved.

Process models are particularly useful in designing and interpreting formative research. Examples are readily available, particularly in symbolic interaction theory. This type of design can also suggest the relative contribution of each part of a program. In addition, the sociologist is skilled in the use of secondary as well as unobtrusive types of data (Webb et al. 1966). Agency records can be a valuable source of data and a contribution of the consultant is not only to use case data as an efficient and cost-saving tool in research but, as discussed below, to help improve agency record keeping to improve its future evaluation efforts.

Program Development

This is an area of impact that follows logically from evaluative research, although this type of consultation is not dependent upon a specific evaluation research project. Our experience in universities and a number of human service organizations is that most evaluation results are not used to guide administrative decision making and have little impact on the work of practitioners in the agency (Smith 1982). In fact, evaluative research is sometimes never communicated to professionals who work directly with clients. A major reason for the nonutilization of evaluative results is that research data and conclusions must be interpreted and sometimes "translated" before they are useful to administrators and practitioners. Thus, a natural extension of the consultant's evaluative researcher role is in program development. To repeat, the sociologist who designed the evaluation with program development in mind is the logical person to be retained for help in using the results.

However, the sociologist can have a continuing role in program development aside from the conduct of evaluative research. This area of impact stems from the consultant's communication and liaison roles as listed in Figure 1.1. In brief, the sociologist consultant can function as a major communication link between the agency and sources of professional and scientific knowledge. First, as noted, most sociological knowledge as well as scientific knowledge from the other social behavioral sciences must be "translated" for use in programmatic decision making and then adapted to the actual problems that are faced on a day to day basis. Second, the sociologist consultant can act as a link in a communication network to the professional associations that represent the agency and its professional staff. Our experience with administrators and practitioners shows that, for a variety of reasons, they do not receive the available research and practice literature in their field.

The problems of *dissemination* and *utilization* of knowledge have received a great deal of attention in recent years. Sociologist consultants are in a unique position to link the agency and relevant sources of information. This is not an easy task, for it requires a great deal of hard work that is not visible to the agency. It means that in addition to keeping up on sociology, one must also read in related disciplines and become involved with professional information networks. This includes joining relevant professional associations, participating in their meetings, and generally becoming a heavy user of their communications. Of equal, or of even greater, importance is the consultant's links in the informal communication networks that cross the field. Trela and O'Toole (1974, 16) summarize the contribution of this role as follows: "Thus, by participating in the professional-scientific communication network, by promoting the linkage of new knowledge with practice, and by drawing out the implications of research for practice, the [consultant] may have a significant impact on program development and the quality of new programs." It is thus easy to see the relationship of dissemination and utilization to the potential impact of the sociologist consultant regarding agency problems in developing and maintaining staff effectiveness.

Staff Effectiveness

In negotiating relationships with agencies the consultant can make the point that a number of his roles have payoffs for the education and motivation of agency personnel. Several latent functions of systematic evaluation should be considered. Evaluation produces in staff greater awareness of the relationship between their work and client progress. If handled properly such research can be a positive growth experience for staff as opposed to the view that they are being "watched" and evaluated negatively. Through participating in data collection, staff are reminded of program service goals and the usefulness of periodic reviews of both individual clients and programs in relation to those goals. There is thus the opportunity for periodic self-evaluation. In this way and in educational programs and seminars the sociologist consultant can help increase not only staff *effectiveness* but also their *job satisfaction*. For example, staff "burnout" and turnover are common problems for human service organizations.

Organizations must train both new and continuing personnel, as well as prepare staff for new programs. The consultant can also link the agency to the educational programs in the community to provide mandated requirements for continuing education for their various professional groups. We have noted that one of the most persistent needs of agency staff is for realistic information about various university programs and requirements.

Organizational Development

The sociological consultant's skills and experience in program planning and evaluation can be of service to the agency in grant writing and other types of proposals to secure funds for agency development. Even though agency staff have a great deal of knowledge concerning programs, they often feel they lack the necessary conceptual and writing skills to develop a fundable proposal. The consultant's role is then to conceptualize the program on the basis of staff ideas and their own contributions, including the evaluative research design when required. Funds can then be made available for program innovation and flexibility in programming to meet client needs. The acquisition of funds for agency development is the most visible and rewarded of the consultant's activities. It is also a role that can result in expansion of the consultant's work with the agency, in part because it often brings in the funds for continued consultation.

Problem Solving and Decision Making

Sociological theory, substantive research knowledge, and scientific thinking that partials out various alternatives are basic to problem solving and decision making. The consultant can help agency staff analyze various alternatives to help solve problems. A major contribution of the sociologist consultant in this process is the production of data, that which is already available or can be assembled easily, to provide information for problem solving. Finally, while not "value free" the sociologist can often offer administrators a more detached perspective in outlining and evaluating policy alternatives. This is personally one of the most exciting and rewarding of consulting activities.

Client Records and Program Accounting

It can be said that probably, with few exceptions, practitioners do not like to keep client records, and have even more disdain for departmental and other types of reports. They feel too much time is spent on such work and are "constantly behind" on these chores, which often take second place because they compete for time with the primary goal of helping clients. Workers cannot see how record keeping helps with the solution of client problems. In fact, often it does not. One principal reason is that agency records were not designed with worker use in client services, organizational functions, or interorganizational uses in mind. Records are incomplete, noncomparable between workers, or over time, and often suffer from lack of organization, making for severe problems in retrieving discrete pieces of data on either individuals or groups of clients. Records often have little or no relation to data categories required for agency accountability purposes with government organizations, accrediting agencies, or third-party payers such as insurance companies. In addition, agency systems often do not take advantage of available computer hardware and software systems. Sociology students who have taken only an introduction to research methods know that data processing and analysis of data are among the major skills of the sociologist.

The sociologist, more than most competitors in the consulting market, is skilled, not only in advanced techniques of data processing and analysis, but in designing a record-keeping system that is relevant to the solution of problems at different conceptual levels of analysis. In addition, the sociologist's skills in handling and analyzing qualitative data should also be stressed when discussing record keeping. While many of the activities of professional workers and clients are quantifiable, others are not. Workers may want to be able to retrieve, assemble, and analyze qualitative data. Sociologists, more than our competitors, have special skills in using qualitative data that we can easily demonstrate. Consulting on record keeping and report writing is a good place to start working with an agency. Because of the interrelationship of records to other agency problems, this consulting role can lead to others.

Support and Resources—Interorganizational Problems

Many of the agency administrators and staff with whom we have had contact were troubled by the requirements imposed on them by other organizations. Increasingly, the resources upon which the agency depends—for example, funds, clients, knowledge—are provided through a complex series of interorganizational networks. They often lacked knowledge of these organizations that could be used as a basis for establishing relationships with them. In short, the consultant sociologist has to understand this system so that the agency can be guided on how to interact with its interorganizational environment.

The sociologist is better prepared to understand the complexities of this interorganizational system because only sociology truly addresses this level of analysis. Thus, one of the major services that the sociologist can offer is knowledge of the system that can be used to meet the agency's needs to establish accountability by reporting information and to gain resources for continued operation and growth. Sociologists who not only have knowledge of the system but also who have a network of consultantships are in a unique position to aid each agency to bring about system change. Of course, conflict between agencies may create ethical problems for the consultant.

Visibility

It has been our experience that human service agencies are particularly good at "hiding their light under a bushel," to borrow a biblical phrase. With few exceptions, human service agencies have not been effective in public relations. Probably only sociologists themselves have been more neglectful of their public relations problems. The tasks of the sociologist consultant in this role are to help the agency communicate its programs and accomplishments to its many and varied publics. For example, the consultant can help agency administrators and staff prepare speeches and brochures as well as secure the support of the media in reporting agency activities. It should also be noted that a number of these activities will also enhance the careers of agency personnel and thus can become either implicit or explicit stakes in the negotiations process. Both the consultant and agency staff can use activities such as the presentation of papers at professional meetings to contribute to the knowledge base of the human services fields.

Contributions to the Human Service Fields

Here we are analyzing the contribution of research, education, liaison, and communication roles to (1) linkage of theory, research, and practice and (2) contributions to knowledge as shown in Figure 1.1. We view the consultant sociologist as a major link between the all-too-separate world of theory and research and the world of practice. Theoretically there should be a great deal of mutually profitable exchange between, for example, university-based scientists and agency practitioners. Practitioners often use ideas that have been developed on the job. Their "practice theory" is thus often unorganized and unsystematic. A crucial role for the sociologist is to help organize and systematize these practitioner ideas. Once stated in a theoretical manner they can be tested and modified. New theoretical and research ideas can be disseminated through in-service education and program planning and development. It has been our experience that only persons with experience in both worlds can effectively handle this liaison role.

Until recently there have been too few means for consultant sociologists to share such knowledge. However, professional associations of sociologists have been devoting a large number of sessions to applied sociology topics. Journals also are now available for the presentation of the work of applied sociology, such as *The Journal of Applied Sociology.*

NEGOTIATING COORDINATION AND COOPERATION THROUGH INTERORGANIZATIONAL RELATIONSHIPS

In the relatively recent past a number of significant advances have been made in the treatment of individual health, psychological, and social problems. At the same time organizational designs and particularly interorganizational systems to coordinate these services and to provide needed structural changes have not kept pace. In fact, such processes as deinstitutionalization, professional and organizational specialization, the aging of the population, the feminization of poverty, as well as budget cutting, make the problems of organizing professional and agency effort even more difficult. Such interorganizational problems are clearly at the heart of sociological analysis and sociological consultants should have an advantage over their competitors in this area of consulting work.

The project we have used for this illustration is taken from our research on the development of a complex of 11 rehabilitation agencies (O'Toole and O'Toole 1981). The goal of the complex was to secure economic savings and programmatic advantages through cooperation and coordination—such as the sharing of physical resources and the coordination of programs that shared the same clients. In this project our major role was research, in which we sought to study the process of interorganizational coordination, so that other agencies could use the results to initiate their own planning. In addition, we helped with the public relations (communication) work on the project, gave advice concerning the development of interorganizational structures that were developed, and consulted on the liaison negotiations that were held with the many public and private organizations that were involved. It should be made clear, however, that we did not possess the knowledge of organizations, negotiations, or the uses of power that were required to develop the complex of agencies. This knowledge was held by the individuals who actually developed the complex.

We present this project as an example of sociological consultation because it demonstrates:

1. The utility of a sociological theory, the negotiated order approach, to consulting work.
2. The mutually beneficial relationship between the practitioner and the sociologist. In this project we learned more from the practitioners and agency trustees than they learned from us.
3. The relationship of the research role to the other consulting roles listed in Figure 1.1. In addition, it demonstrates the importance of the liaison role for the consultant.
4. The need for sociologists to have a great deal of practical knowledge of the social structure and culture—the "structural context"—of the area in which they are consulting.
5. The value of the consultant continually reinterpreting past consulting work in light of new developments in theory and research.

Development of the Rehabilitation Complex

In our first analysis in this project we described the development of the complex using some sociological concepts that specified and clarified the social processes that made the coordination a success. We later reinterpreted the data as a sociological study (O'Toole and O'Toole 1981) using Strauss's (1978) negotiation paradigm, and applied it to the solution of problems in nursing and educational administration (O'Toole and O'Toole 1983). We will first describe the negotiations process that brought about the development of the complex and then discuss this project in terms of what it taught us about consulting.

According to our analysis, the significant aspects of the negotiations were:

1. The characteristics of the negotiation team (the director and two trustees) that represented the agency that initiated the plan. Specifically (a) the team's

commitment to the process over a 25-year period, (b) the team's *theory of negotiations,* and (c) their positions in community power and funding networks.

2. The team's strategies in the negotiations process included: (a) selection of co-negotiators in the agencies they were attempting to recruit, (b) restriction of *issues* to be negotiated, (c) manipulation of *stakes* so as to increase the other agency's rewards while reducing their costs, (d) the strategy of employing *covert* negotiations to handle difficult problems informally with the use of a "peer type" coordinating organization (Mott 1970) as the structure for *overt* sessions.

The plan for the rehabilitation complex and the negotiations through which the other ten agencies were recruited were the work of a team made up of the agency's chief administrator and two influential trustees. Each team member had considerable negotiations experience but perhaps much more important was their dedication to the complex.

The team did not attempt to develop a formal plan for the complex. Instead, they used a *theory of negotiations* that sought limited success to be used as a basis for higher level goals. In what Strauss calls *multiple* and *linked* negotiations they first contacted agencies they believed would be easier to recruit and then, on the basis of these alliances, contacted the more difficult agencies. They selected as co-negotiators their counterparts in other agencies, trustees and administrators, often on the basis of previous relationships. The trustees also held similar positions in other organizations, what Perrucci and Pilisuk (1970) refer to as interorganizational leaders. In some cases they were board members of both agencies involved in a negotiation and could, thus, influence the process from both sides. As interorganizational leaders they could use their positions in community power and resource networks to secure resources to bargain in the negotiations.

The team used what we termed a reward-cost-involvement formula to manipulate the *stakes* for the other agencies. For example, goals that neither organization could achieve separately were offered as rewards. Costs were specified and membership contingencies outlined to dispel agency fears about loss of autonomy.

By selecting people like themselves as co-negotiators they were able to restrict potential *issues* that would come up in the negotiations as a result of their similarities in background and outlook. They also restricted the initial negotiations to financial and physical plan concerns. Potentially conflicting issues such as program or staff sharing would come later after initial cost sharing success had been attained. *Covert* negotiations were used to reach significant agreements followed by *overt* negotiations in formal meetings that served mostly expressive and public relations functions.

Uses of Negotiations Theory in Consulting

One of the major values of the negotiated order approach is its ability to incorporate a number of sociological levels of analysis as well as integrate ideas from other disciplines. The applied sociologist is often required to be more eclectic and to be able to use ideas from other scientific and professional areas. If we are to be able to participate in the negotiations on behalf of an agency or to advise them in the process we must be able to anticipate steps, stages, and potential outcomes. To do this we must have both theoretical and practical knowledge of the properties of the negotiations process. In particular, the consultant must have knowledge of the *structural context* and the *negotiations context* for the negotiations. Much of this knowledge can be acquired only through participation in the day-to-day interaction of practitioners. Sociologists may not have specific knowledge but, through contacts in the liaison role, they should know where to find such information.

This project can also be used to show the relationship of the research to other consulting roles. Our major role in this project was research, but not research in the way the term is used for the most part in academic sociology. The federal funders of our work were primarily interested in the development of ideas that could be used by practitioners in other areas who were concerned with greater coordination and cooperation among human service agencies. They wanted a practical model that could be used elsewhere. They had only secondary interest in the building and testing of theoretical models. Practitioners were interested in research that would document the accomplishments of the agency and show the future potential of the complex they had developed. Thus, for them, research would be useful if it brought public relations value to the complex and made it easier to secure cooperation and the necessary resources to further extend their community service work. The sociologist consultants would be of value if they helped to describe the process and then communicated its results. The practitioners had even less interest than the research funding agency in the theoretical output of the project. Publications in scientific journals would be "nice" but not of primary value to the agency. If the sociologist could offer advice from time to time, that also would be helpful. For the most part, the sociologists learned more from the administrators and trustees than the reverse. Most of the time we were somewhat dumbfounded by the practical knowledge of social structure and process that the administrator and trustees used to accomplish their goals. We "paid our way" on this project, not in terms of sociological knowledge concerning interorganizational relations, but primarily in terms of the public relations value of our research and our ability to communicate our findings.

We should call attention to one of the values of conducting research with practitioners in a project of this nature. Research tends to make practitioners more self-conscious of their behavior. This is particularly true of participant observation, intensive interviewing, and the use of agency records to document past events and behavior. As they reflect on their actions and become part of the research process they begin to learn the sociological perspective and how it applies to their work and agency. They become more willing to see and understand the potential value of sociology. They can begin to see the value of expanding their relationship with the sociologist to include other consulting roles.

Finally, the project demonstrates the value of the sociological consultant keeping up on the literature. We did not have a conceptual scheme that could handle the rich and extremely complex series of events that had unfolded over a 25-year period until we read *Negotiations* (Strauss 1978). However, once we were able to use this paradigm to understand the process we were able to use these ideas in work in other settings (O'Toole and O'Toole 1983).

NEGOTIATIONS THAT FAILED: CONSULTANT NAIVETÉ

This case developed from one of the author's work as the representative from sociology at a research and training center. My duties, in addition to developing my own research program, involved consultation with researchers and practitioners from a relatively wide array of professional and scientific groups. In this capacity I was requested to help a resident physician who was interested in researching the relationship between sexual intercourse and bacterial infections in the female urinary tract. We worked out a good design that varied the independent variable by comparing a control group of nuns with an experimental group of prostitutes. The dependent variable was to be measured using systematically collected urine samples. I was somewhat worried about participation of nuns in the project, but the physician negotiated their cooperation relatively easily through religious health care organizations. Because of my previous research on prostitutes it was assumed that I could best secure the sample of prostitutes. I made an appointment with a sergeant in the Vice Division of the Police Department of the city. I will discuss the interaction that followed in negotiation paradigm (Strauss 1978) terms, but this is hindsight. I made an appointment with the sergeant because it is more advantageous to handle initial negotiations in person. It is much easier to turn down a "nonperson" on the phone or in responding to a letter. The sergeant's first reply to our request was to state: "There is no prostitution in this city." Actually, I handled this statement fairly well. I did not start laughing because streetwalkers did a brisk business not far from the precinct headquarters where we were talking. I realized that for public relations this was a standard comment. I also realized that in terms of *stakes* he had very little to gain and a good deal to lose by helping with our project. For example, sociologists, other social scientists, and journalists have used the research issue to "rip off" the police by writing exposé-type articles. Time and inconvenience were also major stakes for the officer in addition to potential trouble. However, I was able to convince him to take our request for cooperation to his superiors. The resident physician would come to the jail at specified times and get urine samples from the prostitutes who wished to cooperate. I left his office feeling good about the project because it was such a simple request that I was sure that all would go well.

Several weeks later, after several phone calls, I was told that the project had been vetoed by the physician who was in charge of health care at the jail. The project thus died after the investment of a good deal of time and effort. The resident physician redesigned the project using a clinic sample of women and interviews to measure frequency of intercourse. Later I was told that the physician in charge of jail health care did not want another physician invading his "turf." My only rewards were the knowledge that I gained and the fact that I have been able to use this experience in my research methods classes as an example of how not to manage research.

Strauss (1978) states that one of the advantages of the paradigm is its use as a predictive guide for researchers (we add consultants). We use the paradigm to show how several strategies could have been used to achieve probable success for the project. I should have explored the structural context of the negotiations and the properties of the negotiations context to understand what types of negotiations needed to be conducted and with whom to secure cooperation. First is the question of who would negotiate with whom, and what were the stakes. It would probably have been better to have a prestigeful physician from the medical school or county medical society negotiate with the physician in the jail. A physician with a personal relationship with the physician in the jail would have been ideal. Perhaps the stakes for him could have been favorably weighted in terms of reward for his cooperation. A junior physician and a sociologist probably had insufficient power as well as few stakes to manipulate in negotiating cooperation.

What can be gained in regard to consulting strategies from this case?

1. We must know the organization with which we hope to negotiate—for example, its decision-making and power hierarchies. We must have knowledge of the professions that are represented.

2. We must be able to use our knowledge to plan a series of linked negotiations.

3. We must be able to anticipate the stakes in the negotiations and increase the rewards of cooperation.

4. As noted above, we must be observant of the tendency for the number of issues and their complexity to accelerate.

Using this knowledge of the negotiations process and the structural context in which it takes place we are in a better position to anticipate problems in consulting and to plan for their solution. In addition to the insights gained in the two consulting jobs we have analyzed, there are two particular issues we have encountered repeatedly that deserve attention. First is the matter of clients' expectations or, more specifically, their overexpectations of the sociologist consultant. Second, we will briefly comment on the consultants' need for intimate knowledge of the area in which they are working. This may seem self-evident, but a number of consultants seem to feel they can apply a method on technique in an area in which they have little or no experience.

THE CONSULTANT AS ALCHEMIST

As consultants we have often been asked to straighten out a neglected inadequate evaluation of a funded human service program when in reality it is too late to complete the evaluative design as it was originally conceived. The "evaluation" thus far may consist of a few cases on which there is unsystematic data. The staff had been hoping to get started on the research but had spent their time "helping people." As the time to prepare a report on the project approached, something close to panic occurred as the loss of funds, jobs, and needed client services became a reality. When the "data" were first looked at the alchemist analogy came readily to mind. Indeed, one was being asked to change lead into gold! We will use cases of this nature to discuss the consultant-practitioner relationship, the ethical and policy problems this consultation entails, and, particularly, implications for negotiations with clients.

First, sociologist consultants need to know just what they are getting into in this type of problem. If the practitioner-consultant relationship and the expected product are not fully understood by both parties there can often be misunderstandings down the road. Second, there are the ethical problems the sociologist faces if he or she decides to take the job. Third, if the sociologist does take the assignment he or she may be in a very good position to demonstrate the value of sociological consultation and to expand the consultation both in terms of roles performed and continuity beyond the task of completing this initial evaluation.

In graduate school, for the most part, we learn to design and conduct research in ideal settings in which the problems of the real world are often overlooked. We do not learn how to use *anything we can find* to attempt to provide data to evaluate a human services program. Yet this is what must be done, if available data can be assembled, processed, and analyzed to produce an evaluation that will provide some information for policy and program decision making. Moreover, unlike much academic research, it must be done very quickly. The project cannot be redesigned because the report is due in a few weeks.

The sociologist consultant in the initial negotiations with the practitioner must establish just what can be done with the data at hand. The practitioners will hope that the consultant can, in fact, somehow produce an evaluative report that will allow the funded program to continue. On the other hand the consultant will be tempted, for a variety of reasons, including money, to promise too much in order to get the job. Consultant time and the product are important issues to be included in the negotiation of the contract between the sociologist and practitioner and are discussed later. For now it is sufficient to realize that if the initial agreement is not based on the current reality of the data and its limitations, the practitioner will be disappointed later on and may even feel that the consultant has not fulfilled the agreement.

The ethical problems stem from the different points of view and stakes in the evaluation of the practice agency that is retaining the consultant, the scientific and professional integrity of the sociological consultant, and the funding agency. There will be fewer ethical problems and fewer misunderstandings if the "salvage operation" and its products are negotiated by the sociologist with the other two interested parties.

This is a very good time for the consultant to demonstrate the value of sociology to the agency. For example, agency administrators can see the value of having a researcher not only design an evaluation, but advise on administration of the program, and help prepare the final report. At the same time, the consultant will have the opportunity to discuss the uses of the evaluation in program planning. At this time of high visibility of sociological work and its value, the consultant is in a good position to discuss additional roles that can be performed: program planning and design, record keeping, communication, liaison, and education and training.

INTIMATE KNOWLEDGE OF THE PRACTICE AREA

The consultant's working knowledge of the area is essential to secure and maintain the consulting relationship. This point has been made implicitly in the preceding case studies but it is of sufficient importance that it deserves explicit attention. We have observed a number of instances where "experts" have been brought in to consult on specific problems, to design an evaluation, or to conduct staff in-service training programs, which failed to meet objectives because the consultant did not have intimate knowledge and understanding of the area.

In one vocational rehabilitation agency, an expert from a prestigious university was brought in to consult on problems in work evaluation and work adjustment programs. His expertise was in socialization theory. He had little knowledge of the day-to-day problems confronted by the staff or of the types of programs in which they worked. However, the problem that turned off most of the staff was his incorrect use of the standard language of vocational rehabilitation—the culture of the staff he had come to help. Thus he might have been a very learned professor but when it came to their daily work, "he didn't know what he was talking about." In addition, they felt he was talking down to them as he tried to relate his theoretical notions to his understanding of their work. They were particularly incensed because of the amount paid to the consultant. In fact, it was not exorbitant as a consulting fee, but having felt disgruntled by his performance, they began to compare his worth to theirs by computing how much time they had to work to earn a comparable amount of money.

A similar case is the evaluative researcher who feels that he can evaluate any program without knowing its specific content. He can use a type of experimental design, but the evaluation will often fall far short of its potential because he lacks the knowledge to research those aspects of the program that are most amenable to administrative or professional change. He cannot make the evaluation fit in with the regular work of the staff. He may doom the program to failure by selecting evaluative criteria beyond its reach.

Both examples show the value of a working understanding of the everyday world of the practitioner, the client, and the agency. Both of these consultants had much to offer the agencies. However, they did not know how to make their knowledge *relevant*. To make knowledge relevant consultants have to know and speak the language of practice. This is particularly true for sociological consultants since the value of their theory, research knowledge, and methods is relatively unknown. The burden of the "proof of the pudding" is upon them. They cannot expect practitioners to take on the burden of translating sociology into specific activities that will help in their daily work.

REFERENCES

Freidson, Eliot. 1970. *Profession of Medicine: A Study of the Sociology of Applied Knowledge*. New York: Dodd, Mead.

Johnson, Paul L. 1983. "Human Services Planning." In *Applied Sociology*, edited by Howard E. Freeman, Russell R. Dynes, Peter H. Rossi, William Foote Whyte, pp. 106–17. San Francisco: Jossey-Bass.

Mott, B. J. F. 1970. "Coordination and Inter-Organizational Relations in Health." In *Inter-Organizational Research in Health: Conference Proceedings*, edited by P. E. White and G. J. Vlasak, pp. 55–69. Washington, D.C.: National Center for Health Services Research and Development.

O'Toole, Anita W., and Richard O'Toole. 1983. "Negotiating Cooperative Agreements Between Health Organizations." *Journal of Nursing Administration,* (December): 33–38.

O'Toole, Richard, and Anita Werner O'Toole. 1981. "Negotiating Interorganizational Orders." *The Sociological Quarterly* 22 (Winter): 29–42.

O'Toole, Richard. 1982. "Sociology: A Consulting Profession." *The Applied Sociologist Bulletin* 3 (Summer): 3–6.

Perrucci, Robert, and Marc Pilisuk. 1970. "Leaders and Ruling Elites: The Interorganizational Relations Among Public Agencies." *American Sociological Review* 35 (December): 1040–57.

Smith, Nick L. 1982. *Communication Strategies In Evaluation.* Beverly Hills, Calif.: Sage.

Strauss, Anselm. 1978. *Negotiations: Varieties, Contexts, Processes, and Social Order.* San Francisco: Jossey-Bass.

Trela, James E., and Richard O'Toole. 1974. *Roles for Sociologists in Service Organizations.* Kent, Ohio: Kent State University Press.

Webb, E. J., D. T. Campbell, R. D. Schwartz, and L. Sechrest. 1966. *Unobtrusive Measures: Nonreactive Research in the Social Sciences.* Chicago: Rand McNally.

2

Consulting Sociology as a Vocation: Sociological and Societal Conditions and Constraints

JEFFREY K. LANGE

From Comte to Weber to C. Wright Mills, sociologists' career opportunities and professional accomplishments have been considered central sociological topics. Sociologists have not assessed their collective occupational prospects merely out of an interest in the "market" for their services, but—more importantly—to learn something vital about a society that permits and encourages the empirical testing and rational explanation of human relationships and institutional arrangements. Those who have contributed much to an understanding of the occupational role of "sociologist" have generally done so by placing it in a broader social matrix of scientific and professional careers of other kinds and of historically varying magnitudes of demand for social scientific knowledge. Such a comprehensive and holistic analysis is needed again today with respect to the role of "consulting sociologist," a career option that many look to with great optimism (Watkins 1981; Heller 1984).

Today we might well ask: What are the prospects for one who would carve out a career as a consulting sociologist? We would respond by looking to "external conditions" formed by both the discipline of sociology and the wider society in which it is practiced, in order to develop an understanding of the limits that define sociologists' potential for establishing and succeeding in careers as consultants.

From the standpoint of the sociologist, "external conditions" are comprised of, first, characteristics of sociology itself as a basic science, as a form of social criticism, and as a departmentalized academic subject; and, second, broader societal characteristics including attitudes of prospective employers, clients, or other contracting authorities toward the discipline of sociology.

When one takes into account these external conditions—and places them alongside numerous optimistic pronouncements about prosperous times ahead for applied and consulting sociologists (Brown 1984; D'Antonio 1982; Deutscher 1983)—the effect is rather sobering, for the demand for consulting sociologists may be considerably less than anticipated.

In this chapter I will analyze the prospects of consulting sociologists given the sociological and societal constraints; and I will identify and discuss three different occupational roles—the consulting sociologist, the sociologist-who-consults, and the sociologist-in-reserve—that characterize today's consulting sociologist.

CONSTRAINTS ATTRIBUTABLE TO THE STATE OF THE DISCIPLINE OF SOCIOLOGY

Sociology as a Basic Science

Just because an area of human endeavor qualifies as scientific does not necessarily mean that it has immediate, practical applicability to other activities or purposes. Often this is because a science attempts to develop empirically based theoretical explanations of phenomena that are of such scale and complexity that the science does not progress rapidly to a level of scientific "control." This is true not only of the social sciences but also holds for such "natural" sciences as astronomy, geology, oceanography, and meteorology. Theories, measurement techniques and instruments, and descriptions of empirical reality flowing from these fields often have little immediate relevance to humankind's attempts to control various troublesome processes leading to undesirable events. In other words, basic scientific progress may aid in explaining or anticipating atmospheric storms, tidal waves, meteor showers, or earthquakes, but disciplinary knowledge in the corresponding intellectual fields is typically inadequate to permit us to intervene. These examples from the natural sciences illustrate that at least in some cases society permits scientific progress to unfold at a basic level without its members necessarily insisting on immediately practical results—namely, results that specify "handles" or points of control for altering the course of natural events.

It often seems that such institutionalized patience toward some macro-level natural sciences is not extended to the social sciences in similar circumstances. This may be so in part because the phenomena in a field such as sociology seeks to explain in a theoretical way are *already* explained by common sense—however inconsistent, biased, or downright wrong it may be. The natural sciences may even have it relatively easier in that the phenomena on which they focus often carry an aura of mystery to the average person. Sociology's central topics, on the other hand, are aspects of everyday life for which common sense has already provided workable explanations and socially appropriate action guidance. Perhaps no other science faces such formidable pseudoscientific competition, and this competitive situation probably adds to societal impatience or hostility toward (and sociologists' own resulting embarassment with) the state of sociological knowledge and its relatively low level of direct applicability (see comments by Dynes in Watkins 1981).

Max Weber (1958) observed that scientific inquiry involves certain ultimately unprovable assumptions, the acceptance of which, in the case of sciences of complex macrosystems, may serve for a time to insulate science from societal demands for production of control technologies. Therefore, if society allows, as an article of faith for the development of scientific knowledge "for its own sake" in the first instance, it should not demand immediate applicability of such knowledge in the second instance.

Scientists themselves may get caught up in responding to societal demands for a science to justify resources to its "advancement" by pressing prematurely for the creation of an applied science phase, as if it were a moral imperative. Weber (1958, 144) cautioned that "natural science gives us an answer to the question of what we must do to master life technically. It leaves quite aside, or assumes for its purposes, whether we should and do wish to master life technically and whether or not it makes sense to do so."

Accordingly, the science of sociology is in a weak marketing position to supply consulting services because the knowledge sociologists produce either supplies little guidance about intervention points in social process or because the knowledge it produces does not fit with broader value commitments about what, if anything, ought to be done about a given social situation.

Sociology as Social Criticism

The prevailing style of inquiry does not match well with expectations of those who would hire organizational consultants. Returning to Weber (1958, 147) a key element in the situation is uncovered:

The primary task of a useful teacher is to teach his students to recognize "inconvenient facts"—I mean facts that are inconvenient for their party opinions. And for every party opinion there are facts that are extremely inconvenient, for my own opinion no less than for others. I believe the teacher accomplishes more than a mere intellectual task if he compels his audience to accustom itself to the existence of such facts.

An academically based sociology is, quite understandably, likely to take this guidance to heart with respect to research as well as to teaching. The result is a highly inquisitive, almost relentless, mode of inquiry into the realm of taken-for-granted social life. Such study often ranges beyond bounds of "propriety" recognized by the wider society in and about which such studies take place. However, as the science of sociology reveals "inconvenient facts," it can and does go against dearly held beliefs and opinions, some of which are literally party opinions. But the "inconvenient facts" do not merely disturb an intellectual mind set, they also can be personally, economically, and politically embarrassing.

Scientists in other fields—especially the natural sciences—are relatively free to pursue drastically different theoretical problems or probe into "uncharted territory" not traversed by their peers. Sociologists, on the other hand, who engage in unorthodox research are more likely to have their work received as "radical," "irreverent," or "silly," because of the greater familiarity the general public believes it has with the subject matter studied by sociologists.

Sociologists come to understand that the host society often does not widely endorse or appreciate their work and that such support should not really be expected. Out of necessity, sociologists have become highly "inner-directed," to borrow a concept from Riesman (1950), an orientation that poses difficulties when one must shift gears and become "other-directed" according to the requirements placed by an employer or expectations expressed by a client. Such other-directedness may be quite difficult to put into practice on a personal, intellectual level, and it should in some sense *be* difficult at the disciplinary level in order that sociology retain necessary detachment and objectivity about the social matrix it seeks to examine. As Lyson and Squires (1982, 1) put it, "the turn toward non-academic employment for sociologists and the plaudits directed to so-called "applied sociology" may inadvertently contribute to the proletarization of sociologists, particularly those in nonacademic settings, and raises serious questions about the evolving intellectual character of the social sciences generally."

Another reason sociology is particularly difficult to convert into a consulting profession is that, unlike most professions or occupational roles, the role of sociologist makes it difficult for an incumbent to determine when he or she is or is not "at work." Because the entire social milieu is potential subject matter for inquiry, an individual sociologist can be virtually always "on duty," using personal experiences and other information received outside the formal research process as relevant data for theory testing or as a guide for subsequent systematic study. An attorney or physician is familiar with this same nuisance when pressed to offer "free advice" to friends or fellow party-goers. But at least these professionals can clearly detect the approach of a clearly legal or medical *question* with enough warning to head off the inquiry with a suggestion to "call at the office on Monday," when the professional is obviously at work on a fee-for-service basis.

Sociologists, by contrast, may come to think of themselves (and not wholly incorrectly) as *always* "on duty" and never resist contact with an informant or experience that might suggest new insights into the structure of the social system or that might indicate new lines of formalized research. The entire society becomes virtually an office-without-exit. Sociologists' "trained incapacity" to turn off their professional perspective in order to take on other social roles without reservation is a substantial obstacle in the way of realizing extensive consultation opportunity.

Sociology as Departmentalized Academic Subject

The third aspect of the field of sociology with consequences for its ability to produce and achieve occupational placement of consultants is that it typically is an embattled department within the academic setting. Today, sociology is granted a place in the academic market but is challenged by faculty retrenchment, stiffening of tenure requirements, and absorption into interdisciplinary social science or humanities "divisions." Current challenges to academic sociologists as faculty take the form of (1) overall declining enrollments resulting in smaller pie from which to attract majors; (2) student conservatism and careerism leading to their shunning traditional courses in the humanities and social sciences, leading to a smaller slice of an already smaller pie for sociology departments; and (3) administration response to these trends emphasizing that departments are individual profit centers, each of which must justify institutional expenditures to support it. Together, these elements lead to a freeze or decrease in tenured positions in those departments showing serious enrollment declines or lack of enrollment growth.

In the face of these difficulties, it is no wonder that sociology faculty would come to see the emergence of "applied and consulting sociology" as a multifaceted blessing. First, it enables sociology professors to promote a major in sociology by marketing a distinct occupational role and leading students to believe there is a significant payoff to their investment decision to specialize in sociology. Not only are these roles portrayed as existing in the occupational structure, but they are also cast in a context that is nonthreatening to the social order and well "within the system," thereby appealing to today's more conservative and career-oriented students.

Second, increased enrollments from promotion of consulting-sociological careers at studies' end and from processing students through "applied tracks," it is hoped, will legitimize a relatively new *academic* specialty called "applied sociology" (calling for new courses, new textbooks, and new journals). The promise of this new area of specialization is expected to help insulate mid-career, not-yet-tenured faculty members from institutional pressures for faculty retrenchment and tenure delay or denial. It is a rather Simmel-like irony that the successful *internal* marketing *within* academia of applied/consulting sociology—with consulting sociologist the penultimate role—is highly beneficial to academically based sociologists. This holds true—at least in the short run—even if no corresponding demand actually exists for consulting sociology or whether the quasi-profession of sociological consultation is ever marketed as such to the nonacademic world.

A final benefit accruing to sociology faculties is that, to the extent departmental graduates are able to find satisfying nonacademic employment—of whatever kind—they are removed from competing with their mentor cohort for what will likely continue to be a constant or shrinking number of academic positions in sociology.

As a basic science, as an institutionalized form of social criticism, and a departmentalized field of study in colleges and universities, the discipline of sociology throws up considerable obstacles for one who seeks a career as a sociological consultant. However, other characteristics of American society may pose even more formidable constraints.

CONSTRAINTS ATTRIBUTABLE TO THE STATE OF CONTEMPORARY AMERICAN SOCIETY

The discipline of sociology confronts a "host" society that is oblivious at best and hostile at worst to its holistic perspective and mode of inquiry. Most of the field's introductory textbooks contain a rather defensive first chapter in which extensive effort is made to convince the student-reader that the field is neither trivial (because it deals with aspects of familiar, everyday reality and because it sometimes confirms "common sense") nor dangerous (because researchers appear to engage in muckraking, excessively investigative, or disrespectfully radical style of research). These chapters serve as prima facie evidence that a problem exists in the public image of sociology.

A look at one best-selling dictionary further supports such a view. The terms "historian," "psychologist," and "economist" have separate entries, but the term "sociologist" is subsumed under a definition of "sociology" (Morris 1976). This reflects, I believe, that the former terms are far better established in everyday language and the public consciousness that they appear often enough in print to justify individual entries. They appear that often because the occupational roles they name are themselves established as legitimate professions with clearly understood contributions to the good of society. This is not true—or at least not *yet* true—of the role of "sociologist."

The teaching of introductory sociology is commonly considered as familiarizing the student with a discipline he or she may wish to pursue further, either as a major or in fulfillment of graduation requirements. One should also bear in mind that this particular course also serves to promote the field of sociology as a consulting profession to those who, in later life as business persons, government officials, or nonprofit agency managers, might need assistance in resolving interpersonal or organizational problems that arise. The introductory course is rarely conceptualized as serving such a purpose, and I wonder how good a job is actually done in marketing the field to those who may become sociologists' clients or employers and who constitute, in fact, a *minority* among organizational leaders who have had any exposure to the field in the first place.

Even among those with some familiarity with sociology, business and agency managers have completed other courses of academic study, many of which supply theories of professional behavior and problem resolution that have been developed in a scholarly manner and passed along to cohorts of students through other degree programs. Those instructed in the fields of business administration, organizational behavior and development, public administration, personnel and human resources management, social services management, and so on, will not necessarily perceive that sociology has anything to offer them that their own educational preparation has not already addressed. Because of their own professionalism, they are unlikely to relinquish control of a problematic situation to the hands of a consulting sociologist, whose theoretical knowledge and style of analysis are suspect. Such clients are, as a result, unlikely to enter into a subordinate role in the traditional client-professional relationship where the client defers to the professional's technical knowledge and practical wisdom.

To many potential employers and clients of consulting sociologists I would imagine the field of sociology remains what Pavalko (1972, 39) labels a "marginal profession," a category for which the role of chiropractor serves as a convenient example. Despite the fact that chiropractors themselves believe they can diagnose a number of otherwise undetected or miscategorized health problems through the application of their unorthodox theories of health care, this does not mean that chiropractors can displace other health care professionals who have a stronger hold on the public's consciousness and have leveraged far more substantial resources for dispensing and displaying their versions of health maintenance. Chiropractors face a constant threat from other health professions who dismiss their work as quackery (Wendell 1972).

Similarly, sociology is likely to be viewed among relevant organizational problem-solving professions as marginal, subject to the same kind of facile dismissal accorded chiropractors by both their target clientele and their competitors.

The field of sociology does not enjoy a high profile among academic subjects or among consulting professions. One of the few available vehicles for promoting sociological practice, the introductory course, has not been conceptualized in its marketing context, and opportunities have been lost. I have already noted that sociology departments, along with other social science and humanities fields, face declining enrollments, so efforts to make the introductory course serve more of a long-range promotional purpose are likely to meet a diminishing audience.

THREE AVAILABLE ROLES FOR ASPIRING CONSULTING SOCIOLOGISTS

Three distinctly different occupational roles can be discerned with respect to applied consulting work: the consulting sociologist, the sociologist-who-consults, and the sociologist-in-reserve. The genuine consulting sociologist is conceptualized as a professional to whom clients, who have already defined their problems as sociological in nature, approach with a plea to accept their cases and to solve or recommend how to solve problems in line with clearly sociological theories and action prescriptions. By contrast, the sociologist-who-consults (S-W-C) is less likely to be approached to take on "cases" or "projects," but is, instead, sought out to accomplish discrete *tasks* for which a social science education may be a helpful background. The S-W-C may take on these tasks as an aspect of full-time employment or as an independent contractor dealing with customers. The third kind of consulting role is, from the employer's perspective, neither sociological nor consultative. Despite holding undergraduate or graduate degrees in sociology, these sociologist-benchwarmers are not really in "the game" of applied sociology at all, although they may have been convinced through the educational process that their private, unremunerated, unpublished sociologizing (which may go on at or about work) is significant "applied sociology" and that they are, in fact, functioning as "sociologists in applied settings."

The Consulting Sociologist Role

The genuine consulting sociologist is a professional who is sought out when a client has defined an organizational problem as susceptible to sociological analysis and ameliorative action arising from such analysis. The consulting sociologist, in ideal-typical terms, is a trusted practitioner into whose hands a somewhat perplexed, bewildered, or embattled organizational representative places a problematic situation. The consulting sociologist is expected to produce a wise diagnosis, using sociological modes of analysis, and to arrive at effective ameliorative strategies. Hypothetically, the consulting sociologist is seen in the same light as other consulting professionals such as lawyers, physicians, or clergy, who are acknowledged as possessing expertise that the client recognizes he lacks or is not available in the appropriate quantity or type on his or her own regular staff but whose skills are perceived as requisite to respond to a pressing need. In this kind of relationship, clients do not challenge the procedures, diagnostic techniques, or conclusions of the professional to whom the client must, out of necessity, defer. As Greenwood (1972, 7) has expressed it,

in a professional relationship...the professional dictates what is good or evil for the client, who has no choice but to accede to the professional's judgment. Here the premise is that, because he lacks the requisite theoretical background, the client cannot diagnose his own needs or discriminate among the range of possibilities for meeting them. Nor is the client considered able to evaluate the caliber of the professional service he receives.

On the other hand, an academically oriented "learned professional" may find it difficult to adjust to a situation where he or she—in Freidson's (1970, 22) terms—

is not the custodian of a revealed dogma whose job it is to distinguish the genuinely revealed from the spurious, nor is he the repository and elaborator of the theory and imputed knowledge accumulated by a society.... [Rather, c]onsulting professions have to take the test of practical problem solving applied by their lay clientele.

Whether or not sociological theory is the dominant paradigm guiding professional service delivery and whether or not the consultant-sociologist is granted wide discretion in the manner described by Greenwood are central considerations in assessing situations where the consulting sociologist is able to operate effectively. Other pages of this volume may even carry convincing descriptions of cases in which such conditions obtain; but one should bear in mind the inherent weakness of the case method in terms of generalizability and external validity (Babbie 1979, 228). The crucial point here is that these criteria define situations in which social scientists function as true consulting sociologists as contrasted with one of the other roles to be described below.

It is likely that only the more senior of sociologists would even be approached to serve as genuine consulting sociologists. Having reached some degree of eminence within academia for research grants brought in, publications in professional journals, and perhaps a highly popular textbook or two, such senior academicians may find consulting sociology a pleasant diversion from what to them has become the tired routine of academic life, "the grueling, competitive, dreary monotony and the petty politics which constitute so much of that world" (Deutscher 1983, 10). We should not be surprised to find that genuine consulting sociologists are relatively rare—an ironic situation where an endangered species is composed of individuals surviving quite well in a small ecological niche. As elites are wont to do, true consulting sociologists may embrace radical-chic ideas, characterizing applied sociology as a kind of elevated avo-cation rather than vocation—an exotic and exhilarating play-experience. To quote Deutscher again (1983, 14), "For those of you who would entertain applying your sociology out there in other real worlds, I say go for it! It is an ancient and honorable pursuit. More important, as Howard Becker once responded when I asked him why he was doing it, 'It's fun!'"

The Sociologist-Who-Consults Role

While I concede that a handful of relatively established sociologists can be expected to find a transitory or permanent opportunity to serve as consulting sociologists, a potentially larger number of sociologists—primarily those with graduate degrees in sociology—are likely to find quite different working conditions when they attempt to apply their skills as consultants. This second category—sociologists-who-consult—are de-fined by the greater frequency with which they are approached to com-plete limited tasks rather than to design projects or to handle "cases." I'm referring here to such tasks as sampling design, questionnaire con-struction, data collection mode selection, field operations management, computerized data file generation, statistical analysis and interpretation, and oral or written presentation of results and other information. To-gether, these tasks might be a significant part of the consulting sociol-ogist's overall responsibilities. But the S-W-C will typically take on only one or a few of these tasks, either as a paid independent contractor or as an occasional duty within the broader framework of full-time em-ployment. These *are* tasks for which an education in sociology, especially a graduate education, can be a very helpful and relevant preparation. More importantly, the tasks carried out by an S-W-C are *not* accomplished as a rule in a context where sociological theory is the dominant paradigm. Nor is discretion granted to the "consultant" to define problems and to recommend remedies. An S-W-C would qualify as a "nonprofessional" to Greenwood (1972, 6):

A non-professional occupation has customers; a professional occupation has clients. What is the difference? A customer determines what services and/or commodities he wants, and he shops around until he finds them. His freedom of decision rests upon the premise that he has the capacity to appraise his own needs and to judge the potential of the service or the commodity to satisfy them. The infallibility of his decisions is epitomized in the slogan: "The customer is always right!".... [T]he customer can criticize the quality of the commodity he has just purchased and can even demand a refund. The client lacks this same prerogative, having surrendered it to professional authority.

Deutscher (1983) has identified what he feels is an unwarranted characterization of "applied sociology" as "dirty work," in contrast with "clean" academically based sociological teaching and research. But this initial insight can be further specified, for the work of the S-W-C is likely to be just the kind of sociological dirty work envisioned by those Deutscher addresses in contrast with the case-based, project-oriented, "respectable" efforts of the consulting sociologist.

The Sociologist-in-Reserve Role

If consulting sociology is a kind of "clean" applied sociology, and nonsociological task "consulting" by sociologists is "sociological dirty work," then there is a third occupational role that comes into view—one that the greater majority of sociology graduates who work outside academia are likely to take on. I referred to these earlier as sociologists-in-reserve to allude to both sports-related and Marxian usages of the term "reserve." To Marx, the "reserve army of the unemployed" was a group of displaced, rootless persons whose dire straits made the holding of any job, no matter how onerous, seem like a privilege. Borrowing further, although somewhat selectively, from Marx, the sociologist-in-reserve is apt to suffer a kind of "false consciousness," believing that his or her sociology degree has led to job placement and has provided special technical skills that will make possible the application of sociological perspectives in "an applied setting."

Turning to the sports metaphor, then, these lumpen-sociologists' social position is much like that of playground basketball players who see themselves eventually as National Basketball Association stars and who consider athletic achievement to be *the* exclusive door to a successful career track. Viewing themselves as tomorrow's "Dr. J.," "Magic," or "Bird," such youth may forego other opportunities for career achievement, namely, their formal educations. Educators and social critics alike have appropriately criticized a system of athletics that involves unrealistic promises and expectations for career success and diversion from more worthwhile investments of time and effort. But no similar outcry is heard on behalf of today's and tomorrow's sociology students, envisioning a career of sociological superstardom as the next Dr. A., Dr. B., Dr. C., or Dr. D., many of whom urge these students to consider the "promising" prospects of an applied consulting sociology career—and this done primarily to enlist them as students in a course or as majors in the field.

CONCLUSION

It should be clear that the prospects for growth in sociological consulting work are defined and constrained by conditions that exist in the field of sociology itself and in American society at large. What today's conditions call for is greater realism about sociological career paths and about the general lack of awareness of and appreciation for sociology on the part of members of our individualistic, consumeristic, and increasingly conservative society. It may well be that instead of infiltrating the "applied world" through consulting work and other part-time sociologizing that sociologists may have to be content with holding the ground they now have in academia and being honest about the field's macrosystem, basic-science orientation and what such entails for one's career prospects under these conditions.

Those of us who have already chosen the sociological "calling" need to come to terms with the consequences of that career choice and not attempt to make society over into something it is not. Let us bear in mind, as we mull over ways to recruit more students into our courses and programs of study, the potential alienation and greater societal hostility that undeliverable promises can manufacture. Riesman (1950, 120) has accurately depicted the condition of one who has determined a life course and found the "material" with which that work must be accomplished to be inaccessible or not manipulable in expected ways:

There is often tragedy in store for the inner-directed person who may fail to live up to grandiose dreams and may have to struggle in vain against both the intractability of the material and the limitations of his own powers. He will be held, and will hold himself, to his commitment.

The vocation of consulting sociology is still taking shape, and the social and scientific conditions for its emergency currently dictate that the "real world" and "consulting sociologists" remain largely unready for each other.

REFERENCES

Babbie, Earl R. 1979. *The Practice of Social Research,* 2d ed. Belmont, Calif.: Wadsworth.
Brown, William. 1984. "Identification of Specific Non-Research Competencies to Prepare Sociology Majors for Non-Academic Careers." Orlando: University of Central Florida. Mimeographed.

D'Antonio, William V. 1982. Correspondence to ASA Members, December 30. Washington, D.C.: American Sociological Association.

Deutscher, Irwin. 1983. "Sociological Work: The Mystique of Applied Sociology as Dirty Work." Addison Locke Roache Lecture, Indiana University-Purdue University, Indianapolis, April 15, 1983. Akron: The University of Akron. Mimeographed.

Freidson, Eliot. 1970. *Profession of Medicine: A Study of the Sociology of Applied Knowledge.* New York: Harper and Row.

Greenwood, Ernest. 1972. "Attributes of a Profession." In *Sociological Perspectives on Occupations,* edited by Ronald M. Pavalko, pp. 3–16. Itasca, Ill.: F. E. Peacock.

Heller, Scott. 1984. "Bad Market for Sociologists Prompts Efforts to Train Them for Posts Outside Academe." *The Chronicle of Higher Education,* May 23, pp. 21–23.

Lyson, Thomas A., and Gregory D. Squires. 1982. "The Promise and Perils of Applied Sociology: A Survey of Non-Academic Employers." Clemson, S.C.: Department of Agricultural Economics and Rural Sociology, Clemson University. Mimeographed.

Morris, William, ed. 1976. *The American Heritage Dictionary of the English Language.* Boston: Houghton Mifflin.

Pavalko, Ronald M., ed. 1972. *Sociological Perspectives on Occupations.* Itasca, Ill.: F. E. Peacock.

Riesman, David. 1950. *The Lonely Crowd: A Study of Changing American Character.* New Haven, Conn.: Yale University Press.

Watkins, Beverly T. 1981. "The Sociology of Sociology: Fewer Positions on College Faculties, Falling Enrollments, and Budget Cuts." *The Chronicle of Higher Education,* September 9, p. 6.

Weber, Max. 1958. "Science as a Vocation." In *Essays from Max Weber,* edited by Hans Gerth and C. Wright Mills, pp. 129–56. New York: Oxford University Press.

Wendell, Walter I. 1972. "A Marginal Professional Role: The Chiropractor." In *Sociological Perspectives on Occupations,* edited by Ronald M. Pavalko, pp. 40–55. Itaska, Ill.: F. E. Peacock.

PART II

Consulting Activities for Sociologists

The lack of relevance of sociological knowledge to the solutions of contemporary social and political problems has been recognized as an area of concern for the disciple. As aptly expressed by Marvin Olsen (1981), "Be relevant or be ignored!" This is indeed a considerable challenge that faces sociology since theoretical and methodological limitations do exist within the field. Sociology does not have all the answers to today's social problems. But then, neither do psychology or economics have all the answers for problems within their realm of expertise.

Whether or not a discipline has clearly established a set of valid scientific principles for understanding and solving problems is not the issue. Indeed there is no "truth" in science. The validity of scientific principles is only relative to the amount of evidence that substantiates it. Scientists are expected to search continually for new evidence to make yesterday's knowledge obsolete.

What is important for a discipline to be considered viable and an influential science in society is that it represent a "workable myth" (Boros 1984). According to Boros this means that a science (sociology) must be believable in terms of other cultural elements and workable in terms of solving problems of life.

For consulting sociologists it is therefore important to establish that their work has policy implications. They must be able to clarify to users the potentials of sociological theory and methods and how sociological results can be interpreted. However, it is also vital for consulting sociologists to recognize and communicate the limitations of what they are doing.

Part II of this book identifies a number of consulting activities in which sociological knowledge and methodological techniques are applied. The areas identified do not necessarily represent applications solely within the realm of sociology. Indeed there may be consultants with different backgrounds who are doing similar work. Furthermore, the areas of expertise discussed do not represent an exhaustive list of sociological applications. The chapters in this part of the book attempt to establish the relevance of sociology for solving selected problems and the extent to which sociological work can have policy implications.

In Chapter 3, Gilbert Fornaciari and BJ Chakiris discuss the area of organization development (OD) as it relates to the sociologist as an organization development consultant. They examine the components of organization development and how sociologists function as OD specialists. Furthermore, they identify the skills that are necessary to conduct OD intervention and the sequence of OD phases—from initial contact and entry into the organization through reentry. The authors conclude by looking at future trends in the OD field.

In Chapter 4, Bruce Koppel examines the sociological consultant in international development. Important dimensions of the sociologist's role as an international development consultant are described and the implications for professional preparation and development are identified. Koppel argues that sociological consulting in any context raises some traditional issues of applied sociology. In an international context, however, particularly for American sociological consultants, these issues are presented in distinctly different ways.

In another application of both sociological knowledge and methodological techniques, Joseph Mercurio (Chapter 5) describes the suitability of sociologists to conduct store location research. Store location research is an area of expertise within the broader field of marketing research. The underlying function of this research process is to help retail firms make the best possible location decisions and to reduce the risk of failure. According to Mercurio, sociologists can bring to this type of research their understanding of the urban environment as well as their expertise in qualitative and quantitative data collection and analysis. The location or growth concerns of a retail firm are of a spatial nature. Consequently, the elements of urban ecology are relevant elements of analysis. For this practical application, the sociologist must reorient these concepts and view them as the dynamics that influence a retail form in its expansion strategy.

According to William Swatos, in Chapter 6, consulting for churches may well represent the oldest form of sociological practice in America. For today, Swatos identifies two categories of church consulting: complex organizational and local congregational. The first type is sponsored by denominational and interdenominational bureaucracies to address questions of concern to administrators. Local congregational research is often a spin-off from denominational projects. A local church interested in recruitment of new members may well make use of material supplied by a denominational agency. Some congregations, however, also hire sociologists—again, perhaps, through their larger structure—to work with them in addressing specific, immediate concerns in their fellowship or community. Sometimes this person may do little more than work with the congregation to develop an effective survey instrument or alternate data collection technique. In other instances the consultant may actually do the research, analyze its results, and take part in subsequent action strategies. Swatos also identifies another area for sociological consulting within the churches—clinical pastoral sociology. Here the sociologist is normally also an ordained person in some religious body and combines these two roles to address the problems individuals face as a result of the social relationships in which they live. This viewpoint differs from traditional "pastoral counseling" in that it emphasizes the web of social interaction as primary—including divine-human interaction as a form of social interaction—rather than the individual as standing relatively alone over against both divinity and society.

Keith Smith, in Chapter 7, presents a unique possibility for consulting in his discussion of combining sociology with engineering. His discussion is based largely on his own experience as both a trained engineer and a sociologist. However, he also argues that sociologist-engineer teams can prove to be useful in certain organizational settings. He identifies various kinds of consulting work for which these two rather disparate disciplines can be usefully applied in a mutually reinforcing manner. In particular, the combined disciplines can prove useful for organizational analysis and organizational change in complex, high-technology groups, especially in the public sector. To a lesser degree, the combination of disciplines can prove useful in social and policy change situations where applied technology is a dominant characteristic. In concluding, Smith offers some suggestions for organizing sociologist-engineer teams, securing acceptance, and carrying out the work.

REFERENCES

Boros, Alexander. 1984. "Sociology: The Workable Myth." Founders address, Second Annual Conference of the Society for Applied Sociology, Covington, Kentucky, October 13.

Olsen, Marvin. 1981. "Epilogue: The Future of Applied Sociology." In *Handbook of Applied Sociology,* edited by Marvin E. Olsen and Michael Micklin, pp. 561–581. New York: Praeger.

3

Organization Development and the Consulting Sociologist

GILBERT M. FORNACIARI AND BETTY JUNE CHAKIRIS

INTRODUCTION

The continued expansion of nontraditional markets for sociological services offers sociologists choices among emerging careers that are both challenging and rewarding. The focus of this chapter is on one such career: the consulting sociologist in the role of an organization development specialist. While engaged in such a role, the sociologist provides professional services to work/nonwork organizations on either a for-profit or not-for-profit (pro bono) basis. Examples of such OD services include the conducting of applied research projects (needs assessments, climate studies, and organization-wide audits); the facilitation of organizational change through direct and indirect involvement with individuals, work groups, and the organization as a whole; the development of training programs around key issues/problem areas; and the measurement of organizational change through longitudinal research and interventions. The provision of these OD services is both a goal of the consultant as well as a process of continuing to develop one's skills in an experiential fashion. Based on these latter points, this chapter presents both OD goals and processes relative to the sociologist consultant as an OD specialist.

Defining Organization Development

Organization development has been defined as "any planned organization-wide effort to increase the effectiveness and health of an organization through various "interventions" in the organizational

Table 3.1.
OD Intervention Levels and Sociological Units of Analysis

Intervention Level External dimension	Unit of Analysis Macro-sociological level
Organization	Sociological *cultural*
Work Group	Social Psychological *subcultural*
Individual	Psychological *Pyscho-socio Development* *Community* *Family*

Source: Compiled by the author.

processes using behavioral and management sciences technologist" (Lip-pitt 1982, vii).

A significant element of this definition of OD is that organizational (social-structural) *change* is *planned* rather than left to chance. That is, the OD practitioner is working in concert with the management of the organization. As such, he or she is directly/indirectly involved in planning and facilitating the implementation of change.

OD intervention efforts can occur on three systemic levels—individual, group, and organization, which are depicted in Table 3.1. These systemic levels of the organization can be thought of in terms of corresponding units of analysis in the behavioral science. As shown in Table 3.2, each particular level has a specific unifying factor as well as an internal and external responsiveness to action interfacing at that level.

Finally, OD specialists utilize a number of behavioral and management science perspectives and methodologies. OD is an *eclectic* discipline drawing many concepts from the behavioral sciences (including sociology, anthropology, and social psychology). Although both the study and practice of OD are becoming more widespread, there is still a relative paucity of theoretical models existing in the field. However, a variety of concepts have been defined and appropriate research methodologies developed. The theory is emerging out of the practice "grounded" in the field analysis. As a whole, grounded theories are emerging versus grand theories.

History of Organization Development

OD is a relatively new field, having its footing in the work of Kurt Lewin (1947) at the Massachusetts Institute of Technology. Lewin's influence on his colleagues Kenneth Benne, Leland Bradford, and Ronald

Table 3.2.
Levels of Analysis and Internal/External Organizational Responsiveness

Level	Unity	Internal Responsiveness	External Responsiveness
Individual	Identification of my basic beliefs; who I am; my uniqueness; self-concept, perceived self. Values: Am I open and other-oriented or closed and self-oriented?	Awareness of myself, my feelings, my needs, my defenses; freedom to fulfill my wants and needs	Hearing and responding to others; active listening; openness to ideas, experiences, persons; love—ability to enter into and establish enduring relationships; interpersonal attraction and involvement
Group	Identification of team goals and objectives; building the team; group achieves syntality (personality) and synergy (group output is greater than the sum of individual outputs)	Interpersonal skills; facilitation of interaction among team members; process observation; sensitivity and coherence; interpersonal attraction *or* cohesiveness develops	Gathering and relating external information relevant to task of team; linkage with other individuals and groups; cooperation for achievement of common purpose with other systems
Organization	Development of common goals of organization; management; according to purpose and mission	Ways components within an organization react to and affect each other; data sharing; organization development and human relations; linkage between individuals and groups	Organization responsiveness to larger community; social relevance, profitability

Source: From Oscar Mink, James Schultz, and Barbara Mink, *Developing and Managing Open Organizations.* © 1979. Reproduced by permission of the BJ Chakiris Corporation.

Lippitt led to their founding the National Training Laboratory, now located in Bethel, Maine (Warrick 1985, 917). Lewin's work in the area of social psychology included the theoretical construct of *forced field* analysis (whereby any driving force within an organization, group, individual are met by opposing resisting forces) and an emphasis on laboratory techniques for learning. The T-group, or training group, was a principal laboratory technique, emphasizing the use of experiential learning in understanding an individual's influence on the group and the group's influence on the individual.

Another influence on the development of OD was the emphasis on quantities and qualitative research techniques (for example, interview schedules, questionnaires, focus group techniques). Subsequent developments at the Survey Research Center at the University of Michigan led to the development of action research designs (Warwick 1985, 917).

Components of Organization Development

Figure 3.1 is a schematic portrayal of the authors' conception of organization development. The authors believe that these components represent salient characteristics but by no means exhaust all dimensions of the field. Taken together, these seven components integrate the concept of OD and serve here as a heuristic device. Operational definition and concrete examples of these components include:

1. *Organization Renewal:* This is a data-based *planned change process.* It is a participative approach to solving problems, in which feedback goes into the organization, and decisions and actions occur. The renewal process lends itself to a diversity of goals and looks at both the internal and external environment. The renewal process uses a general systems orientation involving and integrating all parts of the organization—human, technical, financial, and structural—*to appropriately respond to and manage ongoing and future situations, both internal and external while maintaining and strengthening the ability of the organization to productively and effectively renew itself... to remain continually viable in the future* (see Lippitt 1982; Rumley and Lippitt 1982).

2. *Human Resource Development* (HRD): "[This] is the activity of an organization that provides organized learning experiences for a specified period of time for the possibility of improving job performance or the growth of employees" (Nadler 1977). Nadler notes that there are three activity areas under HRD: training, education, and development.

3. *Needs Analysis:* This includes study into the structural blocks and opportunities existing within an organization (see National Institute of Mental Health 1977; Steadham 1985). An example would be undertaking a study to determine the need for child care services among employed business and industrial workers in a given country. The business and

Figure 3.1
Components of Organization Development

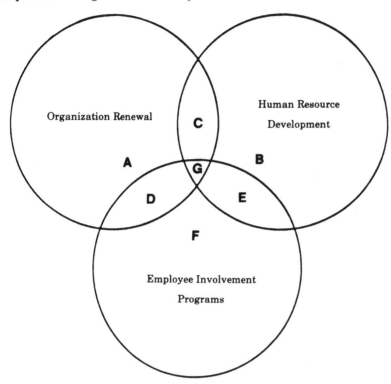

OD Components:

A. Organization Renewal   D. Socio-technical Systems
B. Human Resource Development   E. Climate studies
C. Needs Analysis   F. Employee Involvement Programs
                                      G. Human Resource Audit

Source: Compiled by the authors.

industrial community could then respond to these needs through onsite and or subsidized offsite daycare programs.

4. *Sociotechnical Systems:* This refers to the interaction between people, technology, and structure (see Passmore 1982). For example, bringing new electronic data processing equipment into a company should be

complemented by an understanding of how the organizational structure and its actors will interface with that technology and vice versa.

5. *Climate Studies:* These consist of organizational surveys that focus on the work atmosphere at a given point in time (see Chakiris 1984; Lees-Haley 1985). For example, an OD specialist might look at factors such as morale, communication, and organizational support in a customer service department of a large insurance company. Traditionally these studies *do not have a survey* feedback component.

6. *Employee Involvement Programs:* These consist of developed groups of employees (which can be made up on a horizontal/vertical fashion within the organization) that has as their task the continued growth of individual, group member, work teams, and the organization as a whole (see Beardsley 1985). Quality Circle groups as used in both Japan and the United States are an example here.

7. *Human Resource Audit:* The audit is a powerful tool that can integrate in an ongoing fashion all of the other six elements of OD. It consists of an *action research process* in which organizational members gather data in order to confirm strengths and surface opportunity areas in order to enhance the overall effectiveness of an organization (see Chakiris 1982). For example, a small but growing environmental engineering firm would use a data collection whereby information provided by employees from various work groups is feedback to those groups for action planning and implementation.

THE SOCIOLOGIST AS AN OD SPECIALIST

Not only currently, but in the future, a mark can be made on business and industry by the applied sociologist functioning as an OD practitioner.[1] However, to undertake consulting opportunities, several conditions must be considered. First, whether an internal or external consultant, the applied sociologist needs to become fully aware of the interaction of organizational life and organizational functions. A major flaw in the services of some OD consultants is that they have theoretical knowledge bases but lack practical knowledge and expertise. Hence, when a change is undertaken there may be a lack of information about the implications of that change. In other words, this change may include those who are affected and their interrelationships.

A second condition necessary for the sociologist is the use of language that is readily understood by managers. Given that those who are most affected by the work of the applied sociologist are the managers—technologists in their own right—a commonality of language needs to be developed (and this principally lies on the shoulders of the sociologist). Managers are mainly accountable for getting the product or service out the door and human interaction is a secondary function. Although managers are looking for improved methods of doing work, it must be in a language they can understand and immediately put into practice if it is to have a significant impact on the improvement of the effectiveness of the organization.

In addition, the manager is responsible for the impact on the market community of his or her actions. Indeed, management is not always aware of this impact. In order to assist business people with this problem, the sociologist's principal expertise key must be to develop and utilize skills in organizational structures, systems, and dynamics.

THE CONSULTATION PROCESS

Multiple Roles of the Consultant

The OD practitioner needs to have comfort in using the multiple skills of a consultant (see Figure 3.2). These include both directive and nondirective skills. The consultant influences by his or her competence in the use of these multiple roles using each role appropriately for the situation or the particular consulting phase. For example, given that the client has agreed to administer the human resource audit, the consultant advocates (directive role) that the client choose specific methods of data collecting, training staff members in the administering of the instrument, giving feedback, and conducting action planning sessions. This advocate role, while very directive, is a legitimate role for the OD consultant in that the client initially requires direction and training in how to collect and use data.

The technical specialist roles include informational experts, manufacturing technology experts, and other specialists who are called in as content experts in specific disciplines.

During OD consultation efforts consultants are often called on to perform the trainer/educator and joint problem-solver role. They may be asked to facilitate training and orientation sessions. They may also be requested to design meetings and conferences (such as feedback sessions). As part of these multiple roles OD practitioners are required to perform other such roles as fact finder, process counselor, and objective observer/reflector.

In essence, the continuum of the multiple roles requires the OD sociologist to be skilled in all the roles, choosing the appropriate one to match the given situation and/or consulting phase. Additionally, the consultant trains the client(s) to become skilled in each role.

Figure 3.2
Multiple Roles of the Consultant

Objective Observer/ Reflector	Process Counselor	Fact Finder	Alternative Identifier and Linker	Joint Problem Solver	Trainer Educator	Informational Expert	Advocate

CLIENT

CONSULTANT

LEVEL OF CONSULTANT ACTIVITY IN PROBLEM SOLVING

Nondirective   Directive

Raises questions for reflection	Observes problem-solving process and raises issues mirroring feedback	Gathers data and stimulates thinking interpretives	alternatives alternatives and resources for client and helps assess consequences	Offers alternatives and participates in decisions	Trains client	Regards, links, and provides policy or practice decisions	Proposes guidelines, persuades, or directs in the problem-solving process

Source: From Gordon and Ronald Lippitt. *Consulting Process In Action.* University Associates. © 1978.

Reproduced by permission of the BJ Chakiris Corporation.

Phases of the OD Consulting Process

Each work-related organization is at a particular developmental stage relative to the adoption of organization development; therefore, any OD professional contemplating entry, whether internal or external, must be aware of *where the organization is* when he or she is attempting to diffuse OD-related programs into organizations. Thus both internal/external change agents and organizational decision makers must be communicating at the same awareness level regarding the particular programmatic activity being discussed. Further, there must be certain preconditions within the organization for the possible adoption of programs and activities. This line of reasoning directly follows the empirical and theoretical work of diffusion and adoption researchers (Rogers 1962; and Rogers and Schumaker 1971).

The OD process takes the form of six phases as shown in Table 3.3. Described below are some of the elements and dimensions of each phase.

Phase 1: Initial Contact and Entry. This is the start-up of a relationship between client and OD consultant. Targets of entry include establishing rapport, developing trust and openness, creating clearer expectations about what is to be done, reducing unrealistic dependency, and collecting the initial information about the problem or change desired. There are three kinds of entry and contact: self-initiated by the OD consultant, the consultant is invited in by the client, and the consultant is imposed by another person. The dilemmas of entry include legitimization, power and authority issues, economics, readiness and timing, experience with other OD consultants (positive or negative), and whether the client and consultant perceive they can work together.

Phase 2: Contract Formulation and Relationship Establishment. During this phase the client and the consultant formulate a definition of how they intend to work together. It ranges from informal verbal statements and a shake of a hand to a written formal contract. The elements of contract formulation require looking at what outcomes are desired, role definitions of who does what, and what time perspectives and accountabilities need to be defined. Critical to this phase is looking ahead at how the OD effort will be measured and evaluated. The OD consultant needs to pay close attention to what will be measured and who will measure the results. Contract formulation occurs throughout the consulting process and requires that at regular progress checkpoints feedback is initiated between client and consultant. Again, as in Phase 1 Phase 2 requires trust and openness in the relationship.

Phase 3: Problem Identification and Diagnostic Analysis. This is the data-generating phase in which the problem or opportunity is researched through instrumentation, interviews, questionnaires, observation, focus groups, creative brainstorming, and examining documentation. Critical

Table 3.3
Phases of the Consulting Process

Phases	Decisions and Actions
1. Initial Contact and Entry	1. Initiative of making first contact 2. Indentify and clarify need for change 3. Explore readiness for change 4. Explore potential for working together
2. Contract Formulation and Relationship Establishment	5. What outcomes are desired? 6. Who would need to do what? 7. Time perspective and accountability
3. Problem Identification & Diagnostic Analysis	8. Force-field diagnosis and deriving action possibilities
4. Goal Setting and Planning	9. Projecting goals 10. Planning for action and involvement—what? who? when?
5. Action Taking and Feedback Cycling	11. Successful action taking 12. Evaluation and guiding feedback 13. Revising action and mobilizing additional resources
6. Contract Completion, Continuity and Support	14. Design for continuity supports 15. Completion plans

Source: From Gordon & Ron Lippitt, BJ Chakiris, and Robert W. Pirsein. "The Consulting Process In Action Skill Development Kit." University Associates. © 1978. Reprinted by permission of the BJ Chakiris Corporation.

to this phase is how the data will be collected, who will do the collecting, what skills are required for interviewing, what confidentiality is required, how feedback will be given, and what involvement is needed. This phase projects desired outcomes and identifies both supportive and restraining forces using the force-field techniques. Out of this data/information action derivations are identified as the client and consultant we move toward action planning (in Phase 4).

Phase 4: Goal Setting and Planning. This phase involves action at the appropriate levels of the organization. This can include senior officers, upper- and middle-line management, staff professionals, supervisors, and individual employees. The planning can occur across functions and within functions, departments, and divisions. Often during the planning phase temporary task forces, committees, steering groups, and ad hoc subgroups are formed around specific tasks or projects. During this phase the OD consultant is mindful that multiple goals exist in an organization and attempts to work through this goal alignment required to match the organization's mission, purpose, and direction, while not losing sight of the individual and group goals. Phase 4 has specific pitfalls as well. These include planning without involving the people who will implement the plan. The OD consultant designs interventions and planning sessions with various levels and functions such that ownership, motivation, and milestones of progress are made visible during action implementation (Phase 5).

Phase 5: Action Taking and Feedback Cycling. This phase is at the essence of OD consultation, that is, achievement of results. Here is where it happens or it doesn't. During this phase the OD consultant may need to mobilize additional resources, initiate feedback to see how things are working, provide support, and revise plans where needed. Critical to the action taking/feedback cycling is the careful monitoring of results. Evaluation should include: looking at the client and consultant relationship to see how things are going; looking at the interim goals (such as intervention events and milestone evaluation); and looking at the overall progress toward a goal or desired outcome. Competent OD consultants welcome feedback. They also help clients learn how to initiate and receive helpful feedback. Key to the OD consultation effort is the strengthening of the internal resources. This client development often requires training, education, and orientation sessions. OD facilitation interventions, for example, often include training clients in problem solving, productivity studies, career planning and development, designing human resource management systems, and strategic planning. Often the internal OD consultant initiates contact with the external OD consultant to assist in the OD efforts (such as the development of the executive team, co-facilitating role negotiation across departments, implementing a macroorganization renewal process using the human resource audit throughout the organization, and so on).

Phase 6: Contract Completion, Continuity, and Support. This requires in-depth reflection planning for OD consultants. When well designed, this phase includes reducing the amount of time the OD consultant needs to spend with a particular client engagement. A dilemma of contract completion is when to pull away. The OD consultant asks, "If I pull away too soon will the client be able to continue the effort?" "Are there sufficient resources available to the client without my help?" "How might I keep in touch with the client to provide occasional support visits or establish other linkages to ensure the client gives adequate attention to sustain the change effort?" During this phase clients plan for such events as re-audits, assessment and evaluation projects, new schedules for updating planning, periodic futuring sessions with managers and employees, and reviews of product/service with customers.

We are reminded of a comment Jack Gibb (1978), an OD practitioner, once made: "Help is not always helpful!" Essentially what he was saying is that OD consultation is the act/or/art of giving help to a help-needing client or client system. This means when the consultant, who is a temporary intermediary, gives help he or she should leave the client strengthened and capable of carrying out the change effort. At the same time the client learns in the consulting relationship, so does the OD consultant. One outcome of using the action research model is that there is mutual learning and involvement between client and consultant. Both are involved in the learning and the change processes.

TRENDS IN THE FIELD OF ORGANIZATION DEVELOPMENT

The authors, having both studied the OD field and practiced extensively as professional OD consultants, developed a number of trends for you, the reader and *practitioner*. These trends are cast in the form of a number of management situations with corresponding implications for management training and development on the part of the OD (sociologist) consultant.

Organization Situation	OD Challenge
1. Increased need to unify the organization in terms of its mission and strategy within an ever-changing global market and world environment.	Increased world market exposure for products and services. Skills in global marketing and intercultural communication to work across cultures.
2. Increased need for visionary and total resource management, using "holistic" approach to organization development (human systems development).	Planning skills in goal integration and human systems renewal theory (for example, manufacturing with marketing; organization with world community; employees' work with life goals).
3. Increased need for flexible organizational structures for appropriate organizational responsiveness.	Skills in how to work as both team leader and team member, "teaming" and "peering" across business units.
4. Increased need for participative organizational cultures to enhance creativity, cross business synergy, innovation to solve complex problems.	Skills, knowledge, and criteria in how to form and manage project groups, task forces, and action research teams within the organization.
5. Increased interface of technology and human systems (for example, management information systems, robotics, office automation).	Skills to combine information with human decision systems and an awareness of social implications of technological change.

Organization Situation	OD Challenge
6. Workers' changing values toward the whole notion of work and the increased need on the part of managers to provide worker/job satisfaction, quality of work life, product, and service.	Counseling and consultative management skills in how to conduct a meaningful dialogue and involve employees in planning and implementating organizational vision and mission.
7. Worker/job obsolescence and disappearing jobs, a more static work force, less upward mobility, reduced career fulfillment.	Developing internal study groups to investigate Worker/Job Obsolescence and conducting Proneness Audit for early warning signals in organizations.
8. Concern that upcoming younger workers may have more loyalty to their profession than to the organization.	Increased use of entrepreneurial skills to manage professional interdependence creatively between units.
9. Increased need for meaningful performance appraisal and opportunity for individuals to see how they can be challenged and develop.	Individual development and professional growth plans that factor in life goals, work goals, and organizational goals.
10. The trend of organizations to become institutions of learning with line managers performing roles of change agents, educators, and mentors.	Imparting skills of how people learn, developing effective models of working with and through others to initiate and implement needed change.

CONCLUSION

An integrated or holistic perspective that includes both the sociologists' spheres of theoretical knowledge and his or her consulting expertise of practices provides a more comprehensive understanding of organizational behavior.

Consistent with these ideas, becoming a successful OD consultant demands that sociologists take a look at the totality of their skills in a *holistic* fashion rather than focusing only on those skills learned in an academic setting. This requires that applied sociologists develop an understanding of their own personal acceptance of self in order to interact efficiently and effectively with clients, be they internal or external. In addition, there are organizational constraints that are different from academic constraints. These need to be identified and adapted to if the applied sociologists are to find their niche in the applied community. In this light, we ask the reader to review Table 3.4.

Action research is a viable option for an organization to use in response

Table 3.4
Perspectives of the Sociologist as an OD Practitioner and the Traditional Academic Sociologist

The Sociologist as an OD Practitioner	The Traditional Academic Sociologist
Inclusive orientation	Exclusive orientation
Assertive	Reflective
People oriented	Idea oriented
Synthesist	Analyst
Enterprising	Intellectual
Facilitative leader	Independent thinker
Extrovert	Introvert
Oriented toward action research	Oriented toward systematic investigation
Concerned about business management	Interested in philosophical ideas and values
Results oriented	Seeker of truth
Concerned about client problems and opportunities	Concerned about research problems

Source: Compiled by the authors.

to anticipated challenges and trends in the global marketplace. Action research brings together research and practicality, the academician and the practitioner working together to collect data, analyze and interpret data, develop action derivations, implement action, monitor and recycle the model.

The phases of the action research model provided in this chapter can be used as a framework for data-based organizational change. The sociologist needs to educate and train others, including managers, in the use of the action research methodology in how to gather and use information such that organizations can anticipate and plan for change.

There is a *challenge* for the sociologist today that is even greater than it has been historically. It is the *opportunity* to impact the present and the future in fluid and dynamic organizational systems that have requirements that seek responses. To what degree this can be met is incumbent on sociologists if they want to be absorbed by the business community.

NOTE

1. The Sociologist as an OD Specialist is taken from Gilbert M. Fornaciari and Mary Coeli Meyer, "Generating Consulting Contracts in the Socio-Technical Field." (Paper presented at the 1982 Illinois Sociological Association Annual Meeting, Bloomington, Illinois.)

REFERENCES

Beardsley, Jefferson F. 1985. "Quality Circles." In *Human Resources and Development Handbook,* edited by William R. Tracey, pp. 326–40. New York: Amacom.

Chakiris, B. J. 1984. "Organizational Climate Survey." Chicago: BJ Chakiris Corporation. Offset (Copyrighted).

———. 1982. *The Human Resource Audit Facilitation Manual.* Chicago: BJ Chakiris Corporation. Offset.

Fornaciari, Gilbert M., and Mary Coeli Meyer. 1982. "Generating Consulting Contracts in the Socio-Technical Field." Paper presented at the 1982 Illinois Sociological Association Annual Meeting, Bloomington, Illinois.

Gibb, Jack. 1978. "Current Theory and Practice in Organization Development." Speech given at OD Network Annual Conference, March 16–17, 1978, San Francisco, California.

Lees-Haley, Paul R., and Cheryl E. Lees-Haley. 1985. "Attitude and Opinion Surveys." In *Human Resources Management and Development Handbook,* edited by William R. Tracey, pp. 715–27. New York, Amacom.

Lewin, Kurt. 1947. "Feedback Problems of Social Diagnosis and Action." In *Frontiers in Group Dynamics,* edited by Kurt Lewin, pp. 441–44. London: Tavistock.

Lippitt, Gordon L. 1982. *Organization Renewal: A Holistic Approach to Organization Development.* Englewood Cliffs, N.J.: Prentice-Hall.

———, and Ronald Lippitt. 1978. *The Consulting Process In Action.* LaJolla, Calif.: University Associates.

Mink, Oscar G., James M. Schultz, and Barbara P. Mink. 1979. *Developing and Managing Open Organizations.* Austin, Tex.: Learning Concepts.

Nadler, David A. 1977. *Feedback and Organization Development: Using Data-Based Methods.* Reading, Mass.: Addison-Wesley.

National Institute of Mental Health. 1977. *Needs Assessment Approaches: Concepts and Methods.* Washington, D.C.: U.S. Department of Health, Education and Welfare (Public Health Services—Alcohol, Drug Abuse, and Mental Health Administration).

Passmore, William S. 1982. "Socio-Technical System Interventions." In *Organization Development: Managing Transitions,* edited by Ernest J. Parlock, pp. 73–80. Alexandria, Va.: American Society of Training and Development.

Rogers, Everet E. 1962. *Diffusion of Innovations.* New York: The Free Press.

———, and Floyd Schumaker. 1971. *Communication of Innovations: A Cross Cultural Approach.* New York: The Free Press.

Rumley, Jacqueline, and Gordon Lippitt. 1982. *Organization Renewal* (workbook). Washington, D.C.: Organization Renewal, Inc.

Steadham, Stephen V. and Maria A. E. Clay. 1985. "Needs Assessment." In *Human Resources Management and Development Handbook,* edited by William R. Tracey, pp. 1338–52. New York: Amacom.

Warrick, D. D. 1985. "Organization Development." In *Human Resources Management and Development Handbook,* edited by William R. Tracey, pp. 915–25. New York: Amacom.

4

Sociological Consultancy and International Development

BRUCE KOPPEL

Many more sociologists are leaving graduate school with international interests than there are professional opportunities for them to pursue these interests. Among the opportunities that do exist, it is very probable that limited-term consultancies substantially exceed career-track staff positions. In many other cases, academically based sociologists, whose core teaching and research output will not necessarily be international, spend a small proportion of time periodically as international development consultants. For these two major streams of the sociological pool, as well as any other streams, the practice of sociological consultancy in international development contexts needs to confront the issues of professional preparation and development:

- Is there anything special about applied sociology for international development and international sociological consultancy that needs to be reflected and incorporated in educational preparation of sociology graduate students?

- What is professional development as an international development sociological consultant? What are the problems in maintaining professional development and what are the challenges of verifying that professional development is occurring?

To answer these questions, it is necessary to convey a picture of what sociological consultancy in an international development context is. This chapter will describe important dimensions of the sociologist's role as an international development consultant and then address issues of professional preparation and development of sociologists.

THE ROLES OF THE SOCIOLOGICAL CONSULTANT IN
AN INTERNATIONAL DEVELOPMENT CONTEXT

What is the international development context in which consultant activities by American sociologists typically occur? Here are some examples:

- A World Bank project to rehabilitate an irrigation system that involves identifying, assessing, forming, and strengthening local farmer irrigation associations and improving the capabilities of extension agents to work with farmer associations.

- A project supported by the United States Agency for International Development (AID) to improve local government project identification and implementation capacities through changes in internal organization and personnel management.

- An urban health project supported by the United Nations Development Program (UNDP) that involves the identification of at-risk neighborhoods and households, the design of appropriate support services, and the implementation of program and benefit monitoring systems.

What is different about these examples from a similar list of domestic illustrations may not be the projects per se, but rather interactions between the projects and the contexts in which these projects are functioning. These interactions can give a special twist to questions about the practice of sociological consultancy. What are some examples of these questions?

1. What issues emerge from the often "critical" training that American sociologists receive in graduate school? American graduate students are encouraged to demonstrate "critical" thinking during the course of graduate preparation. In this context, "critical" often refers to specific philosophical and political sensitivities and perspectives, not simply to pragmatic or "questioning" intelligence. Do graduate education emphases on neo-Marxist concepts, political economy analyses, or populist perspectives create special difficulties for the definition and application of sociological knowledge in international settings?

2. Are there limits on the international transferability of what is known in the United States as "good" sociology? To the extent that there are limits, are the limits primarily the result of where sociology is practiced or are they inherent in the concepts and methods of "good" sociology? How does a consultant resolve such questions without having a continuing familiarity with basic *and* applied sociological research within *and* outside the United States? How does a consultant even acknowledge such questions without succumbing to the temptation of treating applied sociology as an "inferior" product?

3. Does the American sociological consultant working in an international setting need to understand why a foreign sociologist has been requested? Does the American consultant have professional responsibilities to ensure that, in some way, the local sociological community benefits from the consultant's presence?

4. What responsibilities, if any, does the consultant have to advocate the adoption of positions supported by sociological analysis? Are these responsibilities "offset" by political and social working contexts that do not expect or reward advocacy?

Social Soundness Analysis

None of these questions are completely unique to the international development working environment. However, these and similar questions acquire special form in the international development environment for the sociological consultant. A good example is social soundness analysis (SSA), which was incorporated by AID into its normal project formulation and appraisal procedures in the early 1970s. The idea was to ensure that the following issues were considered during the course of project preparation: the sociocultural context; the mutual adaptability of project strategy and the beneficiary system; the participation of beneficiaries, especially women and minorities, in a project; the distribution of costs and benefits; spread effects, that is, secondary and tertiary social consequences of a project; and data needed by project management to ensure good implementation and facilitate project evaluation. These issues and what AID expected in the way of answers were described in an AID handbook. In principle, a project could be subjected to considerable modification, delay, or even cancellation if an SSA exercise determined that SSA issues were inadequately addressed in project design or that negative social consequences, in terms of SSA issues, were very probable outcomes of project implementation.

Practitioners of SSA were expected to accept as issues what the handbook identified as issues. Project advocates grew accustomed to expecting from SSA what the handbook promised—no more and no less. In specific situations an SSA that rigorously adhered to the handbook might raise questions that were not relevant (for example, participation of women in settings where this was not a primary issue in the social division of labor) and ignore questions that were (such as whether a project's specification of beneficiaries was appropriate). However, SSA was typically expected by an AID mission ultimately to offer a "yes" or "no" on the major questions. That became AID's minimum need and interest.

Social soundness analyses are typically conducted by sociological (including anthropological) consultants. However, sociologists asked to conduct SSAs are often given relatively short terms (two–four weeks) to complete their work. This has not proven to be enough time to do many things sociologists would want to do to answer the handbook's questions. For example, if a complex rural development project's probable influence area covered several thousand households engaged in heterogeneous economic activities, how could a sociologist do much more than a superficial appraisal of the probable distribution of social costs and benefits or of the incidence of "spread effects?" Time would not permit designing and implementing any survey research, and often time would not permit secondary analyses of surveys that had been previously implemented. Unless the sociologist was familiar with the culture area, time might not permit identification of reliable key informants. Rapid rural appraisal techniques might be used, but the conclusions the appraisals generate are subject to challenge from economists and project advocates, particularly if the conclusions are not favorable to the project. Could defensible conclusions about "social fit" be made and defended in this kind of working context?

The picture is not completed there, however. While AID might be providing the major hard-currency support and many other inputs as well, AID projects do not occur in the United States. They occur in other sovereign countries where there may well be different ideas about project identification, project preparation, requirements to substantiate beneficiary participation as part of project appraisal, and so on. These "different" ideas, particularly as they relate to social soundness, should not be dismissed as "anti-equity." Insisting, for example, that an SSA verify that the roles of women and minorities are enhanced by a project may be counter to deeply held cultural and religious standards. In many cases, countries see the benefits of a project as "self-evident" (such as irrigation to dry areas) and therefore see the time, resources, and potential power assigned to SSA as dubious. Social soundness, as represented by the SSA handbook, establishes a view of and context for sociological input that has been rationalized in terms of AID as an institution and AID's domestic needs to justify and defend its global programming to various constituencies *within* the United States. SSA was not established with the understanding that it could vary with local interpretations of social soundness.

This is not simply a matter of AID imposing the fashions of development thinking in Washington on AID missions and national governments in developing countries. The process is considerably more symbiotic. Both AID and the country need the project, although perhaps for different reasons. Nevertheless, both AID and the country are willing to insist on and ignore different things in order to get the project. SSA will be in the middle, but not always in-between. Unfortunately, one response that many consultants have chosen is to put sociology in their hip pockets and do the superficial and supportive work that everyone appears most prepared to accept with the least thorough evaluation. This is an unfortunate course because it does little to improve understanding of what the roles of sociological knowledge might be.

Multilaterally Assisted Development Projects

Sociological input in multilaterally assisted development projects tends to come later in the project cycle and generally is not nearly as codified as the AID case. For the World Bank, the Asian Development Bank, the United Nations Development Program, and so on, there is no social soundness analysis. Sociological consultancy will arise on an as-needed basis; it is not required. Sociological input of some sort may be requested for education, nutrition, and welfare-oriented projects; for projects that involve local organizations and beneficiary user groups for project services; for projects involving population relocation; and assorted other cases. In the last few years, some of the multilateral institutions (notably the International Fund for Agricultural Development and the Asian Development Bank) have begun to be more systematically concerned with generating baseline information on beneficiary characteristics and to encourage what has been called benefit monitoring and evaluation. The impetus for this interest is primarily a result of frustration with projects that do not work as expected (project completion is delayed, cost overruns are high, disbursement rates on loans are low, and project effects are less than anticipated), largely, it is believed, because the beneficiaries of such projects are not participating (that is, committing local resources) in the ways that were expected. Baseline information would indicate whether prospective beneficiaries understood how they might benefit and what they would have to do for these benefits to occur. Here again, the juxtaposition of multiple criteria can occur—not only between external agency and host government, but between those two and the consultant's insights about why a specific project appears to be mutually acceptable.

As an example, I can report a situation where a multilateral development assistance agency had decided to compel borrowing countries to monitor project benefits by making what is known internationally as project benefit monitoring and evaluation (PBME) a requirement for approving project loan agreements. I was asked to implement a workshop that would provide an overview of how to do benefit monitoring for managers of projects financed by loans from the institution. Preparatory field visits before the workshop revealed only vague understanding of what benefit monitoring was. Often the whole exercise was seen as a waste of time, generating useless and even unwelcome information. Several times, I was told that if the multilateral wanted PBME information, the multilateral should take the responsibility for getting and using that information—but none of that should have anything to do with implementing the project or deciding whether the project was "good" or "bad." Publicly, however, only statements of support and good intentions could be found. The multilateral was imposing its own notions of what was needed. The host governments had not objected, but were doing no more than was absolutely necessary. The governments believed that the need that they and the multilaterals had to "do" projects would not really be threatened by any insistence on compliance with the benefit-monitoring clause of project loan agreements. Some staff within the multilateral itself shared that view.

I was supposed to run a workshop that assumed there were no questions about the "why" of benefit monitoring, or about what benefit monitoring was, who could do it, what use it was, and so on. My solution was to sell all parties on the idea that monitoring information was a management tool. Hence, I would make the workshop a project management workshop and would ask the participants to prepare case studies about management problems from which I could derive some benefit-monitoring issues. The result was positive, in the sense that both my employer and the governments came to their own conclusions about the value (and the limits) of benefit monitoring as a management tool. One point this case illustrates is that sometimes, in fact many times, the solution for the sociological consultant is not to diminish the quality or scope of sociological input, but to offer that input with any other input that helps things happen. In this case, it was project management. In other cases, I have used economic planning, technology assessment, and once, even plant pathology.

Working Directly with a Developing Country Government

The sociological consultant working for a bilateral or multilateral institution in a developing country faces a situation involving a juxtaposition of objectives and criteria. What about the consultant who works directly for a developing country government? Here several issues arise. As a sociologist, why am I there (rather than a local sociologist)? How should I relate to local sociologists who may be on a team with me, perhaps knowing much more but certainly earning much less? How do I relate myself to local expectations about what sociologists have to offer, expectations that often take the form of "support it and defend it; don't be 'anti' what a government wants to do?"

I was asked by a developing country government to evaluate an ongoing project that was developing a social accounting system. I led a team that included two local sociologists, both with graduate training in the United States, and two economists, also well-trained. Nutrition was one of the indicators on which the accounting system was going to report. Data were presented in terms of a single mean number of caloric intake per capita. In that way, the population was seen to be above minimum United Nations daily requirements.

I knew, however, that disaggregated data would show about 60 percent of the population below the UN minimum. In the course of reviewing project files (which my local colleagues could not see), I discovered that a high-level government official had mandated that no "unfavorable" presentations should enter the final social accounting system. As the time for a presentation of our evaluation to a government committee approached, what was I to do? What were we to do? There were various costs to local social scientists if they objected to the indicator. I could say "what I liked" but how would that reflect on the people who hired me? On the other team members? If none of us said anything, where did that leave sociological input? We had to reach a solution as a group and as a group we decided to suggest that disaggregation of social indicators on a spatial basis be considered. This sidestepped sensitivities to distinctions based on income groups—which were the sensitivities we understood to be most problematic. However, since we knew that poverty had regional regularities, and we also knew that budget allocations were done primarily on a regional basis, we concluded that suggesting that the social accounting system report caloric means by region was a reasonable compromise that could constructively influence budgetary resource allocation. The recommendation met a vigorous reaction, but it was accepted.

The consultant's role in an international development context rarely offers "clean" outcomes. The challenge is to achieve balanced outcomes within a working context that is itself a subject of sociological insight. The pursuit of the "most that can be done" outcome, in an international development context, will often mean spending considerable effort to understand why various elements of the working situation are as they are.

THE ISSUE OF PRAXIS

Praxis is the challenge of practice, of using sociological theory in the real world, not to verify theory but to verify application. Among the most difficult issues that applied sociology in any context confronts are those issues that accompany attempts to put popular rhetoric, aspirations, and developmental values to a real-world test. How does the sociologist translate notions of critical theory, political economy, populism, or participatory development into applied positions? The question is not "simply" an issue of "how" to go from theoretical knowledge to applicable knowledge, but a question of "whether" the link can be made.

Participatory Development

An example of the praxis problem in international development is the issue of participation as a cornerstone of development strategy. Sociological insight and considerable development experience suggest that much of the mixed record in development experience can be attributed to inadequate participation by project beneficiaries in project identification, implementation, and management. Irrigation projects are a good illustration. Irrigation projects are among the most delayed and expensive, but also among the most useful and important of international development projects. Most of them cover tens of thousands of hectares each and include thousands of small farmers and tenants, cultivating land parcels that are often as small on average as under one-half hectare each. Sociological research and project implementation experience in recent years suggest the conclusion that large systems with several thousand small farmers cannot be centrally managed with effective or efficient consequences. The argument is increasingly made that it would be better to decentralize irrigation system management and allocate as much responsibility as possible to local farmer water-user groups who can better manage water distribution among themselves. If such groups exist, they should be "strengthened." If such groups do not already exist, then irrigation projects should include components for organizing water-user groups.

Similar characterizations can be found for community forestry projects, for slum improvement projects, and so on. The rhetoric in support of participation is there, but going from rhetoric to intent and from ambition to application is another matter entirely. This is where sociology and sociological consultants enter the picture. Consultants are asked to appraise the status of existing organizational resources among farmers in existing irrigation systems and even among farmers in prospective irrigation systems. Consultants are asked to characterize the capabilities of indigenous farmer organizations to assume certain management roles and to identify forms of technical assistance and external support that can strengthen these capacities. Consultants are being asked to design strategies for organizing groups where none may now exist. Consultants are being asked to consider how traditional civil engineering and agricultural extension systems can be reoriented, in staffing and management terms, to properly participate in development efforts with local groups.

Sociological consultants are asked to address these kinds of issues, but does sociology have enough to offer? The answer is not entirely promising, which presents a difficult and complex challenge for the consultant. Good advice can be given, but how does the consultant communicate the necessarily tentative nature of the advice? One strategy is for the consultant to urge project administrators (and sometimes rural groups) to adopt an experimental attitude. But to what extent is this self-serving? Does it protect the consultant but discount the difficulties most formal bureaucracies would have with adopting such a stance and ignoring the nontrivial nature of resource commitment that organizational activity represents for local communities? One answer, I believe, is that the sociologist who expects to work in this area has an obligation to gain understanding of social processes and dynamics that transcend local groups and agency support systems. How do local groups and external support systems now interact? How does problem identification in the relationship occur? What forms of bargaining predominate and how are the "norms" for bargaining maintained? What are the main stresses in the relationship and how are these addressed? Answers to questions such as these all contribute to understanding the context, to comprehending how objectives and purposes are organized, rationalized, and adjusted. The foundations of any praxis will have to be built there.

Critical Social Theory and Political Economy

Another example of the praxis problem is the issue of critical social theory and political economy. Increasing attention to the role of history and politics, social class, civil repression, and foreign domination all cast an especially difficult light on the praxis problem. The challenge for the sociological consultant who is intellectually oriented this way is how to bring the orientation into a real-world frame where the consultant is more likely than not to be working for, with, or under the watchful eye of the agents of political and economic control. One view is that the consultant should identify the consequences of continuing existing structural arrangements and processes for the security and welfare of these same elites. The problem is that while this can elicit greater sensibility to reform through self-interest, it can just as easily raise the temptation of preemptive repression. An example is provided by land reform projects.

Access to productive assets, particularly land, is a key issue in any agrarian setting. Many agrarian and rural social relations are organized around the distribution of access rights to land. Land reform programs have traditionally been seen as a way to restructure access rights to land and, through that, to restructure rural social relations. Superficially, land reform will therefore mean reforming the legal bases for land access through such steps as financing land acquisition by former tenants, establishing legal support for tenure security, identifying upper limits for individual landholding sizes, and supervising procedures for breaking up large estates.

However, land reform programs are much more complex and subtle than generally thought. They require understanding often complex sub-tenancy and access arrangements that have developed but are not "le-gally" recognized. Land reform typically places a high value on certain forms of property rights, forms that may be unfamiliar to local peasants. Financing and administrative arrangements for land reform can be By-zantine and are subject to both capture and deferral by more powerful and well-connected individuals.

In this difficult context, the sociological consultant may be involved in establishing criteria and procedures for determining who are eligible for land reform awards; evaluating the progress and problems of land reform programs; determining who are benefiting compared to who were supposed to benefit, and so forth. In the actual context in which many land reform programs operate, these seemingly direct tasks can acquire very subtle, elusive, and sensitive characteristics. An effective consultant will have to understand the distinction between perverse out-comes that are the result of deliberate intent and perverse outcomes that occur despite good intent. The consultant will need to understand the many levels and scales at which such programs operate and at which they can be distorted. The consultant will need to distill such under-standings through an appreciation of what can actually be done and who can actually do it. If the consultant overshoots and, in effect, asks for the sky, the consultant's input will never have any influence. If the con-sultant undershoots and assumes, for example, that only minor changes in record-keeping procedures can be accepted easily, the consultant may do more to excuse and even legitimize ills known to be present than to contribute to any incremental improvements. Ultimately, the key is con-textual knowledge, understanding what is happening and why.

Normative Preferences

The praxis issue does not say to the consultant: leave your normative understandings in your hip pocket. In the case of land reform, a con-sultant needs to understand the context of agrarian and rural relations, of relative distributions of power, of historical precedents, and such. Where issues related to the fundamental organization of society are on the table, the consultant cannot deny normative preference. What the praxis issue does is ask the consultant to immerse positivist understand-ing into normative orientation and to seek a resolution.

What is difficult about this course in any working context, but espe-cially in an international development context, is that the consultant is not playing simply a "professional" role as the purveyor of objective knowledge and methods. The consultant is also an advocate, a carrier of values and normative preferences, which refer to the status and role of objective knowledge and methods but also refer to normative perspectives on developmental outcomes that are not clearly or even necessarily derivative of that same objective knowledge and methods. When the consultant argues for normative outcomes, with less than "absolute" linkage demonstrated to what is viewed by the consultant, or those the consultant must convince, as "objective" knowledge and methods, the consultant's role drifts from that of the professional to that of the citizen, but the citizen without civil status.

I believe that one way the consultant overcomes these difficulties is by acquiring enough understanding and acceptance in working social relations that a vision of a praxis solution as an emergent social process can be found. After all, the worse assumption would be that only the consultant has normative preferences. The consultant will work with people who have their own versions of the praxis problem. The consultant can only learn from the experience of comprehending these preferences, but to begin to do that, the consultant also has to be accepted as an individual with normative sensitivity, not simply as a gun for hire.

PROFESSIONAL PREPARATION AND DEVELOPMENT

Educational Preparation

The question of educational preparation for international development consultancy is really part of the larger question of educational preparation for applied sociology. What amount to professional master's degree programs already exist at several universities, often in conjunction with some cross-disciplinary program (such as international agriculture development). In recent years, and particularly within the land-grant university system, discussion continues on what would amount to professional doctorates, as compared to conventional research doctorates. While a few would disagree that applied and basic sociologists operate in somewhat different work environments with associated differences in incentives and rewards, the proposition that these two "types" of sociology are different in some hierarchical way has not helped efforts to integrate educational preparation for international development. Some see applied sociology as a subdiscipline, a sanitized slice of what "real" sociology is about, which emphasizes the kinds of sociological input that are used, or at least are thought to be useful, in applied settings.

I would suggest that explorations in this direction, as either friend or foe of the proposition, are not going to be fruitful, at least not for the question of sociology and international development. The scope for sociological input in international development contexts is so broad that educational preparation for the sociologist who would apply skills to international development issues cannot be less than educational preparation for the academic sociologist who would teach and do publishable research about international development issues; it does to be more. There are practical and conceptual reasons for this conclusion.

The practical reason is that if a sociologist is only marginally literate in what basic sociology is about, that sociologist will be excessively dependent on the bridges others build and verify for going from sociological knowledge to sociological insight in applied circumstances— provided others make such bridges known. Unfortunately, in the discussions that surface on applied sociology and its relationship to mainstream sociology, the issue of the bridge is never really discussed. Who will build the bridges? Who will determine whether the bridges built are adequate? Will communication across the bridge be two-way or is the bridge really a chute—gems from basic sociology come down, but nothing goes back up. In international development contexts, we are nowhere close to having publicly built, verified, and codified transmission channels between the basic and applied sides of sociology. Consequently, when the conclusion is suggested that educational preparation for applied sociology (in international development) is a reduced form of basic sociology, I fear that what will result is a sociologist who is essentially a technologist. That is not enough.

There is a closely related conceptual reason for seeing educational preparation for applied sociology in international development contexts as more, rather than less, of what would be accepted as adequate for academic career preparation. What the sociologist is doing as an international consultant is *not* applied sociology, but *applying* sociology. What is packaged as applied sociology includes in its baggage numerous assumptions about the dynamics of any social context. These assumptions may actually be appropriate for some settings. The problem is knowing when. In the United States, research and research traditions have created complex terms of reference for understanding major social processes in American society. Within those terms of reference, various research derivations can be "applied" without any necessarily enormous controversy about basic contextual assumptions. Can we say the same for many other areas in the world? I believe that the answer is "no."

Consequently, we have a conceptual responsibility to be both more explicit and plural in considering how to characterize social context in other settings. This means that the sociological consultant must understand and continue to understand basic sociological knowledge well enough to recognize the different layers of social context it can enlighten. Given judgments about normative and positive "fits" between sociological knowledge and the social facts of a specific context, the consultant needs to determine the forms of sociological insight that can yield understanding for applied purposes. What all this means is that the international sociological consultant needs to be as good a sociologist, particularly on issues of theory, as the academic sociologist. Where they differ is in what derivations they typically attempt to extract from that knowledge, not in their professional proximity to that knowledge. In terms of educational preparation, this suggests to me a need for serious curriculum development in sociological methodology—what we know as sociological knowledge and how we know it—not simply an expansion or revision of existing courses on sociological methods. There are complex issues of inference, evidence, verification, generalizability, and so on, that reside primarily in the construction of sociological knowledge, not in the refinement of statistical artifacts.

Beyond the sociological, there are other skills that are needed. An international development consultant cannot have a merely casual familiarity with another culture. I am convinced that there is no substitute for investment in language and in specific culture area studies. Without the commitment to learn about another culture in depth, it is hard to believe that we can produce anything other than facile generalists—running around the world applying sociological methods, but having inadequate critical standards to guide when and how those methods should be used. It is necessary to have exceptional sensitivities to the local milieu if the various roles of an international development consultant are to be performed effectively.

A consultant has to be able be communicate effectively to nonsociological audiences. A consultant needs to have other skills, most notably working familiarity with economic and financial analysis, and personnel and financial management. Finally, if a sociologist has specific sector or industry interests (such as agriculture, transportation, human services) then the sociologist has to understand politics, economics, and technologies of that sector. In sum, educational preparation for applying sociology to international development is not a question of doing less. I believe it is quite the opposite. It is a challenge to do more because for the preparation of sociologists who can effectively work as international development consultants, more needs to be done.

Professional Development

Educational preparation is one part of professional development as an international development sociological consultant. Professional development continues throughout an individual's career. However, professional development is not only a characteristic of individual careers; it also refers to the orientation and capability of a profession—as a body of knowledge, methods, and values and as a social system for maintaining that knowledge, methods, and values—to define and accomplish objectives and missions. In academic sociology, professional development of individuals is evaluated through peer judgment processes that include publication in refereed journals and by prestigious presses, promotion to job security and to administrative roles, and various other forms of professional recognition (such as offices in professional societies, citation by public media, and so forth). Much of what there is to be evaluated is public knowledge, both for those who are being evaluated and those who wish to be evaluated and rewarded in the future. The publications are not confidential. The terms of reference for jobs are not secret. In this context, professional development, as both an individual and "group" phenomenon, can be said to exhibit considerable continuity. Cumulative contributions to specialized areas of knowledge are publicly encouraged, acknowledged, and rewarded.

Professional development in applied sociology is considerably different, particularly in international development contexts. Individual careers certainly can and do exhibit professional continuity. Individuals sharpen their insights and skills; innovate on the margins of their own work; grow. However, among sociological consultants working in international development, there is considerably less communication, experience-sharing, and public knowledge of individual achievements than would be the case for academic sociologists. For example, when a sociological consultant works for some of the multilateral development institutions, the consultant will sometimes confront a contractual clause that constrains the consultant from public presentations (through publication or public workshops) of work performed under the contract for periods of several years. Sociologists who attempt to report on applied international development experience at professional discipline meetings often find themselves placed on heterogeneous "residual" panels with other people whose presentations just do not "fit" anywhere else. Consequently, while individuals may exhibit continuity in professional development, the profession exhibits discontinuity. The cumulative work that individuals do is dramatically less cumulative for the sociological profession.

Evaluation of consultancy work is geared to the needs of the employer. However, in the international development arena, this is too much of a simplification. Sometimes the sociologist is not there because the office that employs the consultant actually wants the consultant's skills. The consultant can be there because someone paying the bills (for example, a bilateral or multilateral assistance agency) thinks the consultant should be there. However, as social soundness analysis described earlier suggests, this can create a context in which the sociologist may have some difficulty determining who the employer is and what any of the multiple employers actually want. In other cases, the consultant is there because the consultant is "trusted." This may mean respect and need for the consultant's skills, but it also can mean that the consultant can be trusted to "help" and to respect confidentiality. Professional development as, for example, the deepening of sociological methodology, is not precluded by such characteristics, but how is anyone to know?

Where the consultant is based can make a very important difference for whether, how, and what professional development criteria emerge. The consultant based in an academic setting is accountable enough to the incentive and reward system there that some kind of "open" professional development system can be expected to arise. As it relates explicitly to international development consultancy, it is probably best characterized as emergent, but at least, in principle, it can be there. There will be problems that have to do with the generally marginal status of international interests in most sociology departments and the view that time outside the country is also, in some sense, time outside the profession. Young, untenured faculty know well the trade-offs they encounter in these areas—even when the university has contractual obligations to conduct international development activities.

The consultant who works in a nonacademic setting will be accountable in some way for the professional development expectations characteristic of that organization. These may not be sociological, but in some sense we would expect to see some pressure to relate and possibly even to justify an individual's activities as a consultant with their activities as a staff member. This is the case in my own institution.

The free-lance sociological international development consultant represents a special and challenging case. It is here where concerns about quality of performance have tended to focus. Like other sociological consultants, free-lance sociological consultants will function in some kind of network and, within that network, notions of professional development will be nurtured. However, here more than anywhere, the buyers' market probably predominates in establishing and promoting standards for professional development. Consequently, it is quite possible that the concerns sometimes raised about the status of sociology practiced are expressions about different forms of professionalism and professional accountability more than they are reactions to variations in professional performance.

These are not issues for international development alone; but I believe that the characteristics of international development work exacerbate some of the problems and defeat the intentions of some of the commonly proposed solutions. Improving communication between applied sociologists is one answer, but it cannot be the only answer and perhaps it should not be the main answer. There is too high a risk that this strategy reinforces the "two cultures" in sociology. Academic departments and key professional discipline societies must have a primary responsibility. We can't expect educational preparation to improve if it must occur in a context that is itself split. Nor can we expect educational preparation to lay credible groundwork for building and using bridges that connect basic sociology with sociology that is being applied if the occupational world does not acknowledge that two-way traffic on such bridges is worth defending.

One solution that is much talked about is credentialism—professional "certification" of applied sociologists, for example. For some sociologists who do international consultancy work, sociology does not appear to be in the forefront of what they do. Does that reflect the "sociology-in-the-hip-pocket" phenomenon or the incorporation of sociology into more digestable vehicles? In some cases, method appears to greatly outshine methodology. Does this reflect inadequate commitment to understanding specific social contexts or the limits of effective performance in a given situation? Faced with such variation, credentialism may not create higher sociological standards, but it might protect the potential users of sociological input from lower standards.

I would feel more comfortable with credentialism if I thought we actually had developed an idea of excellence and clearly associated ideas of competence that bridged the many pieces of the picture implied by applying sociology and the many more pieces represented by the addition of international development working contexts. We have not developed such ideas. The dialogue that will be needed to explore such ideas is only beginning. We will need to avoid the pitfall that many economists have confronted—the "right" conclusion (the "market" is always better) is more important than contextually specific substantiation for the conclusion. Credentialism will make sense, perhaps, when the institutional framework within which it should occur appears to be more of a reality that it is now. Until then, proposals for credentialism have to be seen with a cold eye. Too often, they look too much like the dark side of professionalism—exclusivity and privilege dispensed for narrow purposes.

CONCLUSION

Sociological consultancy in an international development context offers what is, in many ways, a sharper version of the issues and themes associated with sociological consultancy in domestic contexts. The international development context also presents issues and themes that are not simply variations on the practice of applying sociology domestically. This chapter has argued that a central professional issue raised by sociological consultancy in international contexts is sociological methodology itself. The relationships between theory, understanding, knowledge, and fact encompassed by sociological methodology need to be visualized as the dynamic core of any sociological effort in the international development field. To do otherwise is to short-circuit a learning process that is necessary for the sociology of international development in whatever working context that sociology appears, including consultancy.

The two-culture climate between basic and applied sociology in the United States cannot be anything other than a millstone for a sociology that concerns international development. The millstone is given; it is also accepted. All this should stop. The sociological consultant working in international development needs to recognize a larger challenge; to see the consultant effort as part of an important learning process for sociology and for sociological methodology. Obviously, it would be nice if many other things also happened, but a good place to begin is among consultants themselves. If consultants can once again think of themselves as sociologists, even when they are international consultants, some of the other desirable steps might just follow.

ACKNOWLEDGMENT

The author wishes to express his appreciation to Irwin Deutscher for very incisive and constructive comments on an earlier draft of this chapter.

5

Sociology in Marketing Research

JOSEPH W. MERCURIO

Store location research is an area within the broader field of marketing research. This chapter focuses on the suitability of sociologists to conduct this type of work. The store location research analyst generally functions as a member of a retail firm's in-house research department, or as an analyst employed by a consulting firm. Store location research positions are occupied by professionals representing a variety of academic disciplines. The most common backgrounds include geography, marketing, and store operations. Sociologists are appropriate, but seldom-employed, candidates for store location research.

This chapter demonstrates the suitability of sociologists to conduct store location research through a description of the urban community and a discussion of the location problems facing urban retailers. It will also examine the sociologist's role as a store location research analyst.

THE URBAN COMMUNITY—A SOCIOLOGIST'S INTEREST

This chapter concentrates on an urban application, but sociological concepts also have relevance and application to rural store location research.

Human Ecology

The application of sociology to store location research is based primarily upon the findings of urban theory and research. The field of human ecology has provided an academic perspective that has practical applications. Human ecology is relevant to store location research because of its concern with the spatial distribution of people and institutions. Duncan (1959) described the ecological system as having four main elements: population, environment, technology, and organization. Sociologists conducting store location research apply these concepts extensively. The following description of these elements is broadly based on Duncan.

Population: Population is always involved in human ecology. The relevant attributes of population include its size, geographic distribution, and density; its growth or decline; and demographic makeup. Movement of the population, whether in a daily commuting pattern or massive relocation, are all of interest to the human ecologist.

Environment: Generally the environment is described in terms of physical properties, including topography, climate, flora, and fauna. Population comes in close contact with the environment, makes changes to it, and is also limited by it. Most urban environments have been substantially changed through the construction of roads and the development of industry and commerce.

Technology: The degree to which the environment is controlled or changed by the population is largely dependent upon the level of technology. Technology refers to the ways in which man uses tools in order to control or change the physical environment. For example, the automobile helped make possible the development of the suburbs, and likewise the availability of air conditioning encouraged the development of the sun belt.

Organization: To the human ecologist this element refers to the social organization of activities on the community level. Primary interest is usually with the organization of economic activities. Cities are physical entities, and their various parts compete for space. Because of the ecologist's economic interest, and the competition for space, human ecology is frequently concerned with two factors that affect cost: time and space.

Retailing and Urban Ecology

Urban ecologists are interested in these four elements and their interrelationships as they exist in the urban setting. Retailing is a major factor of most urban communities and can be understood in terms of the ecological perspective. For a practical application, sociologists must re-orient these concepts, and view them as the dynamics that influence a retail firm in its expansion strategy. It requires the sociologist to apply information on collectivities as they relate to a specific retail firm.

THE URBAN SETTING—A RETAILER'S ENVIRONMENT

Retailers conduct business in the urban environment but may not share the perspective of the ecologist. As a factor in the urban setting, retail firms must compete for space along with other activities of the city. This section describes some of the retailer's basic concerns and challenges. The orientation is with a large, multiunit retail chain, since this type of firm is the most likely to conduct store location research.

Retail Expertise

The primary interest of a retail firm is with retailing. At its most basic level, retailing is an activity that consists of obtaining goods from a wholesaler and selling them to the public. Consequently, the skills and energies of a retail firm are devoted to purchasing, merchandising, pricing, advertising, employee productivity, and so on. Running a retail chain is a complex business, with a focus toward efficient day-to-day operations. Superseding all of these daily concerns is the profit objective, which must be achieved while operating within a competitive environment.

Long-Term Objectives

The most important long-term objectives of a retail firm are profit and growth. Profit must first occur to insure the firm's continued existence. Growth must occur in order to maintain a competitive posture. With few exceptions, retail firms are in a competitive struggle for the consumer's dollar. The more successful chains tend to capture a greater portion of this dollar at the expense of the less successful operators. They accomplish this by doing a more effective job than their competition in purchasing, advertising, merchandising, and so on. The reward for the most effective execution of basic operations is profit.

Profit is also related to size, with the tendency for bigger firms to be more successful than smaller firms. This occurs because of the economies of scale associated with size. Two examples of this are seen in the following trends: First, there is a shrinking number of "mom and pop" stores, the independent retailer, to the benefit of the regional or national retail chain. Second, even among chains, there is a continuous shakeout and consolidation, as some businesses go out of existence (for example, W. T. Grant, Fed Mart, Woolco), and others consolidate through acquisition or merger (for example, American Stores and Jewel Co. or K-mart and Pay Less Drug Stores). While there are also examples of ailing large companies (Montgomery Ward, A&P), retail dominance by the largest firms appears to be the general trend.

Growth of a firm can occur in several ways. Commonly, it is achieved through increased sales in existing stores, but this approach has obvious limits. First, a store is limited by its size, and will eventually reach a maximum capacity. Second, sales increases are influenced by many factors that are beyond the retailer's control. These uncontrollable factors may include the decline of population, an increase of competition, and other environmental changes.

Because of these limiting factors, the more successful retail chains seek growth through additional stores. One approach to adding stores is through a merger or acquisition. This is limited, however, by the availability and suitability of such candidates. More commonly, growth is achieved through construction of new stores.

Risk and the Cost of Failure

Given a competitive environment, retail chains must grow to maintain or increase profits. This usually means growth through the addition of new units. This type of growth, however, entails substantial risk of failure. Although change in any aspect of a retail operation involves some element of risk, none has the long-term significance of a new location. For example, poorly chosen merchandise can usually be sold at a short-term loss; selection of a poor manager can be resolved by replacement; a poor advertisement can be revised; and so on. These all tend to be quickly reversible mistakes that result in short-term losses.

In contrast, the selection of a poor location for a new store can be very costly and have long-term consequences. The high cost occurs because of the inherently substantial costs associated with land acquisition, construction, interest rates, and other factors of store development. In addition, the location choice is usually for the long term. When adding a new unit, retailers either purchase the land and building (through a long-term mortgage), or commit to a long-term lease of the property.

Through store location research, the risk of failure is reduced. As a store location research analyst, a sociologist brings an understanding of the urban environment that can be readily applied to the retail firm. This is knowledge that retailers may not have, since they are preoccupied with "running the store."

Management Decision Making

Because of the large amount of capital involved, long-term leases, and the inherent risk of failure, location decisions in most retail companies are made by members of the chain's top management. While the actual process of decision making varies from one company to another, location research can play a key role in the decision-making process. Given managements' long-term objectives of profit and growth, a prospective location must satisfy individual corporate criteria of profitability. This requires a projection of profitability, which reflects costs such as payroll, occupancy, and inventory relative to store sales, which are estimated by the store location research analyst.

Location decisions are not based exclusively on projected financial performance. Marketing considerations, such as the following, may rule in favor of opening a store even though it has a substandard financial outlook: to help fill out the company's market coverage strategy in a particular city, to improve the level of consumer awareness in the market, as a defensive move to pre-empt a competitor from opening at the proposed location, or in an area of substantial projected population growth the risk of a short-term loss may be worth a potentially profitable long-term opportunity.

STORE LOCATION RESEARCH—AN APPLICATION

Davies (1984, 1) defines store location research as "essentially concerned with identifying the ideal position and site for a new store (or entire shopping centre)." The location or growth concerns of a retail firm are a spatial problem. Consequently, the elements of urban ecology are relevant factors of analysis. The overall goal of store location research is to help management make the best possible location decisions. This involves avoiding bad or unprofitable sites and, conversely, not missing good locations. The underlying function of this entire process is to reduce the risk of failure.

Store location research occurs most often in larger retail firms. It is a relatively young discipline, having its birth in the 1930s and 1940s. The field grew substantially with the post-World War II baby boom, as a result of the rapid expansion of many retail firms that followed population growth and relocation to the suburbs.

Along with other topics, store location research involves an assessment of environmental elements that are familiar to sociologists. In the most simplified case, the analyst's task is to evaluate the adequacy and sales potential for a proposed location. More complex projects might include identifying a new market for a chain in search of more territory, developing a complete metropolitan location strategy with multiple sites, or projecting sales for an existing store to be relocated or expanded. The following description is limited to an elementary case requiring the evaluation and sales projection for a proposed store at a single location.

Research Goal

The primary goal is to provide management with an objective sales estimate for a proposed store to be located at a particular site. A secondary objective is to inform management of relevant area characteristics that may influence their location decision. These goals require the analyst to prepare a sales estimate that includes the current year and is projected out several years into the future. This estimate is be based upon an understanding of the nature of the retail business and the nature of the specific location. It also includes the analysis of area characteristics consisting of population and demographics, transportation systems, physical barriers, market potential, and the retail environment. The following sections describe the basic elements of a trade area analysis. Trade area analysis is highly descriptive in nature; however, the information collected in this process is subsequently used in the more analytical phase of making sales estimates, described later in this chapter.

Trade Area Analysis

The first major undertaking of a store location analyst is an identification of the proposed store's trade area. A trade area is the homogeneous geographic area from which the store will derive the majority of its sales. For each location, the analyst defines a trade area and measures its potential. This is accomplished through an evaluation of the following major elements.

Nature of the Business

Trade areas vary among firms according to the basic nature of their business. Generally, stores offering a highly differentiated product or service will have a physically extensive trade area. For example, a furrier or exclusive jewelry shop would be capable of attracting customers from a much greater distance than would a convenience food store or drugstore. Consequently, the analyst must develop an understanding of the nature of the company's business before attempting to identify the area from which the store will draw its customers.

Nature of the Location

The size or shape of a trade area is influenced by the general nature of the location. For example, a convenience food store in midtown Manhattan would probably have a trade area significantly different from a location on suburban Staten Island. The Manhattan trade area would probably closely reflect employment patterns and follow commuter lines or include the working population of nearby office buildings. In contrast, the suburban location might encompass a highly localized residential population base.

A detailed evaluation of the specific location is also undertaken and requires the analyst to make an on-site visit. If the location is currently undeveloped the analyst must visualize the location via an architect's rendering. A few of the most salient physical site characteristics to be evaluated include the ease of getting into and out of the location, proximity and adequacy of parking, visibility of the location for motorists or pedestrians, and appropriate signing. The degree to which these characteristics are present in a positive or negative way will enhance or detract from the sales projection for the proposed store.

Population and Demographics

Human ecologists are interested in population size, its density, growth, and decline. To the store location analyst, population represents a potential customer base. To be successful, the store must generate a sufficient sales level from this trade area population. The analyst's job is to measure accurately the populations' current size, its geographic distribution, and project likely future changes.

The location analyst is primarily interested in population density, which is of significance because the larger the base of potential customers in the smallest geographic area the greater the probability of achieving a given sales level. The interest in density will be expressed differently among different retail types. For example, a drugstore that is primarily convenience oriented may require a specific population level within a one-mile radius of the location, while a discount department store, because of its broader geographic customer draw, may measure its population requirements with a three-mile radius.

Demographics of the population are important in two ways. First, areas of significant demographic difference tend to delineate store trade areas. This occurs as groups of similar demographic composition tend to shop in similar areas. Second, the analyst must understand the suitability of area demographics to the nature of the company's business. This is important since different retailers each have their own unique demographic appeal.

For example, even within an industry as basic as food retailing, substantial demographic segmentation has developed. This can be demonstrated by comparing Byerly's, a small chain in Minneapolis nationally recognized for its service and quality orientation, with Cub Foods, a warehouse/discount price operator, in the same city. Presumably, Byerly's would be most appealing to a shopper characterized by white-collar employment and a higher level of income and education than the Cub Foods shopper.

Demographic considerations become even more apparent with the more highly specialized retail types, ranging from department and apparel stores to sporting goods and toy stores. Each chain has its own unique consumer appeal, which can be measured in demographic terms. It is the analyst's task to identify and measure the relevant demographic variables for his or her company in any given trade area.

Sources of information for population and demographic data are well within the *province* of most sociologists. They include personal observation, extensive use of U.S. Census documents, and information prepared by local city or county planning departments. The type of demographic characteristics frequently of interest to the analyst include income, family or household composition and size, and ethnicity.

Transportation Network

Human ecologists are interested in the transportation systems of urban communities. To the location analyst, this means evaluating ways in which customers will come to the proposed store. In evaluating transportation patterns the analyst's considerations include speed limits, the number of traffic lanes, turn lanes, the placement of traffic signals, areas of congestion, commuter versus local traffic, and such. Essentially the analyst determines how well the site is positioned relative to the flow of traffic. A location with a good transportation network will have its sales potential enhanced. This could mean a location at a major freeway interchange for a department store, or being situated at a bus stop for a drugstore.

Information about the transportation network is gathered through first-hand experience including extensive driving and/or walking in the area. Secondary sources may include data ranging from bus route schedules to traffic flow maps.

Physical Barriers

Certain physical features can act as barriers to the smooth flow of people through or into the site's trade area. These barriers may include rivers, hilly terrain, major highways, or railroad tracks. It is essential to identify any such barriers, because they diminish the probability of attracting customers from the population affected. Failure to recognize a barrier would lead to overestimating the potential for the proposed site. Consequently, the analyst has to understand the area's land use patterns. Extensive observation is needed to identify these physical barriers to trade. Local planning agencies may assist in providing land use and other maps.

Market Potential

The location analyst estimates the trade area sales potential for the company's type of merchandise. Market or expenditure potential generally refers to the amount of money the population has available to spend on the merchandise sold by the proposed store type. Naturally, some types of merchandise like basic grocery items may have little variation among demographic variables, others like prescription medicine, toys, or building supplies may have substantial variations among items like age, income, and family size.

This type of expenditure information is obtained through secondary sources including the *U.S. Census of Retail Trade Market Guide* (1982) and the *Survey of Buying Power* (1985). Expenditure data may also be obtained through any number of survey methods employed by the analyst, ranging from focus groups to telephone interviews.

Retail Environment

With the trade area's total dollar potential estimated, the analyst deciphers patterns of the retail environment. This includes identifying those stores in which the population is making its purchases. It also means estimating the level of sales at each relevant competitor. The analyst also identifies the current and past location patterns of area retailers. Since the proposed store must obtain its sales either by taking business away from these existing stores or by generating new business, it is important to understand the retail environment in terms of these location and expenditure patterns.

This requires the analyst to make a comprehensive evaluation of the current retail setting. This evaluation is based upon secondary sources including *U.S. Census of Retail Trade* and other published material. It also includes the first-hand experience of taking a physical inventory of major competitors. This may involve surreptitiously interviewing the employees of the competition to gain performance information.

Sales Estimates

The above trade area information is primarily descriptive in nature. By applying certain more analytical techniques to the trade area information, the analyst makes an estimate of sales for the proposed store. Sales estimates are the single quantification that reflects the analyst's evaluation of the site. These figures are used by management in their decision to approve or reject capital allocation for any particular site. The following is an overview of some of the most frequently used sales forecasting techniques.

Analogs

This is the oldest and most elementary of the quantitative sales forecasting methods. Developed by William Applebaum in the 1930s while he was at the Kroger Company, it remains the bedrock of more sophisticated techniques (Applebaum 1968). Essentially, it compares the proposed location to the performance of existing stores with similar site and trade area characteristics. Existing stores are analyzed through in-store customer surveys. The data from these surveys are calculated to produce market share information for subsegments of the trade area. These figures are then used as the basis for making estimates of the proposed location.

Regression Models

Regression modeling here refers to the technique of the same name with which most sociologists are familiar. When used in sales forecasting, the independent variable is some indicator of sales potential, usually total store sales. The dependent variables consist of those factors that best predict store sales in a sample of the firm's existing stores. These usually include the variables of competition, population, demographics, transportation systems, and so on. Similar to the analog approach, regression modeling requires extensive data collection from existing company stores, their trade areas, and customer composition.

The analyst must measure those variables used in the model for the proposed location. For example, if the total square footage of competition within one mile of the existing company stores is included in the model, then similar measurements must be made within one mile of the proposed site. After collecting the required information for each variable, they are multiplied by their respective coefficients and added or subtracted to calculate the total sales estimate.

Gravity Models

Gravity models are based upon the work of geographers, including Reilly (1931) and Converse (1949). The basic factors in a gravity model are distance between consumers, competition and the site, size and quality of the competition, and the image or acceptance of each individual store rated by the trade area population. Gravity models are based upon spatial relationships. Given existing relations, they attempt to allocate sales to a proposed store at any given location.

Communication of Results

All of the pertinent trade area and sales forecasting information must be effectively communicated to management. This is accomplished through some combination of written and verbal presentation. Communication is one of the most crucial parts of the research process, since management must be convinced of the analyst's findings before acting on them. This requires the sociologist to adapt a communication style that is most effective to the company's management. It usually entails an emphasis on clear, brief, and practical reporting.

APPLIED SOCIOLOGY—PERSONAL REQUIREMENTS

The concepts of human ecology provide a perspective easily applied by sociologists in store location research. This research requires additional skills, some already in the sociologist's repertoire and others that must be acquired. Some of these skills are summarized below:

- *Communication skills.* Strong written and verbal skills are essential in effectively communicating research findings with management.

- *Quantitative abilities.* Store location research demands a personal ease with numbers, and an understanding of elementary statistics.

- *Observation skills.* The nature of store location research emphasizes personal observation as a key data collection technique.

- *Understanding spatial relationships.* Since store location research has a strong spatial orientation, the analyst must be comfortable working with variables of time and space.

Freeman and Rossi (1984) describe the personal characteristics of those most likely to succeed in applied work to include the ability to work under tight time constraints, a high level of self-confidence, a willingness to take risks, and the ability to achieve professional job satisfaction without substantial personal recognition. These attributes apply equally well to sociologists who conduct store location research.

The most succinct description of the requirements for success in the field of store location research is Freeman and Rossi's (1984, 574) comment distinguishing applied from academic sociology. They note that "in addition to conceptual acumen and technical virtuosity, there is a premium on moving quickly, accepting trade-offs that value some data over best data, gauging the level of precision and accuracy required, and communicating clearly."

REFERENCES

Applebaum, William. 1968. "The Analog Method for Estimating Potential Store Sales." In *Guide to Store Location Research*, edited by C. Kornblau, pp. 232–43. Reading, Mass.: Addison-Wesley.

Converse, P. D. 1949. "New Laws of Retail Gravitation." *Journal of Marketing*, 14: 379–84.

Davies, R. L. 1984. "Introduction." In *Store Location and Store Assessment Research*, edited by R. L. Davies and D. S. Rogers. Chichester, England: John Wiley.

Duncan, O. D. 1959. "Human Ecology and Population Studies." In *The Study of Population*, edited by P. M. Hauser and O. D. Duncan, pp. 681–684. Chicago: University of Chicago Press.

Freeman, Howard, and Peter. H. Rossi. 1984. "Furthering the Applied Side of Sociology." *American Sociological Review*, 49 (August): 571–80.

Reilly, W. J. 1931. *The Law of Retail Gravitation.* New York: Knickerbocker Press.
Survey of Buying Power. 1985. New York: Sales and Marketing Management.
U.S. Census of Retail Trade Market Guide. 1982. Washington D.C.: U.S. Department
    of Commerce, Bureau of Census.

6

Consulting for Churches

WILLIAM H. SWATOS, JR.

Sociological consulting for church organizations may well represent the oldest form of sociological practice in America. One major stream of early American sociology was the "alliance for progress" of this new human science with institutional religion (Reed 1981). Both the *American Journal of Sociology* and *Social Forces* in their early years carried a large number of religion articles of an applied nature. "Modernizing" church structures to deal with the social problems at the turn of the twentieth century was one of the major concerns of early American sociology (Swatos 1984). The work that was done in this period covered a wide range. Much was merely descriptive, reporting on specific projects undertaken by churches or interchurch bodies to alleviate local social problems or redirect administrative energies. Some, however, had lasting value. Walter Laidlaw, an urban Methodist minister-researcher, for example, is to be directly credited with the construction and ultimate government adoption of census tracts during a New York City Federation of Churches study of neighborhoods in 1902 (Green 1954). Laidlaw's work is particularly important to contemporary value-application debates in sociology, because it demonstrates that applied sociology of religion can have impact on general social science knowledge and is quite independent of dogmatics.

The breakdown of the sociology-and-religion alliance was part of a much broader process in sociology that, as Janowitz (1978) puts it, separated the profession into "intellectuals" and "doers," with the former reaping the greater intradisciplinary status honor. One of the stigmatizing strategies of the movement from "practicalism" to "the pussyfooting sociologist...sneering at 'reformism' and condemning 'value judgments'" (Ross 1936, 180) was a lumping of practically all applied researchers from its early years under such labels as "do-gooders" and "preacher's kids" (Reed 1982). As academic sociologists increasingly adopted William F. Ogburn's stance (in his presidential address to the American Sociological Society in 1929) that sociology "is not interested in making the world a better place to live," religionists were particularly singled out for criticism as relics of a bygone era (see Bernard 1934; Barnes 1929).

This did not end sociological consulting for churches—though it certainly did not advance it—but, rather, sent it underground, primarily into seminaries and agency-sponsored research institutes. Foremost among these was the Institute for Social and Religious Research, whose urban department was headed by H. Paul Douglass, with a town and country department under the direction of Edmund deS. Brunner. In his early fifties, after an accomplished career of almost 30 years as a pastor and missionary, Douglass soon became the foremost religious researcher in American social science. "Combining field research with survey data...Douglass never conducted a survey without spending at least some time on-site to gain firsthand knowledge" (Hadden 1980, 72). After the Institute closed in 1934, Douglass moved to various Council of Churches tasks. During the 13 years of the Institute's existence, it published 78 volumes of applied religious research. An inventory of the Harlan Paul Douglass Collection of Religious Research Reports housed in the Department of Research, Office of Planning and Program, National Council of Churches in New York contains several thousand "fugitive" studies, primarily from the 1950s to the present, that rarely found their way into published format. A microfiche edition of 2,270 of these prior to 1970 is now available from Research Publications, Inc., under the title "Social Problems and the Churches" (Brewer and Johnson 1970). These materials provide both a measure of the continued demand for social science research on the part of religious audiences and a resource tool for those contemplating this venture.

During the 1950s the Religious Research Association (RRA) was founded primarily to provide a professional association and communication for workers in applied sociology of religion. The membership consisted of two groups: an older cadre of trained social scientists who had found niches in seminary or occasional university settings and a newer group of "bootstrap methodologists," who often lacked professional training in sociology but were recruited to serve pressing denominational needs (Thorne 1974). The RRA addressed four interrelated themes: a concern about greater methodological sophistication, a desire to use academic expertise, a perception of a need for professional standards and symbols, and an ecumenical response to move beyond the Protestant mainstream (Hadden 1974, 130). The second of these items largely addressed the first, as sociologists like Charles Y. Glock led a group of solidly trained methodologists into the association. The *Review of Religious Research* began publication in 1959 and continues as a quarterly journal addressing both basic and applied issues in religious research. Interfaith ties began with Roman Catholic members, such as Joseph Fichter, and soon included Jews, Mormons, and, more recently, Islamic scholars. That this has redounded back to the religious traditions may be illustrated by the formation of such organizations as CARA, the Roman Catholic Center for Applied Research in the Apostolate, whereas earlier the Roman hierarchy had suppressed the continuation of Fichter's monumental Southern Parish research.

CONSULTING FOCI

Specific consulting projects with churches have run a wide gamut over the century. Early studies often focused on how the churches might serve particular "needy" groups in society. More recently there has been a shift toward intrainstitutional studies. Fichter (1951, 1980, 1982, 1984) has completed projects for CARA and other Roman Catholic agencies on such topics as clergy alcoholism, clergy burnout, and Catholic hospitals. This does not mean that religious groups have necessarily become more introspective. Much of the work on the "needy" that religious groups once sponsored is now done under governmental or other secular auspices. The results of this work can be used by organized religion for a variety of ministries to target groups as effectively as those data supplied by the earlier studies.

For purposes of the potential church consultant, however, perhaps the most useful conceptualization of clientele and their needs can be drawn from Roof's (1976) cosmopolitan-local distinction, which has been an important theoretical tool in explaining religious behavior generally. What I am suggesting here is that there are two major audiences for consulting in applied sociology of religion and two relatively different styles to accompany these. The first is in research conducted by denominational and interdenominational bureaucracies to address questions of concern to administrators—how to educate pastors most effectively for stewardship development, for example—or to the membership at large. This type of consulting is similar to much work done for formal organizations in our society. The second type is local congregational research. This is sometimes a spin-off from larger projects, but local churches also identify needs—or can be assisted to identify needs—within their immediate fellowship or community in which a consulting sociologist can be of value. While all religious organizations in the United States are technically voluntary associations, most church bureaucracies work like bureaucracies. Congregations, by contrast, have unique local circumstances to which the consultant must be sensitive.

Cosmopolitan Consulting

Most denominations have developed an awareness of the value of the survey as a planning tool. Some have in-house research staffs. Some contract out or do both. Peter Berger's early work in the sociology of religion (1961a, 1961b) grew out of research for the Lutheran Church. Glock, Ringer, and Babbie's *To Comfort and to Challenge,* published in 1967, is actually a secondary analysis of data collected in 1952 by the Bureau of Applied Social Research of Columbia University for the Episcopal Church. The Office of Review and Evaluation of the Presbyterian Church in the United States was established largely as a result of constituent demands for accountability on the part of leadership in program implementation. Members who were funding programs wanted to have some impact assessment data for subsequent budgeting. The United Methodists also have an in-house research staff. CARA both commissions research associates and undertakes direct involvement. Groups once considered too "fundamentalist" to tolerate social science also are increasingly open to applied research, particularly in regard to such topics as new membership development and stewardship.

To some extent research and consulting for denominational and interdenominational organizations has been a reflection of the churches' perceptions of their own standing vis-a-vis society at large. The Glock study in 1952, for example, was concerned with church social policies and community action. The 1950s represented a period of church growth and a concern on the part of leadership for program development. More recently there has been a considerable decline in membership—particularly among the so-called mainline denominations—and with that research interests have focused more on membership issues, perhaps best exemplified by the essays in Hoge and Roozen's *Understanding Church Growth and Decline* (1979). Churches want to know why some denominations are growing and others are not, what motivates the church member to stay with or leave the church, how church members make decisions about financial support, and so forth. One characteristic of the voluntary-associational character of American religious organization that does persist at the cosmopolitan level is an intimate relationship between membership support and occupational survival. Regardless of organizational polity, most religious organizations actually operate on a bottom-up principle, so that the financial pinch often hits at the top first. Whereas many formal organizations' administrative staffs remain relatively untouched by financial ebbs and flows (while "labor" is laid off), most local ministers remain in place, while a managerial staff member is cut.

What church bureaucracies want from a sociological consultant are: strong quantitative skills, expertise in questionnaire design, clear and relevant data analyses, and an absence of either theoretical or methodological mumbo jumbo. The greatest difficulty many sociologists face in coming into church consulting that is unique to the job is sufficient familiarity with church teaching and practices to execute good research. Regardless of their personal religiosity, sociologists often lack substantive training in religion as a set of organizational structures related to some more or less explicit goal statement. This can lead to naively constructed instruments that either are rejected by the contracting agency or are used and then found wanting. This is partially the reason that many organizations have begun to develop in-house staffs. The sociologist who wants to consult for a religious organization must show a degree of sophistication and interest in that group to make the services proffered attractive to the client group. I do not mean that consultants need to be either pious or theological scholars. Ironically, sociologists who are taught to be "value free" far too often focus on values rather than structure in approaching religious organizations. Certainly a theological ignoramus is going to be at a deficit in approaching church clients, but a theological "expert" who doesn't know how clergy are placed or administrative leaders chosen in a particular denomination may be almost as bad off.

How an understanding of structure can be used creatively can be illustrated by looking at two books attempting to deal with problems of attendance for mainline Protestant denominations during the 1960s: Jeffrey Hadden's *The Gathering Storm in the Churches* (1969), which focuses on the increasing divergence of clergy and laity on theological, social, and political issues, and Dean Kelley's *Why Conservative Churches are Growing* (1972). Kelley holds an applied position with the National Council of Churches; Hadden is a competent research sociologist. The two books can be tied together inasmuch as Hadden shows wide differences on core issues between clergy and laity in mainline denominations (that is, being a Christian means different things *within* the same group), while Kelley argues that consistent meaning systems are what characterize conservative versus mainline groups. All of this may be true, but I would argue that neither author pays sufficient attention to the fact that the liberal churches by and large are much more bureaucratic and exercise far greater bureaucratic hegemony over the placement of clergy into local cures. Not only *how* the clergy are placed, but also *who* may be placed is increasingly removed from local hands, apparently, as denominations "liberalize." The same is generally true for clergy removal. This structural difference between conservative and mainline churches is often overlooked in analyses that focus primarily on values.

I would suggest that to these analyses the following kind of model be added: Whereas church organizations in the United States are voluntary associations dependent upon a local base of support, denominations in which clergy are assigned to local cures or called to cures with permanent tenure or called only after the completion of a hierarchically approved curriculum of study are more likely to experience clergy-lay dissensus to a greater extent than those in which the choice of a pastor is primarily congregational, in which professional training is minimized, and in which the line between lay and clergy roles is diffuse. This model emphasizes primarily the social structure of the religious organization—at both its cosmopolitan and local levels—over against the meaning systems of the participants. The fact that in recent times these happen to be conservative churches probably reflects more of a rejection of the bureaucratic style of administration and its attendant life-style than an *a priori* value commitment. Antibureaucratic nonestablishment liberalism usually also rejects organized religion. I would hypothesize, however, that to the extent that such a group could be formed, it too would be growing (Swatos 1981).

A consulting sociologist using such a model as this with denominational executives might be suggesting some surprising alternatives to contemporary programing. Data from organizational mergers in the business world, for example, might be included to raise questions about the long-range prospects of interdenominational mergers at the formal organizational level. Corporations that merge do not necessarily show greater profitability, though they do show greater concentration of power at the top. How valuable this is to organizations whose ultimate power lies at the bottom should be studied very carefully. Although the Roman Catholic bureaucracy has a remarkable history and, indeed, could well be studied under the rubric of the transition from empire to transnational corporation, there is no assurance that mainline American Protestantism can ape this model successfully. Here values return again to the analysis, but from a structural perspective: To what extent can an organizational form founded on localism (the American denomination) structure itself upon cosmopolitan principles, when those principles have no clearly operative control mechanism for their enforcement? What the Protestant denominations lack in contradistinction to both historic Roman Catholism and the modern corporation is clout over their members, and this is becoming increasingly true for Roman Catholicism in spite of its authoritarian tradition. This example is offered to illustrate how a consulting sociologist who understands both the intraorganizational structure of religious groups and the relationships between forms of organization and societies generally can develop analytical tools for church clients at the cosmopolitan level.

Local Consulting

The discussion of the structures for pastoral deployment will help us to segue from the cosmopolitan focus to that of the local church. Many local church projects develop from larger denominational concerns. Often the parent body will provide consultants from its own ranks or provide training for consultants appointed by regional judicatories that serve as mediating structures between denominational headquarters and the local congregation. A local church interested in evangelism (that is, recruitment of new members) or stewardship (fund-raising) may well make use of materials and personnel supplied by a denominational agency. Denominations also may attempt to require local congregations to engage in specific quasi-research activities. The Episcopal Church, for example, recently promoted such a program under the title of "The Next Step." Congregations were to engage in "self-evaluations" according to prescribed formulae with respect to five different areas of ministry, designated SWEEP: service, worship, evangelism, education, and pastoral care. The Next Step in Mission program followed upon a fund-raising program known as Venture in Mission, promoted by the church's hierarchy largely to deflect attention from internal denominational divisions.

Some local churches, however, also hire sociologists—again, perhaps, through their larger structure—to work with them in addressing concerns in their own congregation or the community within which they operate. These may be general, such as "planning for the future," or specific, such as where to relocate (if at all) the church building in light of neighborhood change (Bartholomew 1969). It is studies of these sorts that make up the bulk of the Harlan Paul Douglass Collection of the National Council of Churches. Such studies can have continuing relevance and be applied across a variety of denominational lines, for example Samuel Kincheloe's "The Behavior Sequence of a Dying Church" (1929). Here a first principle for the local church consultant can be articulated: Local churches must be understood primarily in terms of local rather than cosmopolitan (that is, denominational) context. A major difference between working with the local church versus a denominational organization is that the consultant must know the locality within which the work is to be done. Survey instruments of wide generality can be used, for example, only if they are interpreted in light of local circumstances. It may be far more important to know the social status of Presbyterians versus Methodists in a given community than it is to know how a national sample of Presbyterian or Methodists responded to a questionnaire.

Neighborhood change is one of three areas in which sociological consultants can share considerable expertise with local congregations. Church members will readily tell you, "Churches are people," and so they are. But church people rapidly, amazingly rapidly, build buildings, and from then on "the church" is more and more likely to refer to a piece of real estate than a group of people (with a "big C," of course, "the Church" is often used by individuals to refer to some administrative entity, local or cosmopolitan—since capitalization is difficult to see in spoken language, a sociologist must be careful in distinguishing uses of this term in research). The real estate, in turn, is likely to be subject to demographic change. Local congregations form primarily around ethnic, status, or age lines. As demographic change impacts upon a neighborhood, the building remains while the congregation moves. Increasingly congregations are sensitive to this possibility and seek to determine the best strategy to couple real estate and people. A sociologist who can bring expertise in demographics, cultural differences, and affiliational behaviors can contribute substantially to this decision-making process. The consultant should remember, however, that the church building is an affectively charged setting. Critical life events have been solemnized and symbolized within its walls. An executive who would think little about relocating a company's headquarters if it better served the goals of the corporation may shed tears over the destruction of the altar at which a marriage was solemnized or from which a parent was buried. A special problem under this rubric is that of churches placed on the National Register of Historic Places—a designation eagerly sought after by many congregations when it first became available, only now to become a proverbial albatross as it limits development and change.

A second area for sociological consultants to churches is that of expansion of membership. Congregations are increasingly becoming aware that there may be reasons why people do or do not choose to affiliate with them that extend beyond theology. It is no accident that this problem has occurred for churches nor is the desire to address it merely Machiavellian. Historically local congregations—denominations, in their original nonbureaucratic sense—functioned to fit people into local communities (Swatos 1981). A person's profession said something about social status and ethnic background. Transportation restrictions limited the range within which church selection could be made. Vertical social mobility often brought denominational mobility, at least intergenerationally. Otherwise, however, congregations were multigenerational collectivities of families. Geographic mobility has radically changed this situation, and churches cannot appeal to the same familistic attachments that once undergirded their programs. Churches must now appeal to "new" people in a very different sense than ever before. A very creative example of how sociological factors can be brought to bear on new member ministry from the standpoint of the structure of the existing congregation is the work of Arlin Rothauge (1983), which operates from the simple, but effective, "basic hypothesis" that "the most effective means of carrying out a new member ministry varies with the size of the congregation" (p. 5). Using four categories based on the active membership categories of under 50, 50–150, 150–350, and 350–500 +, Routhauge shows that the size of the church (as people) affects interaction patterns and that these, in turn, are of critical importance to the attraction and retention of new members.

A final locus for sociological consulting in congregational settings is on the occasion of clergy turnover. Regardless of denomination, the church pastor exercises office charisma (except for the rare cases of genuine charisma). Regardless of the reason for turnover, something of a crisis atmosphere occurs or can erupt with clergy turnover. This is minimized, but not by any means removed, in churches that operate on the assignment system. A pastor's leaving, or a church's difficulty in attracting a new pastor, or differences in the new assigned pastor's style from a predecessor's can signal a need for self-study and evaluation. Here an outside consultant can prove useful. Some denominations *require* this activity prior to new pastor placement; although here the consultant is usually provided by the denominational structure. The outside consultant may work with the congregation to do little more than develop an effective survey instrument or other data collection technique. In other cases the consultant may actually do the research, analyze its results, and even take part in the subsequent hiring process. Such a consultant may also design and implement a format for interviewing prospective candidates. At other times a church may wish to learn, prior to advertising its position, how it may most effectively minister to the community in which it is located, given both its human and technical resources. A sociologist can make an assessment of both factors and provide a profile for action.

In marketing to a congregation, sociologists should be able to make clear what unique talents our training and perspective bring to the assignment. We know that the general population tends to think psychologistically. This can come out in such taken-for-granted assertions in the hiring process, for example, that since extended pastorates correlate with church growth, the church should seek a pastor who wants to "stay around a while." The psychologistic assumption here is that the individual pastor makes the difference in church growth. A sociologist, by contrast, can point out that there is an alternate explanation for the pastorate-growth association; namely, that congregations who work well together as groups *both* attract pastors to extended ministries and members to their fellowship. This specification of the relationship emphasizing the *group* can not only show the significance of a sociological perspective but also may open the door for continued consulting as the congregation decides it wants to learn more about how to work well together as a group.

A final note: Congregational consulting is not a particularly lucrative activity. For income purposes the consultant sometimes can at best hope that good work in this arena may create contacts in other sectors of the community. Many professionals who would not bat an eye on spending $6,000 for a consultant to make recommendations about where to put the water coolers in a plant may well balk at $600 from the church budget. Clergy, frequently underpaid, also are likely to recognize that a consultant's fee today may mean no raise tomorrow. Consultants should bear in mind two specifics: the overall size of the church's budget and the importance of communicating clearly to the congregation what it is getting for its money. Saying you are going to do "a 100-hour research project" is likely to get farther than saying you're going "to do a survey." The average layperson, religious or not, has little idea of how long "a survey" takes. In no case, however, should you fail to communicate the market value of your services, even if you discount or contribute them.

CLINICAL PASTORAL SOCIOLOGY

A final area for sociological consulting within the churches that needs to be explored further is what I term clinical pastoral sociology. Here the sociologist is normally also an ordained person in some religious body and combines these two roles to address the problems individuals face as a result of the social relationships in which they live. Pastoral psychology has enjoyed considerable popularity in American churches; sociology has not (Balswick 1979). Some of the reasons for this may be found in Protestant theology's emphasis upon individual salvation, some in sociology's tendency to be standoffish about application. Regardless of the background factors, here, as in many other areas of professional practice, sociologists have been largely "certified out" of the field. "Clinical pastoral theology," the formal name and structure under which pastoral psychology has been institutionalized, has created a self-perpetuating certification and accrediting system in which sociological training and theory find little place (Van Wagner 1983). Yet pastoral counselors are ready not only to practice their art in the churches but to market their trade (Lageman 1984).

Clinical pastoral sociology as I envision it is clinical sociology applied within the specific context of the religious institution and the pastor-congregant role relationship. This may occur either in the local church or in a religious counseling center. This viewpoint differs from traditional "pastoral counseling" in that it emphasizes the web of social interaction—including divine-human interaction as a form of social interaction (Swatos 1980, 1982)—rather than the individual as standing relatively alone against both divinity and society. Clinical pastoral sociology also differs from clinical sociology, however, in that it accepts and develops upon specific principles of revealed religion. With regard to Christianity, for example, clinical pastoral sociology can affirm that God is not a *deus solitarius* but a *deus triunus,* that the Godhead itself is persons-in-relationship and humanity is created in this image. Sin is the breaking of the image—imperfect relationships. In the incarnation we are told that the *Word* became flesh; language as constitutive of humanity can be explored in unique ways by those with sociological expertise. The importance of the charismatic band to the mission of the charismatic leader is another salient theological theme. A Christian doing clinical pastoral sociology uses these themes along with sociological theory to counsel the client in ways that would not necessarily be appropriate to a secular context.

As clinical pastoral sociology addresses aspects of client's lives that relate to immediate everyday activities, the practice is likely to verge more closely to that of clinical sociology in general. As questions about the client's relationship to deity are raised, the approach will bear a more theological cast. The important point to be remembered, however, is that regardless of the theological or pragmatic valence attached to a given application, the theoretical structure is fundamentally sociological: *social* variables are given explanatory priority. Not "One Solitary Life" but "One Charismatic Relationship" is the text to which our drummer plays.

REFERENCES

Balswick, Jack. 1979. "The Psychological Captivity of Evangelicalism." Paper presented at the combined annual meeting of the Society for the Scientific Study of Religion and the Religious Research Association, San Antonio. Photocopied.

Barnes, Harry Elmer. 1929. *The Twilight of Christianity.* New York: Vanguard.

Bartholomew, John Niles. 1969. "A Study of Planning Techniques for Local Congregations." *Review of Religious Research* 11:61–65.

Berger, Peter L. 1961a. *The Noise of Solemn Assemblies.* Garden City, N.Y.: Doubleday.

———. 1961b. *The Precarious Vision.* Garden City, N.Y.: Doubleday.

Bernard, Luther L. 1934. *The Fields and Methods of Sociology.* New York: Long & Smith.

Brewer, Earl D. C., and Douglas W. Johnson. 1970. *An Inventory of the Harlan Paul Douglass Collection of Religious Research Reports.* New York: Department

of Research, Office of Planning and Program, National Council of The
Churches of Christ in the U.S.A.

Fichter, Joseph H. 1951. *Southern Parish: Dynamics of a City Church*. Chicago:
University of Chicago Press.

———. 1980. *Religion and Pain*. New York: Crossroads.

———. 1982. *The Rehabilitation of Clergy Alcoholics*. New York: Human Sciences.

———. 1984. "The Myth of Clergy Burnout." *Sociological Analysis* 45:373–82.

Glock, Charles Y., Benjamin B. Ringer, and Earl R. Babbie. 1967. *To Comfort
and to Challenge*. Berkeley: University of California Press.

Green, Howard Whipple. 1954. "Serving the Urban Community." In *Methodism
Looks at the City*, edited by Robert A. McKibben, pp. 43–50. New York:
Division of Missions, Board of Missions—The Methodist Church.

Hadden, Jeffrey K. 1969. *The Gathering Storm in the Churches*. Garden City, N.Y.:
Doubleday.

———. 1974. "A Brief Social History of the Religious Research Association."
Review of Religious Research 15:128–36.

———. 1980. "H. Paul Douglass: His Perspective and His Work." *Review of
Religious Research* 22:66–88.

Hoge, Dean R., and David A. Roozen, eds. 1979. *Understanding Church Growth
and Decline*. New York: Pilgrim.

Janowitz, Morris. 1978. *The Last Half Century*. Chicago: University of Chicago
Press.

Kelley, Dean M. 1972. *Why Conservative Churches are Growing*. New York: Harper
& Row.

Kincheloe, Samuel C. 1929. "The Behavioral Sequence of a Dying Church."
Religious Education 24:329–45.

Lageman, August G. 1984. "Marketing Pastoral Counseling." *Journal of Pastoral
Care* 38:274–80.

Reed, Myer S. 1981. "An Alliance for Progress." *Sociological Analysis* 42:27–46.

———. 1982. "After the Alliance." *Sociological Analysis* 43:189–204.

Roof, Wade Clark. 1976. "Traditional Religion in Contemporary Society." *American Sociological Review* 41:195–208.

Ross, Edward A. 1936. *Seventy Years of It*. New York: Appleton-Century.

Routhage, Arlin J. 1983. *Sizing Up a Congregation for New Member Ministry*. New
York: Education for Mission and Ministry Office, Episcopal Church
Center.

Swatos, William H., Jr. 1980. "Liturgy and Lebensform: The Personal God as
a Social Being." *Perspectives in Religious Studies* 8:38–49.

———. 1981. "Beyond Denominationalism?: Community and Culture in American Religion." *Journal for the Scientific Study of Religion* 20:217–27.

———. 1982. "The Power of Prayer." *Review of Religious Research* 24:153–63.

———. 1984. *Faith of the Fathers*. Bristol, Ind.: Wyndham-Hall.

Thorne, Charles. 1974. Reaction to Hadden (1974). *Review of Religious Research*
15:155–56.

Van Wagner, Charles A. 1983. "The AAPC: The Beginning Years, 1963–1965."
Journal of Pastoral Care 37:163–79.

7

Combining Engineering and Sociology

KEITH L. SMITH

People tend to think of sociologists and engineers as poles apart with respect to their work interests, personalities, and value orientations. To a certain extent this is borne out in psychological research (Melton 1982; Teevan et al. 1983). The primary dimension in Holland's personality types theory (1973) places sociologists and engineers at opposite extremes ("Social" versus "Realistic"). However, the second-level dimension, "Investigative," is the same for both occupations.

Be that as it may, I have enjoyed consecutive careers as an engineer and as a sociologist, and now combine both disciplines in my professional work. Quite unexpectedly, I have found that the two disciplines complement each other very effectively in certain types of work. This chapter discusses opportunities for sociologist-engineer teams in applied consulting work. It also explores possible future demand for interdisciplinary sociology-engineering generalists.

TRANSITION TO SOCIOLOGIST-ENGINEER: A PERSONAL EXPERIENCE

At the time of graduation from engineering school my interests closely resembled those considered typical of engineers, focused upon physical phenomena and mathematical relationships. I was concerned with developing practical solutions to technical problems, very little interested in political or social policy issues or organizations. Fortunately, however, I found myself in a geographic area awash with social and economic problems, with very few organizations actively seeking their solution. As my career in industrial research developed, I became aware of the avocational opportunities presented by this situation. Over a very long time (about 20 years), as I became more involved in civic, welfare, and lobbying efforts, my interests greatly broadened. In the fullness of time it became apparent that my effectiveness in social change activities was seriously constrained by lack of training, skills, and credentials. It was necessary to choose one career direction or the other. I opted for the sociology route and obtained a doctoral degree in the field.

At the time I entered the field of sociology it seemed clear that I would of necessity need to leave engineering, since the two fields differ so markedly from each other. But this view did not reckon with the obvious fact that high-technology organizations wrestle with organizational dynamics, organizational and social change problems, and technology transfer requirements. These issues are all deeply embedded in engineering technology and practice. I found there are some unique advantages inherent in the ability to practice sociology and engineering simultaneously.

Since graduating with a degree in sociology, I have worked in both nonengineering and engineering settings. In the former I served as a sociologist on the faculty and in the administration of a medical school, and conducted field research. More recently, I have provided sociology-engineering professional services to a high-technology federal laboratory, to the Department of Energy, and to an organizational unit of the United States Armed Forces.

OVERVIEW AND SOME CAVEATS

The first part of this chapter will focus on the immediate and near-term possibilities for sociologist-engineer teams. In this part I assume that such teams would approximate my own experience. Opportunities for such teams to meet some clearly evident and important needs are identified. Suggestions are made for securing work of this kind, and for carrying it out.

The final section of the chapter explores the possibilities for training and developing sociologist-engineers as a multidisciplinary specialty to meet some high-technology society needs. Opportunities to enhance the scope and challenge of engineering careers are also discussed.

Some qualifiers are in order. To the extent that the presentation has to do with interdisciplinary sociology-engineering, a case could be made that I am dealing with a sample of one. It could perhaps be concerned with a *population* of one, since I know of no one else trained and practicing this combination at the present time. Further, the literature on the subject is rather sparse. Many organizational and management analysts and a few practicing sociologists, however, have had undergraduate training in engineering; to varying degrees they have likely incorporated this training into their work. In short, the base for interdisciplinary work is somewhat larger than it might appear to be. It is hoped that the material presented here will prove suggestive and useful.

The great majority of the applications identified in the next section are areas in which I have worked. I am personally acquainted with sociologists who have worked successfully in the remainder of them.

I do not believe that either sociologists or engineers possess any all-encompassing characteristics, ascribable to each and every member of the respective groups. In fact, much of what I have to say assumes considerable variation in interests within each group. If, in the interest of brevity, my words convey the notion of stereotyping, please discount it.

CONSULTING OPPORTUNITIES FOR SOCIOLOGIST-ENGINEER TEAMS

Opportunities for professional work by sociologist-engineer teams fall into three functional areas: dynamics of technology-oriented groups, organizational change, and technological-social policy development.

To Analyze, Plan, and Make Recommendations Concerning Organizational Structure and Dynamics in Technology-Oriented Groups

Objectives Definition and Measurement

Statements of objectives, at least in engineering technology-oriented groups, tend to take the form of a function statement: "Carries out research in...." Such statements are of little use in the formulation of objectives, or to assess the achievement of organizational objectives. For high-technology organizations, both sociology and engineering skills are needed to identify realistic group objectives (through interviews and analysis), to state them in a form that guides evaluation, and to develop practical instruments to assess group or organizational performance.

Quantification and Characterization of Organizational Inputs and Outputs

Where the resource inputs to an organization and the products from the organization can be measured as the properties of physical objects (composition of a chemical mixture, machined parts, chemical analyses), the productivity and the quality of organizational output can be characterized by well-developed engineering techniques. Where the input or output of a group cannot be meaningfully characterized by its physical properties (such as a research report or an engineering analysis), productivity and quality assessment techniques are nearly nonexistent. Yet, for many high technology organizations (for example, research laboratories and environmental analysis groups), these intangibles may be their only significant product.

Characterization of the quality and volume of organizational inputs and outputs is essential if a research or analysis group is to carry out any kind of meaningful quality assurance or productivity improvement program. In addition, such measures may be useful in the assessment of individual staff performance. Another application: Federal government agencies frequently undertake what are termed A–76 studies, to determine whether a particular government function could likely be carried out more efficiently by the private sector. Such studies require that the quality and volume of organizational inputs and outputs be carefully specified. When the organization studied deals with high technology, then the applicable engineering specialty should be carefully integrated with organizational sociology to carry out the study successfully.

Management/Monitoring Plans for Relatively Complex Organizational Functions

Certain functions of sizable high-technology organizations prove to be rather complex, involving many diverse inputs and outputs and a variety of interfaces. Maintenance functions are a prime example, but environmental protection and safety or emergency functions might also be included. Here, too, I have found that both engineering and organizational dynamics skills and knowledge are needed to develop, document, and provide quality assurance for these complex functions.

To Help Bring About Needed Organizational Changes

Resolution of Organizational Conflict Situations

Group and intergroup conflict that reaches dysfunctional or destructive levels is probably no more or no less prevalent in high-technology organizations than in any other kinds of organizations. These conflict situations do not differ qualitatively in any important respect from those of other organizations. Therefore, their resolution calls into play the same well-known social science skills that would be required for organizational conflict resolution in any other setting.

Destructive conflict and other morale problems often arise (or intensify) as a result of sharp changes in the direction of technology development, cutbacks in funding support, or periodic reorganizations. These events happen quite frequently in enterprises on the leading edge of high technologies. It is usually not too difficult for outside consultants to learn about them and offer to help.

Given the prevailing attitudes of engineers toward the social sciences, gaining acceptance in an organization may prove to be a problem. In my experience, engineering credentials can be helpful, but only if they are used to demonstrate that you have acquired a thorough understanding of the technical situations and problems your client encounters in such functions as research, design, plant operations, and the like. It will prove helpful if engineers in your consulting group are among those who interface directly with the client. In general, your team's engineering credentials can often be helpful, sometimes necessary, but not necessarily sufficient. Demonstrating your capacity to facilitate the solution of group conflict situations will likely prove to be at least as important.

On occasion, opportunities will arise to help resolve conflicts in an informal way in the course of providing other services. It is worthwhile to keep a lookout for such opportunities.

Facilitation of Productivity and Quality Improvements

Publications having to do with productivity and quality improvements, such as Peters and Waterman's *In Search of Excellence* (1982) are exerting an important influence upon many managers of high-technology organizations, at least in the government sector. Many of them sense the importance and the need to improve productivity and quality. A number of them are receptive to competent outside help to attempt to undertake such improvements.

Both sociology and engineering skills are needed to improve productivity and quality in technologically oriented organizations, because barriers to improvement may reside in either the technology or the organizational dynamics or both. It is important to become well acquainted with both the technology and the organizational dynamics. This is needed to unify these seemingly disparate concerns by carefully establishing consensus on objectives and how to measure them. It is also important to use each bit of acquired information to gain further insights into the nature of the problems. Typically, such effort begins with predominate focus on the technology issues, and then moves steadily toward greater concern with organizational dynamics and change.

Help Bring About Needed Organizational Change

High-technology organizations on occasion have need to upgrade or change certain functions that affect almost the entire organization. They include safety, security, quality assurance, emergency programs, control of environmental emissions, or the quality and productivity improvements as noted above. Generally, change in these areas will be the result of purposely planned efforts, rather than a response to crisis. The change process ideally should have begun with the identification of objectives and the structuring of the change process itself. An individual or team with credentials and skills in both sociology and engineering can in effect enjoy the benefits of two worlds: identification with and understanding of the position of the engineering and technology professionals who are experiencing the change on the one hand, together with the broad view of organizational dynamics provided by the sociological prospective on the other. On another level, the combined disciplines provide insights into the interaction of the physical technology with its organizational manifestations.

To Analyze and Help Develop Policy with Respect to Technological/Social Interactions

Sociologist-engineering teams can perform useful work to identify, analyze, and help develop policy concerning the social impacts of technology, social direction, and constraints upon technological change. They can contribute to development of policies for the wisest use of technology in the public interest. They can do these things, but whether they actually do get to carry them out is another matter. This is probably the area of greatest competition from other occupational groups. Some examples of possible opportunity areas are cited below.

Socioeconomic Aspects of Environmental Impacts of Large Technology Projects

Sociologists have worked with engineers and other professionals in this kind of activity for some time now. To some extent the work has become routinized, and will probably address a smaller number of new projects in the near future. Whether opportunites will materialize for newcomers in the field is somewhat problematical.

Facilitation of Transfer and Application of New Technology

For several years, the Stevenson-Widler Act has required that federal government groups who generate new technology must devote a certain part of their budget and staff effort to facilitate the dissemination of this new technology to potential users. This activity can take a relatively passive and conventional form, utilizing technical journals, professional meetings, and seminars to convey the information to persons and groups who are interested. Such efforts could be supplemented by a more pro-active program, to solicit potential user needs, to determine whether the information disseminated is in fact received and used, and to identify any previously unknown roadblocks to utilization. The latter course of action could utilize sociologist-engineer teams to advantage, working closely with generators of new technology.

A very large amount of new technical information has been and is being generated by federal government groups. Much of it is not even in a form that could be effectively communicated. Efforts are under way to disseminate it, largely by conventional means. Whether the Congress intended a more active effort than this is not evident from reading the Stevenson-Widler Act. Presumably a more active effort falls within the scope of executive decision making, if agencies can be convinced of the value of such effort.

Facilitation of Consensus Concerning Environmental Waste Problems

Sociologists have been involved to some degree in attempts to develop a basis for resolution of very contentious issues surrounding disposal of wastes, cost assessment decisions, and the adequacy of technical and administrative solutions to specific problems. Planning, development, and assessment of the control technology of course falls within the province of engineers.

To hold controversies in this area at least within reasonable limits, it is necessary to interpret the usually inadequate technical information competently and objectively. Much more difficult and critical, it is necessary to win the confidence of oftentimes mutually distrustful groups, to find some common grounds for risk management principles and a policy that represents the public interest. Sociologist-engineer teams appear well suited to tackle this kind of problem and have at least on occasion been used for this purpose. A recent approach proposed by William Ruckelshaus (1985), to assess and manage risks associated with environmental hazards in a certain way, could make effective use of sociologist-engineer teams.

Development of Organizational and Interorganizational Aspects of National Industrial Policy Issues

National industrial policy and the heated controversy surrounding it have until now remained largely the preserve of economists and political scientists. Just below the national policy level, however, industrial policy must be concerned with the prospects for cooperative action among antagonistic groups, the possibilities for decisions that reflect the larger public interest, and critical influences upon organizational productivity. All of these issues are firmly embedded in engineering technology. They could be appropriately addressed by sociologist-engineer teams. At least one nonprofit organization is active in this field (Zager and Rosow 1982). Most of the recent work in the area has been done by business management professionals, sometimes teamed with industrial engineers. Two basic needs must be met to work effectively on these problems: a sponsor perceived as unbiased, and efficient means for social and organizational change that go beyond superficial organizational rearrangement and public relations campaigns.

Areas of Sociology That Appear Most Useful in Association with Engineering

The particular areas within sociology that I have found to be most useful in association with engineering include organizational sociology, industrial sociology, organizational change, social change, program evaluation and organizational assessment, and policy analysis. Other areas I have found useful but not quite so central are occupational sociology, survey research, and methodology in general. In other circumstances the list could well have been different.

SUGGESTIONS FOR SECURING AND CARRYING OUT WORK IN THE SOCIOLOGY-ENGINEERING AREA

To Secure Engineer Collaborators

It is not at all certain that just any professionally qualified engineer will prove to be an effective collaborator on a multidisciplinary team with sociologists. Differences in perspectives, interests, and analytical approaches between engineers and sociologists are substantial. Many engineers regard the work of social scientists (with the possible exception of economists) as without value. Even with the best of professional relations, communication can be a problem.

Fortunately, engineers are by no means homogeneous in their interests and backgrounds. Effective collaborators are more likely to be engineers who have completed a liberal arts curriculum before beginning engineering school, have participated in an engineering curriculum enhanced by a substantial number of liberal arts courses, or have had broad avocational experience in civic or other social concerns.

Locating Clients for Sociology-Engineering Services

Organizations likely to use the services of a sociologist-engineer team are probably deeply involved in medium- to high-level technology. They are frequently required to deal with complex organizational and interface problems. They may well already deal with several diverse disciplines, both within and outside their organizational boundaries. Characteristically, they are concerned with (or are a part of) government, or are otherwise unusually oriented toward the public interest. In short, they are concerned with changing social and organizational situations as well as technological innovation.

The client organization's staff typically will include engineers. However, if engineering and engineering activity totally dominate the organization, then it is likely that the organization has defined its purpose in such a way as to exclude many of the problem areas that sociologist-engineer teams are equipped to handle. They are less likely to provide consultation opportunities.

These comments simply identify some characteristics of organizations more likely than others to experience an extraordinary number of situations in which a sociologist-engineer team could provide useful service. Having targeted likely clients, then it is essential to carefully identify and characterize those particular needs or problem areas in which your team can be useful to the client.

Gaining Acceptance

You will, in effect, be competing not only with engineering consulting firms but also with engineers on the client's staff. It is important to demonstrate that you can provide engineering *plus* a unique addition: sociology integrated with engineering.

Like it or not, your potential contribution probably will be assessed from an engineering prospective. There are several things you can do to increase your chances for acceptance. Organize your services around problem solving, rather than performing research or carrying out a study. Problem solving is a venerable and demonstrably valuable tradition in engineering. Objectives and proposed actions will be most readily understood if framed in terms of solving problems.

Sociology and engineering do have some basic concepts in common. The idea of an organizational system, with resource inputs and outputs and the need for net imports across system boundaries to maintain the organization, has an energy counterpart in the engineer's thermodynamic system, and a physical counterpart in the engineer's material balance calculations. Empirical correlations and curve-fitting, as well as graphic solutions are common and well understood. Many of the characteristics of organizational analysis, for example, can be presented in terms and systems concepts with which engineers are quite familiar.

Engineers reputedly exhibit a relatively low tolerance for ambiguity. All too often engineers and physical scientists view the content of social sciences as vague and too imprecise to be practical. The social sciences technical literature requires a very different approach from that needed to understand engineering literature. This is reflected in the often-negative reaction that engineers experience in dealing with social sciences subjects. Therefore, it is especially important to explain to engineers what you can do for them in the most concrete and explicit terms possible. Bear in mind that concepts that sociologists find very useful may strike engineers as vague, an embellishment of the obvious, or "fluff."

Effecting Change

Among the most unique and valuable services you can provide, helping your client to bring about needed organizational or social changes ranks near the top. Your interviewing, small group dynamics, conflict resolution, and communications knowledge and skills—in fact, virtually everything you have learned about social change—will be used and needed. It is indeed essential to involve all kinds of participants from an early point in the change process. Professionals and management in high-technology activities are very much accustomed to work activities that involve frequent small-group meetings, formal and informal. They appreciate and respond well to carefully planned and efficiently conducted group and two-person discussions. In the complex, highly segmented organizations that characterize much of high-technology activity, the extent of internal communications breakdown is often quite surprising. If you can identify these broken or malfunctioning links, gain some insights into their causes, and help reestablish communication, you will have performed a valuable service.

When you convey information, either orally or in writing, it is important to use the organization and style that engineers and high-technology management most clearly understand. As noted previously, this kind of communication emphasizes problem solving, relationships between variables, "how to" explanations, concise descriptions. Flow charts and other graphic presentations, if well designed, are readily comprehended and well received. You will not need to worry about the comprehension of mathematical or statistical materials. You may well find that the language of mathematics and statistics constitutes one of your most important links in common.

OPPORTUNITIES FOR EDUCATION: ENHANCEMENT OF ENGINEERING AND THE DEVELOPMENT OF INTERDISCIPLINARY GENERALISTS

The discussion thus far is based on the very plausible assumption that the supply of interdisciplinary sociologist-engineers is very limited at the present time. Any substantial amount of interdisciplinary work in this area will need to be carried out by sociologist-engineer teams.

On the other hand, I find that substantial advantages can be realized when at least a major part of each discipline is resident in the same person. These advantages may not be fully achieved by interdisciplinary teams, particularly when it comes to the day-to-day operations of a high-technology organizations.

Another objective can be realized by combining the two disciplines. A case can be made for the usefulness of postgraduate education of engineers in the social sciences as a means of solving some persistent problems in engineering careers.

This section will primarily interest educators, students, and professionals contemplating a midcareer change. It should also prove useful to the consultants addressed in the previous section, by providing additional insights into the nature of the problems and the motivations of those with whom they will deal.

First, some developing problems and concerns for career engineers will be discussed briefly. Then two directions for possible change will be discussed. One direction would have as its objective to help engineers enlarge the scope of their skills and concerns, somewhat in the manner in which the Master of Business Administration is now used by engineers (see, for example, Fowler 1985). The other direction explores the possibilities for development of truly interdisciplinary generalists.

Some Developing Concerns and Problems in Engineering Careers

For several decades during and since World War II, engineering has provided expanding, stable, and challenging career opportunities for individuals with the mathematical and analytical aptitudes needed, plus the capacity to meet the rather demanding engineering school curriculum and subsequent on-the-job training. Engineering provides an important means for upward mobility. To a very large extent these qualities still characterize engineering. Starting salaries and employment opportunities for most branches of engineering are clearly greater than those for other college graduates. There is every reason to believe that engineering will continue to provide challenging opportunities at the cutting edge of proliferating technology developments on into the foreseeable future.

The careers of individual engineers are by no means free of substantial problems, however. Most of these problems arise from the characteristic pattern of technological advances, and from the increasing social impact of the technology that engineers develop.

First, new technology areas tend to develop in spurts and to proliferate in different directions: Rapid engineering development builds on the discovery of some new scientific knowledge, followed by a relatively static nature phase, perhaps eventually superseded by technology developed in another area. The rapid development phase requires substantial engineering manpower; conditions encourage engineers to become highly specialized in the details of this particular technology area. Unfortunately, fewer and fewer new technology developments continue in their active, growing phase for the lifetime of an engineering career. As a result, the engineer's job frequently becomes dead-ended, routine, unchallenging, and may evaporate altogether (Gutteridge 1978; Greenwald 1978). Some available evidence suggests that the most satisfying careers in engineering are characterized by frequent change and the capacity to make changes quickly (Bailyn and Lynch 1983). Often such change is not possible, however, because of the nature of hiring practices for older workers, and the difficulty in keeping abreast of new basic engineering knowledge and skills over a career lifetime. Despite the relatively high starting salaries for engineers, employers often find it more productive and cost-effective to hire new graduates than to retain or hire older engineers. Even where career changes can be arranged, the individuals involved are often reluctant to undergo the geographic and status changes required. In short, the number of disillusioned middle-aged engineers in the ranks is fairly substantial.

Second, most practicing engineers have adopted a relatively narrow definition of their professional concerns, compared with the very wide social, environmental, and political impacts of the technology they develop. Engineers frequently see themselves as the instruments rather than the instigators of change (Knepler 1977). They frequently assume that the societal advantages of their new technology are or should be self-evident; the social and political impacts of such developments are considered to be not their concern: Negative environmental and social effects can be cured with the application of more technology. The public expression of antitechnology sentiments characteristically leaves them puzzled, and perhaps angry and estranged.

Third, in order to advance in the organizational hierarchy engineers must frequently cease to practice engineering. Strictly within the traditional functional areas of engineering—such as design, research, production, and technical sales—the hierarchical ladder is characteristically rather short. To advance beyond a certain level the engineer must enter the managerial ranks. For many engineers, who are primarily oriented toward problem-solving on physical systems, a managerial position is not really engineering. Many make the transition and are satisfied with their work; many others are not.

A variety of explanations has been offered to account for these problems. The highly focused pattern of interests of those who characteristically choose to enter engineering is given as one cause. Others have documented a significant reduction in engineers' expectations for their job over time (Kopelman 1977). Engineers' job dissatisfaction has been ascribed to the conflict between professionalism and work bureaucracies

(Alexander 1981). Whether engineering meets the full requirements to be defined as a profession continues to be debated. The accuracy of these observations, and the various ways in which these problems can or ought to be dealt with, go beyond the scope of this chapter. I would like to focus on just one possibility: To expand the scope of issues and concerns to which the engineers could optionally apply their problem-solving abilities.

Some Relevant Trends in Engineering Education

Much of engineering education has in fact been concerned with enlarging the scope of interests and knowledge of their graduates beyond technology for many years (Knepler 1977). Most engineering educators have long since concluded that technological and economic feasibility are not the sole or even the main determinants of what engineers do. Enrichment courses in the humanities and the social sciences have long been required in engineering curriculums, usually as required electives. Some teaching projects to bridge the gap between engineering and sociology have been reported (Kolak and McDougall 1982).

Such efforts usually encounter tough going in turning out "technological humanists." Much like the parallel effort to introduce social and behavioral sciences into the medical school curriculum (in which I have had some personal experience), many students perceive such course work as not important to career success or even short-term academic success, and therefore assign it a very low priority.

If and when practicing engineers see themselves as headed toward a management position (or perhaps if their interests change or they see their current career approaching a stalemate) many of them secure a Master of Business Administration (MBA) degree. This may conflict with their further development in engineering. However, the MBA may help to redirect their interests and concerns into more fruitful channels, and to develop new skills.

MBA curricula at different colleges vary enormously, so it is difficult to generalize. On the one hand, it is possible that this course work redirects, but does not broaden, the interests of engineers in the most needed directions. More particularly, it may not enlarge those concerns in which engineering skills and experience can be used in a challenging way. Some such course work may provide only cut and dried rules and procedures, without developing a real theoretical base and understanding of organizational problem-solving principles. On the other hand, many of the most effective analysts and advocates for change in business and industrial organizations are engineer graduates of business schools.

Why Sociology Combined with Engineering?

Combination of engineering with sociology (or, more broadly, with social sciences) could accomplish two purposes. First, it could increase the opportunities and challenges of engineering careers by enlarging the range of technology-related problems to which engineering problem-solving could be applied. Second, such a combination could produce multidisciplinary generalists to help bridge across the extremely wide range of concerns of a high-technology society.

To Enlarge the Opportunities and Challenges for Engineers

In a very real sense, engineers as an occupational group restrict their participation in the full complexities and challenge of technology-driven change by limiting themselves to just the physical and economic dimensions of such change. Granted, this traditional preserve of engineering can be decidedly challenging, particularly when a new technology is developing rapidly and its acceptance seems assured. However, when the engineers' product encounters organizational or societal resistance and misunderstanding, adverse environmental or public policy controversies, or when the technology simply matures to the point where additional engineering inputs become highly routine, then the self-imposed restraints can become very frustrating.

The action suggested here is really rather modest and limited. Briefly, practicing engineers would have access to opportunities at any time in their careers to expand their capabilities and credentials to include the organizational, social, and policy aspects of technology. It is hoped that this would enable engineers to extend their traditional problem-solving action mode laterally into these other key manifestations of technological change. This in turn could serve to maintain the challenge of engineering work throughout most of the course of a technology cycle. It could provide engineers with more options to shift to new technologies or functions throughout their careers. Much of an engineer's technical knowledge and problem-solving skills could continue to be applied, but in different ways and for somewhat different purposes. They would not need to leave their engineering behind to move to management positions. In fact, the broader skills and credentials could redefine what constitutes a "management position."

The proposal is limited, primarily because it is likely that only a minority of practicing engineers would want to move in this direction. As noted previously, engineers choose their occupation on the basis of quite different interests. However, the interests of individual engineers are by no means homogeneous, and they often change markedly over the course of a working career. It is likely that at least some engineers would be interested in moving in the suggested direction at some time in their career.

The proposal is a relatively modest one because most of the formal education that would be needed is already in place in bits and pieces in various graduate-level programs. Most of these programs are oriented toward graduate education for occupational groups and academic specialties other than engineers, but they could be reassembled to meet career engineers' needs. It is important, however, that the issue of credentials is effectively addressed.

When engineers restrict themselves to technological and economic feasibility considerations, they have very sound reasons for doing so. To venture into the social-organizational-policy areas of technological change is to be criticized for exceeding the bounds of one's professional competence. To enable engineers to expand into social and policy dimensions of technological change, they will need access to a credentialing mechanism, as well as to knowledge and skills. Such credentials can be acquired by experience or by position, such as election to a legislative body; but usually credentials will be most effectively acquired by meeting the requirements of a well-defined graduate education program. It may, seem strange that the social sciences, whose credentials often receive only qualified acceptance in the public area, can provide credentials to a more highly accepted occupation such as engineering. Nonetheless, a large part of the hurdle for engineers consists of overcoming the assumption that they are *only* knowledgeable in physical technology.

Engineers can probably expand into the social and policy areas of technology more effectively by means of a Master's Degree acquired some time in midcareer, much as they acquire and use an MBA degree at the present time. Undergraduate engineering school coursework in the humanities and social sciences can perhaps lay the groundwork for broader concerns throughout an engineer's career. However, undergraduate course work will very likely fall short of providing the necessary credentials. In addition, the intense competition with mainline engineering for students' attention will inevitably keep it in a second- or third-class position.

An effective graduate-level program would not only deal with social science concepts and structure, but would also develop skills in the use of investigative and analytical techniques, such as interviewing and evaluation methodologies. An eclectic curriculum, which would include selected concepts and methodologies in economics and psychology, would prove useful. Practical means of bringing about organizational and social change would be important. Real-world analysis and problem-solving projects would round out the curriculum and contribute to the credibility of credentials associated with the degree.

To Develop Interdisciplinary Sociology-Engineer Generalists

A social sciences-enhanced engineer (or an engineering-enhanced social scientist) is not necessarily the equivalent of an interdisciplinary generalist. If our already complex, technologically oriented society continues to become more intertwined with technology and its social-political impacts, there may well develop a growing need for at least a few such generalists.

Social scientist-engineer generalists would have sufficient understanding and experience with the methodologies of both disciplines to be able to assess the overall quality and implications of the intellectual outputs from both disciplinary areas. They should, for example, be able to identify and analyze the interactions between engineering and social-policy developments. Most importantly, they should have developed a genuinely unitary conceptualization of technological development and change in all its principal ramifications. They should be able to address the theory and mechanisms of the change processes themselves. Finally, their credentials should be sufficiently acceptable that they can move freely in both disciplinary areas, and can provide the analyses and recommendations that will influence the direction of technological and social change.

Almost all of the work in both engineering and sociology (and the other social sciences) will of course need to continue to be carried out by professionals who are primarily qualified in a specialty or subspecialty in a particular field. But this very fragmentation into subspecialties and narrow subject areas increases the need for technological change generalists who can bridge across what is essentially a unitary process in the real world.

At the present time, a few eminent physical scientists and social scientists have undertaken to bridge across the entire technological change area, usually after spending most of a highly successful career in a particular field. Their stature in their particular field usually helps them gain credibility in the much broader area, but most of them are nevertheless subject to the criticism that they try to speak outside the boundaries of their expertise. (Granted that much of the criticism may be motivated by a desire to preserve turf. Even so, the criticism is usually effective.)

Doctoral-level degrees in two different disciplines can often provide the knowledge and credentials to enable a person to effectively bridge across a large subject area. Some people combine the MD degree with another doctoral degree to successfully bridge a sizable subject area. Law degrees are often used in a similar manner. In these instances, however, the diversity in subject matter may not be very large, and in any event both the medical and law degrees are backed by a widely acknowledged licensing system. Licensing is not nearly so strong in engineering, and it is of course essentially nonexistent in most social science fields.

It appears likely that those who could work successfully as generalists across the full range of engineering and social science aspects of technological change would have carried out credible professional work in both areas. They would hold a doctoral-level degree in one or both areas, and would have worked a substantial number of years at the leading edge of technological or social change.

To summarize, it does appear quite feasible to bridge across disciplines even as diverse as sociology and engineering. A case can be made for the need to do so. Professional credibility may be a problem, but it very likely can be conquered.

REFERENCES

Alexander, Kenneth O. 1981. "Scientists, Engineers and the Organization of Work." *American Journal of Economics and Sociology,* January: 51–66.

Bailyn, Lottie, and John T. Lynch. 1983. "Engineering as a Life-Long Career: Its Meaning, Its Satisfactions, Its Difficulties." *Journal of Occupational Behavior* 4: 263–83.

Fowler, Elizabeth M. 1985. "For Engineers: The M.B.A. vs. the M.S." New York *Times,* Sec. 12, March 24, p. 63.

Greenwald, Howard P. 1978. "Politics and the New Insecurity: Ideological Changes of Professionals in a Recession." *Social Forces,* September:103–18.

Gutteridge, Thomas G. 1978. "Labor Market Adaptation of Displaced Technical Professionals." *Industrial and Labor Relations Review,* July: 460–73.

Holland, John L. 1973. *Making Vocational Choices: A Theory of Careers.* Englewood Cliffs, N. J.: Prentice-Hall.

Knepler, Henry. 1977. "The New Engineers." *Change,* June: 30–35.

Kolack, Shirley, and John McDougall. 1982. "Teaching with Engineers and Scientists: What Role for Sociology?" *Humanity and Society,* May: 162–75.

Kopelman, Richard E. 1977. "Psychological Stages of Careers in Engineering." *Journal of Vocational Behavior,* June: 270–86.

Melton, Willie. 1982. "Equality and Freedom: Exploring Social Values and Social Issues Among Engineering Students." *Michigan Academician,* Winter: 273–83.

Peters, Thomas J., and Robert H. Waterman, Jr. 1982. *In Search of Excellence.* New York: Harper and Row.

Ruckelshaus, William D. 1985. "Risk, Science, and Democracy." *Issues in Science and Technology,* Spring: 19–38.

Teevan, R. C. et al. 1983. "Conflicts and Defenses in Engineering and Psychology Undergraduates." *Psychological Reports.* 53:554.

Zager, Robert, and Michael Rosow, eds. 1982. *The Innovative Organization.* New York: Pergamon.

PART III

Training Professionals for Consulting Practice

With limited opportunities for employment of sociology graduates and the decline in academic positions for sociology Ph.D.s, sociology departments have been reassessing the content and direction of their programs. An increasing number of applied programs are being developed and with this there has been an emphasis on training students in specialized areas for the practice of sociology. Student sociologists are now being introduced to nonacademic job opportunities and acquiring the skills that are needed for entering a variety of job markets. While these programs represent a beginning, the field could benefit from more systematic thought and action on the issues of training.

Within the field, though, there is considerable disagreement concerning the purpose and content of sociology programs. This controversy is directly related to the debate concerning the development of sociology's applied side. On one hand, the traditionalists feel sociology should remain "pure," while others recognize the need for developing an applied sociology if the discipline is to survive.

This debate cannot be resolved, but the development of sociology's applied side has already begun and it is gaining legitimacy. The American Sociological Association has recognized the importance of applied sociology and has initiated a number of activities associated with its development. Furthermore, other professional associations—the Society for Applied Sociology and the Clinical Sociology Association—have formed over the past ten years; these groups have as their explicit aim the development of sociology's applied side. All of these groups have been seriously addressing the issue of training and trying to delineate the skills and knowledge necessary for a practicing sociologist.

No doubt, the applied sociologist employed in an agency or organization may have different experiences from the sociologist who acts as a consultant. The consulting sociologist will have numerous "employers" rather than just one, since each consulting activity is contracted by a separate client. Regardless of this distinction, however, both are employed in a situation that requires the practical application of their sociological knowledge and skills. Thus it is critical to know how sociology programs can best prepare students for the practice of sociology. In addition, it is important to know what additional skills consultants need that relate to their self-employment status.

This part of the book addresses a number of issues related to the training of practicing sociologists. Howard Garrison, in Chapter 8, indicates that the demands of the marketplace should be considered in designing new curricula but that narrow vocationalism should be avoided. According to Garrison, at the baccalaureate level, writing, computing, and analysis skills should be emphasized. While on the Master's level, methodological skills should be stressed. At the Ph.D. level, Garrison argues that the student should have a broad intellectual preparation, but should prepare a dissertation that will serve as a bridge into the marketplace. He suggests that the emphasis should be on policy-relevant topics and analytical skills. To improve the job prospects of sociology graduates he emphasizes that demonstrable research and report skills are essential. Sociology programs must put more emphasis on the basic skills such as quantitative techniques, historical methods, interviewing techniques, and observation skills.

Earl Jones, in Chapter 9, argues that consulting is an increasingly complex enterprise calling for sociologists to expand their skills in evaluation, training, and general advisory services. Also, consulting sociologists are expected to be knowledgeable not only in their own discipline, but in related fields, other subjects, and always in entrepreneurial activities. Jones identifies the opportunities for sociology consultants at various degree levels: baccalaureate, masters, and doctorate. He also identifies avenues for learning, beyond the formal degree requirement, that will enhance the success of a consultant. These are formal study, self-study, and experience.

In Chapter 10 Raymond Adamek and Alexander Boros present findings based on 16 years of experience in training and supervising intern consultants in an applied sociology M.A. program. They describe a training model, give an overview of the consulting experiences of 75 interns, and discuss two dimensions of consulting roles. The students in their roles as consultants acted as researchers, program developers, evaluators, and field educators. Adamek and Boros found that the students could adequately cope with the problems encountered in the different settings, advance their practice-oriented skills, and contribute to problem solving; they further provided validating experiences of the practical value of the sociological perspective for human service organizations.

Mary Evans Melick, in Chapter 11, discusses the consulting work of sociologists with preparation in two fields. She identifies a number of advantages to dual preparation that include increased opportunity for obtaining consulting work, facilitation of work in a second field, securing cooperation of respondents, and acting as an advocate. Disadvantages include failure to identify the consultant as a "real" sociologist, problems of overrapport and bias, and posing a threat to respondents. These issues are investigated, in part, through an exploratory survey of sociologists with prior preparation in nursing or divinity. Among the outcomes of this exploratory work is the finding that there is considerable mobility between fields in both the consulting work and full-time employment of sociologists with preparation in two fields. In conclusion, she suggests systematic study of the employment choices, identity, perceived advantages and disadvantages of dual preparation, and the actual consulting work of such sociologists.

8

Preparing Students for Nonacademic Employment

HOWARD H. GARRISON

Sociologists are becoming increasingly concerned about the poor employment prospects for new sociology graduates. In 1982 a task force was established by the American Sociological Association (ASA) to study the employment problem (Bonacich 1982). Projected declines in college enrollments (Bowen 1981) and declining interest in sociology will probably limit the number of new academic positions for sociologists. Indeed, the period of declining enrollment has already set in; some schools have begun to report declines in the size of their freshman classes (Feinberg 1982). In sociology, the declines have been particularly steep. Undergraduate sociology majors have dropped from a peak of 4.0 percent of all 1972 graduates to 1.7 percent of all 1982 graduates (U.S. Department of Education 1948–82). These declines are likely to continue. Data from the Annual Freshman Survey (conducted by UCLA's Higher Education Research Institute) show a continuing drop in freshman preferences for social science majors. In 1974, 12.7 percent of the freshmen planned to major in the social sciences. By 1979 the percentage had dropped to 9.0 percent. In 1983 only 7.6 percent indicated that they planned to major in the social sciences (Green 1984).

The nonacademic job market will not be a panacea for sociologists' employment problems. It offers the prospect of increasing employment opportunities, but only to the extent that sociologists are able to successfully compete with statisticians, psychologists, economists, and political scientists. It will not be easy; all of these groups have strong and well-established claims on some segment of the nonacademic research market.

The question of how to prepare sociologists for the competition for nonacademic jobs is a good and timely one. Much of the discussion revolves around the development of special curricula for applied sociology, but this is a mistake for several reasons. First, the growth prospects for the government and social service sectors are not great. While there is a need to compete aggressively for the available jobs in these sectors, it would be a mistake to make a drastic shift in our emphasis to the pursuit of this market. Second, most academic sociologists do not practice applied sociology and, as a result, may not be able to prepare students for this endeavor.

THE PH.D. LEVEL

The depressed academic job market is particularly significant for the Ph.D. holder. (Master's degree holders are already excluded from all but the most marginal academic jobs.) In the last few years Ph.D. sociologists have started entering the nonacademic job market. In the past, sociologists (unlike economists, psychologists, and political scientists) have been reluctant to pursue these options. In 1975, 84.3 percent of all Ph.D. sociologists were academically employed (Huber 1985). Only 70.6 percent of the Ph.D.s in nonclinical fields of psychology were academically employed in 1975 (Institute of Medicine 1985). There is no reason why sociologists could not perform much of the applied social science work currently done by members of these other professions.

Nonacademic employment opportunities seemed quite promising a few years back, but recent developments require the qualification of some of the intitial optimism. Several areas of nonacademic employment have been hit hard by cutbacks in federal research and development funding. While the percentage of nonacademically employed sociologists rose from 1975 to 1981, unemployment and underemployment also rose (Huber 1985). More current data (combining sociologists with anthropologists and a small number of "other" behavioral scientists) present a mixed picture of nonacademic employment growth. Employment in government and in the nonprofit sector decreased in 1983 while unemployment rose (Institute of Medicine 1985). However, there was a modest gain in total nonacademic employment as a result of large increases in self-employment and hospital employment.

The best course for the Ph.D. candidate seeking to enter nonacademic employment is to develop a series of research projects that demonstrate research abilities—the more, the better. The dissertation in particular should be seen as a bridge into the labor market. It should establish the candidate's ability to define and execute research on a topic of policy relevance.

Internships and summer fellowships can provide exposure to current policy issues and topics. The Presidential Management Internship Program operated by the Office of Personnel Management can provide M.A. or Ph.D. candidates with experience in federal agencies. Other associations and agencies also sponsor summer programs for graduate students. An ASA publication (Howrey 1983) contains advice on internship programs. Some federal agencies, such as the U.S. General Accounting Office, provide financial support for students working on dissertations related to the agencies' mission. Issue-oriented associations and policy symposia may also provide valuable exposure to current policy issues.

Research projects emphasizing policy-relevant topics and analytic skills are the most crucial step. Many agencies collect large amounts of data in the process of carrying out their mandated functions, but rarely is this data thoroughly analyzed by social science standards. In many cases surveys are conducted and only the most basic tabulations are generated. Vast quantities of policy-relevant data are gathered every year. Typically underutilized, much of this data could support high-quality sociological analysis. Agencies may be unable to make full use of this data because of limited resources or lack of personnel. They may be very supportive of proposals for analysis from outsiders. In the event that they are not, researchers have recourse to "freedom of information" procedures. Most data collected with public funds can be obtained through administrative or legal channels. Ph.D. students seeking dissertation data should carefully scan agency publications. Published statistical summaries may provide clues to the existence of much larger data sources.

At the Ph.D. level, there is no need to sacrifice the broad intellectual training that sociologists receive. In the course of the four- or five-year doctoral program, however, serious candidates for nonacademic employment should be establishing connections to policy research via research projects, internships, and professional meetings.

THE BACHELOR'S LEVEL

Much of the discussion of applied sociology curricula centers around undergraduate education, in part because the problems are most severe at the undergraduate level. Unemployment, while rising, is not a pervasive problem for Ph.D. holders. Concern about the job prospects for undergraduate sociology majors is much greater and may have contributed to the steep enrollment declines noted above. The decreasing number of sociology undergraduate majors, in turn, represents a further threat to the academic employment prospects of Ph.D. sociologists. Academia is still their major source of employment and it is still the source of most of the basic research in sociology.

Reject Narrow Technical Training

Most disturbing about the proposals for applied sociology curricula are the suggestions to orient undergraduate students to specialization in institutional content areas (for example, education, aging, environment, recreation). The focus is too narrow at the undergraduate level and the employment demand for various specialties is subject to frequent fluctuation. Fifteen years ago we created a flood of education specialists; ten years ago programs were devised to create environmental specialists. Now job prospects in these areas are slim while the call goes out for military manpower specialists. Today's hot issues may have low priority tomorrow. While some students may move directly into specific jobs, in the long run this match may prove to be a very elusive target.

Over time, the options for the broadly educated baccalaureate students are greater than those of their narrowly trained counterparts. Students, whose postbaccalaureate life span will average more than 50 years, will be seriously shortchanged by narrow technical programs. Entry-level positions in many social service occupations, like corrections work, have high turnover rates. One may ask whether people with brief careers in these fields have profited more from their college educations than the students who come away with a lifelong appreciation of the plays of Shakespeare or the poetry of Milton. Narrow technical training violates the spirit of a liberal education. It will be a serious setback for higher education if we silently submit to the view that the purpose of a college education is to prepare students for specific, lifelong career slots.

Emphasize Basic Skills

Failure to surrender to the rising tide of vocationalism does not, however, require that we be callous and insensitive to the employment prospects faced by our graduates. One compromise strategy is to encourage students to take marketable minors in accounting, business, and other professionally oriented fields. Kinloch (1983) reports that there is already a discernible trend toward these minors among sociology undergraduates.

There are other options for enhancing the marketability of sociology students without recourse to newly created technical programs or the professional programs of other disciplines. Educators should begin by asking, "What are the employers seeking?" Most of the entry-level positions in federal and state agencies do not demand extensive substantive expertise. When positions are open, an agency looks for competent people capable of being trained to do its work. Substantive policy-making positions requiring detailed institutional knowledge are rarely open to outsiders with bachelor's degrees. They are usually reserved for those with years of service within the agency or related experience on the outside. At the entry levels, most agencies and organizations are willing to hire people to write, calculate, and program. They are willing to hire people with skills they recognize as valuable.

An examination of survey data on recent social science graduates might help to illustrate the type of entry-level positions that sociology graduates might be likely to obtain. Periodically, the National Science Foundation (NSF) conducts a sample survey of recent graduates in science and engineering fields. The results of these New Entrants Surveys (NES) are projected to national totals (see NSF 1984 for a description of survey methodology).

In 1982 a sample of 1980 and 1981 master's and bachelor's degree recipients was interviewed. Sociology and anthropology graduates (combined into a single category in the NES) were employed in a wide range of jobs and in a variety of economic sectors. Those who were employed in science or engineering jobs (which, by NSF definitions, include sociology and anthropology jobs) earned an average of $15,100 in 1982. This was $3,100 more than those employed in jobs outside of science and engineering. It would be interesting to learn how these graduates in science and engineering jobs were able to command higher salaries, but these data are not available. It is, however, informative to view the primary work activity of those employed in science or engineering jobs as a guide to preparing students in the future. Table 8.1 presents data on the primary work activity of social science graduates. (In these tabulations, the small number of cases per cell makes it necessary to group sociology and anthropology with economics and other social sciences.) For the recent baccalaureates employed in science/engineering (S/E) jobs, the modal category is "reporting, statistical, or computing activities." Nearly one-quarter of the social science students employed in science or engineering jobs cite this as their primary activity. This category includes report and technical writing. Research and development work is the primary activity of another 14.7 percent. Together, the two research-oriented categories contain nearly 40 percent of the total employed in S/E. Among recent master's degree recipients, the predominance of the two research categories is even greater. Research and development is the modal category with 28.0 percent. The reporting, statistical, or computing activities category contains another 18.0 percent. Together they account for 46.0 percent of the total.

Social science graduates in science and engineering jobs earn more than their peers in other jobs. A substantial portion of the social scientists employed in science or engineering jobs are involved primarily in research, report writing, or computation. Their peers in jobs outside the sciences are far less likely to be involved in these research-oriented activities and are much more likely to be in administrative or sales positions.

Table 8.1
Primary Work Activity in 1982 for 1980 and 1981 Social Science Degree Recipients

	Bachelor's Degree Recipients				Master's Degree Recipients			
	Science/ Engineering Jobs		Not Science/ Engineering Jobs		Science/ Engineering Jobs		Not Science/ Engineering Jobs	
Primary Work Activity	Number	Percent	Number	Percent	Number	Percent	Number	Percent
Research and development	5,000	14.7	2,900	4.5	1,400	28.0	200	4.5
Management/administration	7,300	21.5	19,100	29.5	1,100	22.0	1,500	34.1
Teaching	1,400	4.1	6,600	10.2	500	10.0	500	11.4
Production/inspection	4,800	14.2	3,800	5.9	300	6.0	600	13.6
Reporting/statistical/computing	8,400	24.8	4,000	6.2	900	18.0	300	6.8
Sales/professional service	5,200	15.3	19,200	29.6	200	4.0	400	9.1
Other (including consulting)	1,500	4.4	6,100	9.4	600	12.0	800	18.2
No report	300	0.9	3,100	4.8	—	—	100	2.3
Total*	33,900	99.9	64,800	100.1	5,000	100.0	4,400	100.0

*Due to rounding, totals may not equal 100.0.

Source: 1982 New Entrants Survey (See NSF 1984 for details).

One reasonable course of action for those concerned with improving the job prospects of sociology graduates would be to see that they had demonstrable research and report writing skills. More emphasis should be placed on the basic tools that we use in our work: quantitative techniques, historical methods, interviewing techniques, and observation skills. Terry (1983) recommends three or four statistics/methods courses for students who anticipate government careers. These research methods should not be isolated in special courses, they should become integral parts of every course.

The most critical skill is writing—the skill most likely to be appreciated by the broadest range of potential employers. When asked what skills needed greater emphasis in the preparation of students for employment, writing ability was the overwhelming choice of the employers responding to one recent survey (Brown et al. 1983). We should emphasize to our students the importance of writing skills in the development as well as the presentation of ideas. To many undergraduates, the gulf between their thoughts and a published argument may seem unbridgeable. Students are not always aware of how ideas are refined through expression and revision. We should help them learn how it is done by requiring written projects in every course.

Many sociology courses do not have major written assignments. It might be enlightening (though embarrassing) to learn how many students receive bachelor's degrees without writing a single term paper. We do our students and our discipline a great disservice by dispensing with major written assignments. These provide students with tangible products to bolster employment applications. A series of well-written research papers creates a strong impression. The best example, of course, would be a senior thesis.

Stress Core Concepts

Employers know that statisticians work with numbers; if those numbers include money or employment figures, then the relevance of an economist is acknowledged. For questionnaires and survey research, employers frequently turn to psychologists or market researchers. They seek writers and editors when they want to communicate verbally. One reason for the infrequent use of sociologists is the lack of familiarity with what we do.

Economists present themselves as masters of a specialized body of knowledge suitable for application to a wide range of human concerns. We should do the same. We should spend more time stressing the core ideas of our discipline rather than their many substantive derivations. At a minimum, we ought to be able to expect a sociology degree holder to be familiar with the following core areas of our field: stratification, social psychology, complex organization, demographic processes, and social change.

All departments offer courses in these fundamental areas, but they are rarely required for a degree. In most cases the requirements for a degree are minimal: a theory course, a statistics-research methods sequence, and electives. Students can (and many do) complete a program with a haphazard selection of elective courses in specialty areas such as sociology of law, sociology of medicine, sociology of sport, sociology of religion, and juvenile delinquency. While these courses have legitimate content, little thought is given to the student's overall understanding of the field. While a bright student could derive an integrated perspective on stratification from courses in the sociology of law, medicine, and the family, this would be unusual. It would be much easier for a student with a strong foundation in demography, complex organization, and stratification to derive reasonable hypotheses about the distribution of legal services to the poor.

Some teachers argue that they use their courses on family or medical sociology as vehicles for teaching structural themes. If this is the case, then students are not missing key sociological concepts. However, it is redundant and wasteful to reteach these concepts in every topical course. Teachers must either assume a common core of knowledge—which, at present, students are unlikely to have—or risk repetition.

Our elective courses are often designed to be popular and to reach out to nonmajors; they do, but at a cost to the integrity of sociology programs. In few other disciplines does a single introductory course enable a student to take any upper-level course. It is hard to believe that this practice does not have a deleterious impact on the quality of education that we offer our majors. We may gain a few warm bodies at the price of alienating the more serious students.

Our curricula need to be more integrated and sequential, less segmented. It would be beneficial to start undergraduate students with courses in social psychology, complex organization, and stratification. They would thereby be exposed to core concepts of the discipline at the three levels of analysis. Elective courses should have one or more of these courses as a prerequisite. Many students also delay taking their statistics and research methods courses until late in their program and, as a result, teachers are limited in their ability to present and require research in the classroom. Sociology majors should be exposed to the fundamental methods of research by the end of their sophomore year.

The choice of elective courses outside of sociology should not be ignored by undergraduate advisors. The ability to speak a foreign language may improve job prospects. Students should be encouraged to take quantitative courses; mathematics and statistics courses (beyond those required in the research methods sequence) are desirable. Computer science courses are also recommended. Exposure to one or more of the physical sciences would improve access to jobs in the technology-intensive industries.

Make Courses More Challenging

Rigor in our curricula should be matched with increased rigor in our courses. We have tried to lure students with topical courses and in the process have gained a reputation for "fun and games" rather than intellectual stimulation and challenge. These courses have contributed to a negative image of our students and our discipline. There has been a growing perception of sociology as superficial and trendy. Sociologists are frequently seen as intellectual gadflies. Far too few people come away from sociology courses with the impression that sociology is a challenging discipline.

We need more rigorous standards in all of our courses, but especially in introductory sociology. This is the primary (and often sole) vehicle through which people are exposed to our discipline. Many sociologists on the job market are judged by the perceptions of sociology formed in introductory sociology courses. We should dispense with the traditional introductory course, taught as a "sampler" of the discipline because it tends to be superficial. Students should begin with a specially designed course in social stratification or social psychology. Like courses in macroeconomics or microeconomics, these courses should emphasize general principles rather than dwell on specific institutions.

The image of our courses and the image of our students is an important matter. In the long run, the quality of our majors is crucial for the survival of the field. The image of our discipline and the image of our students are irreversibly linked. Their fate in the job market is also influenced by these perceptions. Mathematics majors encounter more success in the job market than sociology majors, even though mathematics, like sociology, is not a professional program. Recent graduates with bachelor's degrees in mathematics and statistics have lower unemployment rates than recent graduates in sociology and anthropology. According to the 1982 New Entrants Survey, 1980 and 1981 recipients of bachelor's degrees in mathematics and statistics have an unemployment rate of 4.3 percent (NSF 1984). The rate for comparable sociology and anthropology graduates is 10.0 percent. The difference is not due to the greater availability of "mathematics" jobs. Only 14.7 percent of the mathematics and statistics graduates were employed in these fields. The comparable percentage of sociologists and anthropologists employed in sociology or anthropology was 17.2 percent. The advantage held by mathematics graduates is their ability to obtain jobs outside of their field of concentration.

A few years ago, mathematics majors were prime candidates for employer-sponsored computer training programs, despite the fact that the actual mathematics content of most programming is small. More employers are willing to take the time and energy to train them because they assume that a mathematics major can master a rigorous course of instruction.

With more integrated and more rigorous curricula, sociology programs would turn out better students. Unfortunately, unlike a course or two in applied sociology, this is not an endeavor that can be turned over to one or two assistant professors and forgotten. It will require a serious commitment to improved undergraduate education and a concerted effort on the part of entire departments.

THE MASTER'S LEVEL

The position of master's degree students is complicated by their peculiar status in the discipline. While trained beyond the undergraduate level, they lack the doctorate degree, which, for several years now, has been the credential necessary for full acceptance into the profession. The sociology master's degree has become an intermediate step and has lost much of its status as an independent level of professional expertise. Like many other master's degrees, its role has been diminished by the rise of the doctorate degree.

Nonetheless, hundreds of students each year terminate their graduate education at the master's level. While prospective graduate students should be cautioned about the limitations of the master's degree as an educational goal, many of the students who decide to leave school at this point do so for sound personal or academic reasons. Some guidance on our part can help to insure that their educational investment is put to its most productive use.

Students who find employment in the social sciences after receiving a master's degree are very likely to be employed in research-related activities. The most frequently reported activity of social science master's degree recipients in science and engineering jobs (jobs that include social science positions) is research and development (see Table 8.1). In addition to the 28 percent in R&D jobs, another 18 percent describe their primary activity as report writing, computing, or statistical analysis. This contrasts markedly with the social science graduates employed outside of science and engineering.

While science and engineering jobs are not the only jobs that master's-level social scientists can perform, those master's degree holders interested in finding work related to their area of graduate study should be well versed in research techniques. Employers will be looking for people to perform a variety of research tasks, including data collection, statistical analysis, computing, and report writing. Survey research methods are now being applied by a wide range of people in a diversity of settings. Experience in survey research and examples of completed survey projects would greatly increase the marketability of master's level sociologists. Coursework at the master's level should emphasize research design, methodology, and presentation. Familiarity with statistical computing and graphics packages is essential. Internships can also help the master's student make the transition to nonacademic research by introducing him or her to issue areas, data sources, and professional colleagues. Like the dissertation of the doctoral student, the master's thesis should be viewed as a demonstration of relevant research skills and abilities. The elimination of thesis requirements or the tendency to view them as archaic academic exercises may not serve the best interests of the students.

CONCLUSION

Sociologists cannot and should not try to guarantee students a narrowly defined occupational niche. Students will be more marketable if they are perceived as having an education that is rigorous and has given them valuable skills. This requires both an educational and a public relations effort. We must improve the quality of our students and the public's perception of their intellectual tools. Ultimately, it is up to the students themselves to seek their fortune. If, through our sociology curricula, we have given them a program of study that is challenging and intellectually honest, then we have met our responsibility as educators.

NOTE

The views expressed in this chapter are those of the author. An earlier version was presented at the Annual Meeting of the Southern Sociological Society in Atlanta (April 1983). The author wishes to thank Ellen Greenberg, Maxine Atkinson, Susan Arnold, and Linda Kemp for their comments on an earlier draft.

REFERENCES

Bonacich, Edna. 1982. "Task Force To Study Employment and Other Issues." *ASA Footnotes* 10 (August): 3.

Bowen, William. 1981. *Graduate Education in the Arts and Sciences: Prospects For the Future (Report of the President)*. Princeton, N.J.: Princeton University Press.

Brown, William R., John T. Washington, and Allyn M. Stearman. 1983. "Perceptions of Central Florida Employers Regarding the Competencies that

Need Greater Emphasis." Paper presented at the 1983 Annual Meeting of the Southern Sociological Society.

Feinberg, Lawrence. 1982. "American U. Faces Financial Squeeze as Enrollment Declines 5% This Fall." *Washington Post*, September 4, 1982, p. B1.

Green, Kenneth C. 1984. "Talent Migration and Major Field Preference Among Entering College Freshmen." Paper presented at the Council of Graduate Schools Conference in Washington, D.C.

Howrey, Carla B. 1983. *Teaching Applied Sociology: A Resource Book*. Washington, D.C.: American Sociological Association.

Huber, Bettina J. 1985. *Employment Patterns in Sociology: Recent Trends and Future Prospects*. Washington, D.C.: American Sociological Association.

Institute of Medicine. 1985. *Personnel Needs and Training for Biomedical and Behavioral Research*. Washington, D.C.: National Academy Press.

Kinloch, Graham C. 1982. "Undergraduate Sociology Majors and the Job Market: A Case Study." *The Southern Sociologist* 14 (Winter): 20–21.

National Science Foundation (NSF). 1984. *Characteristics of Recent Science/Engineering Graduates: 1982*. Washington, D.C.: U.S. Government Printing Office.

Terry, Geraldine B. 1983. "Developing a Program of Study for Sociology Majors Who Anticipate Government Careers." *The Southern Sociologist* 14 (Winter): 20–21.

U.S. Department of Education (formerly Office of Education), National Center for Educational Statistics. 1948–82. *Degrees and other Formal Awards Conferred (HEGIS)*. A computational data file. Washington, D.C.

9

Education of the Sociology Consultant

EARL JONES

The use of consultants is by no means a recent innovation but its amount and complexity are relatively new ingredients.[1] In earlier, simpler times, professionals were hired or contracted to exercise their specializations: agriculture, economics, education, sociology. Those applications engendered considerable success on limited problem-solving topics but they left many difficulties unresolved, especially those involving general improvements in the human condition.

The social emphasis on improving the human condition resulted in three principal educational thrusts. First, there was the Michigan State University (East Lansing) developmental specialization for sociological work by U.S. and foreign students, contributing to an enormous body of information on many areas of the world and especially on Latin America. A second manifestation was the sociological training of people from many fields as an adjunct to their work; Peace Corps training was easily the most widespread example of this approach. The third phenomenon was the retooling of many specialists to work in or incorporate the social sciences into their consulting—and the reverse, the broadening of sociologists' operations into agriculture, management, industry, and health, to name but a few. The Montana State University Kellogg Fellowship program of the late 1950s and early 1960s was one of these models. Texas A & M University wildlife students minoring in sociology have shown unusual aptitudes in the combined fields. All of these multidisciplinary professionals have been a potent force in the consultant field in the last two decades.

These historical perspectives would appear to indicate a well-developed educational system for consultants but that is not the case. Concrete training programs are few and far between. Further, there is substantial controversy about whether anyone can be trained to become a consultant, ranging from the adamant denials of Bermont (1982) to the highly commercialized seminars by some institutions to create consultants within any specialization, including sociology. The probability is that neither opinion extreme regarding education will produce consistent, long-term utilitarian results, although each has important reasoning to substantiate its claim. Nevertheless, knowledge and skill are required in the application of sociology, or any other field, to the consulting business.

CONSULTANT KNOWLEDGE AND SKILLS

The explosion of knowledge in sociology and the partial dissemination about some of the applications of that science have created at least a fairly solid set of expectations about the products to be derived from consultations (Gallessich 1982). Generalized scopes of work have given way to quite specific and sequenced tasks to be performed.

Most consultants will be required to apply their knowledge in a variety of content and settings (Jones 1982, 1976; Jones et al. 1980, 1984; Jones, Berkowitz, and Roussell 1981; Munoz, Jones, and Wardlaw 1978; Young, Romashko, and Jones 1982). Furthermore, consultants must often provide general advisory and training services. Also, most will be involved in nearly all phases of contract preparation: assessing bid possibilities, writing proposals, calculating budgets, and accounting for expenditures—definite entrepreneurial skills. In addition to these general areas of expertise, there are a number of specific knowledge and skill areas that can be identified.

Social Science Knowledge

Knowledge in the various social sciences is often required in consulting contracts. Knowledge of the historical background of the problem, the political implications, the psychological bent of the targets of a development program and those that manage it, the economic aspects, and the cultural variations that may determine outcomes may be demanded of a single individual (Kelley 1981). While no one should expect to be an expert in all these fields, basic concepts that enable the consultant to discover these perspectives through other sources are imperative.

Special knowledge in sociology is especially useful in consultative applications. The foundation information, however, is less evident (Chinoy 1970). Obviously, the ideal would encompass the full sociological spectrum, even though that is rarely if ever attained. As a generality, the minimum informational base includes:

- the dynamics of social organizations—families, groups, communities and their relationships with affiliate extensions
- the social functions of group members—leadership and followership
- the nature and mechanisms of change
- the roles of change agents
- the directional interactions when goals coincide or are in conflict

This short list will appear simplistic to most sociology professors, and overly practical at the expense of theory. Consultation is, however, almost exclusively pragmatic in function; only rarely are theoretical frameworks brought to bear the problems (Colamosca 1981).

Social psychology and psychology play integral roles in the way consultants apply their interpersonal skills in the conduct of assigned tasks. Such obvious methodologies as working with people instead of imposing upon them, participatory techniques, acceptant consideration of their contributions, and convincing participants when substantive modifications are required need only be mentioned. Program employees and community members are rarely prepared to accept recommendations in their totality without skilled and reasoned communications efforts (Marsh, Jameson, and Phillips 1983; Schein 1969).

The nature and assessment of attitudes is easily the most frequent social psychological component in consulting (Freeman et al. 1983). Informal determination of the attitude sets of personnel is less often neglected by experienced consultants with high interpersonal skills than are those involving the population to be affected (Schein 1969). Even though a considerable body of knowledge exists on attitudes, generally, and changing them, specifically, few agencies attempt to determine them as a part of the project process. The remedies for social, health, educational, and economic improvements are intrinsically "good" and acceptable; the literature is replete with failures caused by this misconception. Consultants who are concerned with success will incorporate attitude measurement and strategies for modification within their applications to the problems.

Anthropological concepts and techniques, formerly in high regard, are often largely ignored in current consulting work. These must still be applied in most projects (Guba and Lincoln 1981). The misinterpretation of traditions and customs, for example, causes these to be seen as lack of information; when so treated, almost insurmountable obstacles are sometimes encountered. The neglect of ethnic, cultural, and language variations usually leads to differentials in operational success (Jones, Berkowitz, and Roussel 1981; Jones et al. 1980).

Economic implications are today the watchword of most consultations—cost-benefit analyses, management versus programmatic expenses, recurrent costs, secondary residuals, and impacts on various strata within an economic system are demanded much more frequently than before. These are highly technical and require the services of an accomplished economist; team leaders from other disciplines, nevertheless, must at least understand their basic nature and implications (Marsh, Jameson, and Phillips 1983). Bare economic projections can obscure long-term developmental goals (Guttentag 1977); on the other hand, outside financing of expensive projects, if it ignores local contributions and ultimate funding capacity, often culminates in designs predestined to partial implementation and/or failure. The combination of expertise in the economic calculations and the broader comprehension of the anticipated outcomes is much more likely to produce salutary results.

Surely no contracted work is exempt from political considerations. Local, state, and national laws plus the regulations of the institutions always impinge in some way on the design, operation, and results of a project. The usual basic government courses are seldom sufficient to provide the needed framework (Jones et al. 1984). Court decisions require special attention. In other countries, the political system may be so different as to negate U.S. concepts of how government works (Vaughn, Massey, and Rudishule 1983). Whether in the United States or elsewhere, consultants must know the political background or consult with political experts, lawyers, or institutional administrators to obtain the information.

Many professionals approach consultant problems as if the past were remote and of negligible influence on present affairs. Contracting personnel and many agency employees reinforce present conditions (Blake and Moulton 1983; Gallessich 1982), yet the present phenomena may be consistent with the past (O'Neill 1982). No consultant can acquire all the historical insights needed, but with readings, advice from local experts, and discussions with counterparts, the essentials can be gleaned.

Project Design Preparation

Preparation of the project design has many of the same methodological characteristics of thesis and dissertation preparation but is less straightforward. Data are usually incomplete, may be questionable, and do not necessarily point out the direction to success. A few organizations offer training in this difficult task; the World Bank and the U.S. Agency for International Development do but participation is limited to their project personnel. A few universities conduct seminars and special conferences. Self study is normally the major avenue available. The best sources are project proposals and reports, evaluative studies, and some articles on findings. Conferring with knowledgeable professionals helps a great deal.

Curiously enough, despite its incidence in consulting, monitoring is seldom formally taught. Detailed evaluation studies that include methodologies for interim examinations give valuable insights. Manuals on self evaluation (Munoz, Jones, and Wardlaw 1978) are usually the best and most direct sources. Monitoring in a participatory fashion, considered ideal, was fully described by Blake and Moulton (1983). Experience gained under competent monitors improves the tactical procedures for such an operation.

Design modifications flow from monitoring, external evaluation, and examinations of interim results. Business consulting guides (Bermont 1982; Lant 1981) and those for a few other specialized applications (Jones 1982; Young, Ramashko, and Jones 1982) outline the processes and these can be adapted for variations in projects.

Training Skills

Consultants as trainers are increasingly requested. Specialists who have taught in schools and universities may have a foundation for conducting seminars and workshops. The essential skills are:

- organizing the material for the level of the students
- devising the outline or syllabus
- determining the methods for best imparting the information or skills
- selecting or preparing the supplements to texts, handouts, or articles
- deciding on interim measures for success of the teacher and the students

Teaching methodologies courses in departments of education will be helpful, especially those designed for older youth and adults. Vocational education methods are particularly applicable because they generally tend to be more step-by-step oriented. A few universities and some companies offer instruction in the conduct of workshops and conferences. When taking a course is impossible or impractical, study of the methods texts will assist in the preparation for this work.

Methodological Skills

Conducting evaluative studies is easily the most common type of consultation methodology at the present time. The conduct of pure research is rarely offered to consultants nowadays. Consultants may be called upon to give advice and technical assistance to research personnel. In addition, evaluations contain a great deal of research even though they have characteristics that distinguish between the two. Since all universities offer substantive graduate courses on research methods, the general body of information need not be repeated herein.

Sampling has become an important qualification in consultant contracting. General sampling techniques taught in practical methods and statistics courses are enough for most occasions. Where greater complexity exists, the use of a sampling expert is strongly recommended. Most sampling texts are difficult to comprehend through self-study; every consultant hiring out for evaluations today should take at least a basic sampling techniques course.

Instrument design is crucial to any study. All the fancy research designs, complicated samplings, and statistical analyses will not save inadequate data from improperly selected or prepared instrumentation. Some excellent texts, many quite readable, are available on the formulation of questions and the overall design of questionnaires (Bart and Brankel 1981 is a good example). Many technical articles on the subject appear in sociology and psychology journals. Review procedures, field testing, and revision strategies are clearly outlined in most. Instrument design is always included in university research courses but it is sometimes squeezed down to such a few hours of presentation that it receives short shrift. Specialized courses are preferred.

The conduct of the fieldwork is described adequately in several textbooks, many of which are found in most university libraries. College courses offer some help. Experience in thesis and dissertation research is of assistance but usually lacks the dimension of managing a team of interviewers. This auxillary personnel must be objective, careful with details, speak the language and level used by the interviewees, and, if possible, be from the same ethnic and enterprise group. Self-study of pertinent textual instructions, reviews of other field procedures in reports, and experience under a high-quality supervisor materially advance the necessary knowledge and skills.

Professional staff and interviewer training on the sampling procedures, the instruments, and the specific interview techniques is mandatory regardless of qualifications. Exhaustive study in a classroom, including practice, is required. Subsequently, a field exercise—usually as the field test of the processes and instruments—not only extends the practice but provides the opportunity to observe the interviewers in action, facilitating final selection of them.

The analyses of the data take two basic forms: descriptive presentations of the variations found among segments of the population on different items, and interactive statistics that point out the interrelationships among the variables. Both types are well covered in university research and statistics courses. Very complicated statistical treatments require strong, advanced university statistics courses for mastery. In addition, there is a plethora of methodological treatises in the professional journals today.

The generalist consultant can, through courses and readings, develop the statistical skills to perform the difficult analysis tasks. The minimum requirement is to comprehend what can and should be done—then leave the calculations to specialists. In either case, experience builds the capacity to determine which procedures are the most applicable for the study, to design the instrument items so they lend themselves to the analyses, and to examine the results to assure statistical accuracy and study practicality.

Computerization of the data and the conduct of the analyses comprise an important avenue for carrying out complicated evaluations. University and computer company courses abound; consultants utilizing this facility must know at least the basics of the processes in order to guide their performance. A few consultants have acquired the necessary skills through self-study of the manuals and practice. For most, though, courses are highly recommended (Bart and Brankel 1981).

Sociologists and other specialists, whether conducting analyses themselves or via statisticians and computer experts, are not absolved from the necessity to apply their professional knowledge and skills to the results. Sorting through the voluminous output, spotting anomalies, and deciding the utility of findings is the investigator's job. Computer courses will not perfect this ability. Working under an experienced practitioner in sociology and computers is strongly recommended for those just beginning with this form of data treatment.

Writing Skills

Writing skill deficiencies are termed by universities and private employers as the single most limiting ability in prospective consultants (Freeman 1983). While some complain about grammar, spelling, and vocabulary, they all agonize over the illogicality of exposition. In an informal survey for this chapter of eight administrators, I found that four have part- or full-time editors to correct the writing of others.

Colleges and universities offer excellent courses to improve writing skills; handbooks offer valuable assistance—both are recommended. Mutual editing among colleagues is a good measure. Working from a detailed outline helps most people. When all else fails, hire an editor.

Foreign Language Skills

Foreign language requirements have substantially increased in recent years as a prerequisite to bidding on contracts. Consultants who expect to make a full-time career of the business are well advised to learn another language. Discussions with a wide variety of consultants emphasized this necessity, even for many U.S. contracts.

Surprisingly, almost all of the consultants surveyed reported that they had begun their language training in college. They noted that those early classes gave them entry to contracts and, additionally, allowed them to progress more rapidly in later training or from experience. Most recommend intensive courses for gaining further competence in a language.

SOURCES FOR CONSULTANT EDUCATION

When money is plentiful, almost anyone with reasonable specialization and some experience can earn at least a part-time livelihood from consulting. When the economy is weak, every professional and entrepreneurial skill must be brought to bear. Specialists and younger graduates hoping to enter the consulting field must seek opportunities to enhance their preparation for the work if they are to succeed.

Formal Course Work

Formal course work in sociology is still the most important qualification for entry into consulting. It's a vital part of the sales pitch. Degrees, the more advanced the better, are and should be seen as preparation for contracting work. Minors as well as majors have utility; combinations that particularly fit a consultation task increase the possibility of qualifying.

Requests for proposals sometimes specify very narrow specializations or may insist on broader, even multidisciplinary, preparation. Persons interested in the practical application of their studies need to decide which route most appeals and then seek the university program that will further that end. A study of catalogs, correspondence with university officials, and conversations with graduates are the best information sources.

Equally important is the amount and variety of practical experience that can be gained during the pursuit of the academics; some expect, and even allow, only the research experience while others require students to participate in training and evaluations. Departments in which some of the professors work actively as consultants are attractive possibilities; their knowledge plus their experience can profit the student. Some disciplines, and sociology is one, periodically publish review summaries about university departments; these furnish a guide to offerings, specializations, and staff.

University course work should not be viewed uniquely in terms of degrees. A course or courses added to an already completed degree program may furnish the consulting skills or enable the professional to qualify for work. Instruction on languages, computers, politics of an area, social change, measurement, and many other subjects is usually open to nondegree students. The search for the course that will most adequately meet the consultant's needs follows the same pattern as for a degree.

Formal instruction offered by organizations utilizing consultants sometimes offers utilitarian opportunities. Private companies are getting into the training business, too, and in some disciplines, especially business and computers, rival the traditional education institutions. Articles in *Business Week* (1981) and *Successful Farming* (1982) emphasize this approach.

Theoretical inputs accompanied by step-by-step practice further the skills acquisition. When catalog descriptions mention little application, a candidate can sometimes arrange for individual study with a professor that can be designed to fulfill both theory and practice needs. Readings and individual discussions are often more satisfactory for mature, experienced professionals than sitting through a course with neophytes in the field. A word of caution: individual study with a conscientious professor usually entails more total work than does a regular course. Nevertheless, when these can be tailored to the exact needs of the consultant, they frequently offer the best approach to adding knowledge.

Self-Study

Self-study encompasses two types of preparation: increased information in a field or new fields, and special preparation for accomplishing work in a geographic, ethnic, or political area. Highly qualified professionals always pursue both vigorously. Some, however, and, curiously enough, many young field workers, neglect these facets of their preparation. Except for experience, Bermont (1982) considers self-study to be the only effective education for consulting. Many other authors barely mention this aspect (*Business Week* 1981; Lant 1981; O'Neill 1982).

The first endeavor, that of adding new knowledge, is not difficult to attain with some probing. Textbooks, particularly those with accompanying workbooks or other practical application exercises, are available in many disciplines. Sociology and social psychology are well represented among these. Computers, statistics, accounting, small business practices, and horticulture are known for providing these opportunities for self-study. Even when texts do not include the more pragmatic aspects, reading them and discussing the content with specialists furnish much the same education.

The selection of professional journals must be done judiciously. The articles in the *American Sociological Review,* for example, are often so complicated that they advance only highly specialized theory and methodology practitioners. *Social Forces* and *Human Organization,* on the other hand, are more likely to report the practicality of research but at the same time summarize the methodology. Evaluation journals are inclined more toward pragmatics but the level of sophistication also varies. These differences appear among the journals of nearly every discipline. A careful review of several recent issues will enable the consultant to choose applicable content and presentation. Well-selected journals are unique sources for professional improvement.

General-information books also can aid materially. The volume of such publications in most disciplines is enormous. Checking with librarians and bookstore clerks helps. For specific disciplines, some of the review publications save a great deal of time. *Contemporary Sociology* is an excellent source for determining what a consultant should purchase or borrow in that field. The critiques normally indicate the level as well as the content, enabling wise choices (Bart and Brankel 1981; Chinoy 1970).

Evaluation Studies Review Annual is of great assistance because it contains briefs on reports not easily available otherwise. Some reports also review materials pertaining to the subject; the literature review chapter in a bilingual education study (Jones et al. 1980) is cited more often than the results. Reference librarians are of inestimable help to a newcomer in the field by locating the reviews and other materials of utility to anyone embarking on self study.

The Education Research and Information Clearinghouse (ERIC) computerized and hard-copy services are unusually thorough and include many social field studies. Few other subjects have so much material collected but some systems do exist. The *Reader's Guide to Periodical Literature,* although indexing mostly popular type, nonfiction magazines, should not be neglected. *Dissertation Abstracts,* found mostly in university libraries, is a good search source.

Reports by government agencies are useful for direct application. Some are listed and abstracted in the *Federal Register;* lists from the U.S. Government Printing Office give additional sources. The Library of Congress receives many reports; some agencies maintain file copies that can be borrowed or viewed on microfiche.

Proposals, interim and annual reports, manuals, and handbooks for operations describe the framework within which a project or other action is conducted. They are vital self-study materials. They furnish important background information, changes in design and conduct, and often the concepts on which the project was based.

Finally, reference lists and bibliographies, whether separate publications or appended to articles, books, and reports, are of special utility. They generally contain the most pertinent treatises that have guided the thinking of the author or project personnel; frequently they are more important to the comprehension of the mental set that guided the formulation of the project than are the routine reports. These lists comprise useful self-study materials.

Experience

Experience is, without doubt, the most salable consultant commodity. Evidence of the same or similar work in the type of task offered, with the agency, and in the geographic area is acceptable proof of capability to contractors. A corollary ability is that of describing the experience to demonstrate that it matches the requirements. Many business schools and other professional organizations offer assistance and/or instruction in writing appropriate resumes.

Internships are one avenue for beginners and persons adding a field to gain experience. Many university offerings preclude students who have not acquired their preparation through that institution and department; state and accreditation rules sometimes forbid entry. In others, however, evidence of adequate preparation may allow participation, although sometimes on a noncredit basis. Few universities actually list a consulting internship program. The University of San Francisco, Antioch University, and the University of Alabama are notable exceptions. In many others, suitable practice can be arranged via individualized instruction or special topics courses. In either event, in-depth discussions with the department head and professors are necessary to assure that the work will fit the needs of the candidate.

Although they are less frequently available at the present time than in earlier decades, some government agencies have internship provisions. The U.S. Department of State intern program is an excellent example for furnishing practical experience. Some state, county, and city governments have such opportunities. Fellowships are another possibility, both in the United States and abroad. Government publications and professional journals often list these. *Footnotes,* of the American Sociological Association, and announcements in *Science* are useful sources. In most, but not all, the pay is low and the person contemplating such a venture may have to supplement the expenses from personal funds or via sabbatical arrangements.

Internships in private consulting companies probably offer a greater variety of experience but they are difficult to obtain except through university sponsorship. Internships are said to be somewhat easier with nonprofit corporations. Bidding procedures complicate the inclusion of noncontract staff but this problem can sometimes be overcome. Office work such as proposal writing, data coding, and analysis are more easily managed than field responsibilities.

Most books on consulting list junior-level entry as a viable educational experience (Lant 1981). Some companies have work for absolute beginners but the opportunities are almost always severely restricted in scope. There is a rapid turnover among juniors; some seek additional learning experiences and others turn to other employment to forward their careers.

Unfortunately, economic vicissitudes and changes in the topics for consultation frequently weaken the experience of the junior consultant. Those who continue in the business find ways to expand the skills in their specializations, to add new ones. An engineering consultant described his decades progress from mechanics, through physical environmental impact studies, to population influences on many kinds of projects. He emphasized that even as a senior in the firm, he worked as a junior in the new fields, under recognized experts, and devoted many, many hours to self-study.

Any discussion of experience would not be complete without relating the changes in employment evident among most consultants. Almost no one begins a career in consulting. They start as employees in schools, agencies, or businesses, or are self-employed as technicians or entrepreneurs. This historical perspective is nearly so absolute as to suggest that route as the most promising for consulting. First acquire some expertise in a field and then seek a position. Experiential learning while an employee of a business, university, or government agency adds to the specialization.

Undue emphasis in the literature, however, on experience as the crucial qualification for consulting obscures the basis for acquiring it:

- A solid university preparation is evidenced in every successful consulting career; the majority possesses the doctorate.
- An unusually high proportion of practicing consultants added a second field via a university, either during their early education or in supplemental courses afterward.
- Self-study is also considered as a vital facet of the training for consultations and for progressing into higher categories of the enterprise.

The consulting business is complex, varies greatly over time, and is highly competitive. Aspirants to the profession and those expecting to progress in it are well advised to map out their educational program and apply themselves vigorously to the acquisition of the knowledge and skills required for full participation.

NOTE

1. Perhaps the most complicated consultant task ever was the study contracted by the U.S. Government during World War II of the Japanese by a team of

social scientists, headed by Ruth Benedict, which led to her book, *The Chrysanthemum and the Sword*. (New York: Houghton Mifflin, 1946).

REFERENCES

Bart, Pauline, and Linda Brankel. 1981. *The Student Sociologist's Handbook*. Glenview, Ill.: Scott, Foresman.

Bermont, Hubert I. 1982. *The Complete Consultant: Roadmap to Success*. Washington, D.C.: Consultant's Library.

Blake, Robert R., and James Moulton. 1983. *Consultation: A Handbook for Individual and Organizational Development*. Reading, Mass.: Addison-Wesley.

Business Week. 1981. "Consulting Springboard." August 17, pp. 101–102.

Chinoy, Ely. 1970. *Knowledge and Action: The Role of Sociology*. Northampton, Mass.: Smith College.

Colamosca, A. 1981. "White Man's Burdens: American Consultants Selling Services to the Third World." *New Republic*, April 4, pp. 12–15.

Freeman, Howard E., R. R. Dynes, P. H. Rossi, and William Foote Whyte, eds. 1983. *Applied Sociology*. San Francisco: Jossey-Bass.

Gallessich, June. 1982. *The Profession and Practice of Consultation*. San Francisco: Jossey-Bass.

Guba, Egon G., and Yvonne S. Lincoln. 1981. *Effective Evaluation: Improving Responsive and Naturalistic Approaches*. San Francisco: Jossey-Bass.

Guttentag, Marcia, ed. 1977. *Evaluation Studies: Review Annual*. Beverly Hills, Calif.: Sage.

Jones Earl. 1976. *An Instrumentation Study of the Purdue Social Attitude Scales for Primary Children (English and Spanish Versions)*. San Antonio, Tex.: Development Associates.

———. 1982. "Process Evaluation: Documenting Project Management." In *Guide to Bilingual Program Evaluation*. Washington, D.C.: Evaluation, Dissemination and Assessment Center.

Jones, Earl, Sarah Berkowitz, and Robert Roussel. 1981. *Evaluation of Title II Food for Peace in Ghana*. San Francisco: Development Associates.

Jones, Earl et al. 1980. *Evaluation of California's Educational Services to Limited and Non-English Speaking Students*. San Francisco: Development Associates.

———. 1984. *Baseline Survey of the Honduran Small Farmer Titling Project: Descriptive Analysis of the 1983 Sample*. San Francisco: Development Associates.

Kelley, Robert E. 1981. *Consulting: The Complete Guide to a Profitable Career*. New York: Scribner.

Lant, Jeffrey L. 1981. *The Consultant's Kit*. Cambridge, Mass.: JLA.

Marsh, Lawrence C., Kenneth P. Jameson, and Joseph M. Phillips. 1983. "Production Conditions in Guatemala's Key Agricultural Product: Corn." *Land Economics* 59(1): 93–106.

Munoz, Adolfo H., Earl Jones, and Barry Wardlaw. 1978. *Self Evaluation Guide for Health Projects*. San Francisco: Development Associates and Region IX Office of Public Health.

O'Neill, Patrick I. 1982. *Community Consultation*. San Francisco: Jossey-Bass.

Schein, Edgar H. 1969. *Process Consultation: Its Role in Organization Development*. Reading, Mass.: Addison-Wesley.

Successful Farming. 1982. "Hired 'Gun' Pulls the Sell Triggers." November, p. 21.

Vaughn, Jack, Parke Massey, and Donovan Rudishule. 1983. *An Administrative Analysis of the National Agrarian Institute: Honduras.* Arlington, Va.: Development Associates.

Young, Malcolm, Tania Romashko, and Earl Jones. 1982. *Evaluating Cooperative Development Projects: A System for Planners, Project Staff, and Evaluators.* Arlington, Va.: Development Associates.

10

The Applied Sociology Intern as a Junior Consultant

RAYMOND J. ADAMEK AND
ALEXANDER BOROS

In the early twentieth century, American sociology emerged as a promising science, facing challenges from a rapidly changing social order to provide useful information for solving critical problems. In response, sociology generally preferred an academic detachment, avoiding the direct confrontation and accountability of actual community involvement in decision-making processes (Janowitz 1971). With diverse research and theoretical perspectives, however, academically based sociologists did make useful contributions to the understanding of social problems (Lazarsfeld et al. 1967).

In the past decade, a definite movement within the discipline sought to develop an applied sociology with direct community involvement and impact (Freeman et al. 1983). Without adequate applied training, many sociologists found themselves losing out to the practice professions, already more attuned to the exigencies of public policy making (Komarovsky 1975). Although applying sociology may now be one of the cutting edges of the discipline, sociologists need to be better equipped for the multidimensional process of fitting their perspectives into ongoing community problem-solving activities. In short, applied sociologists must sharpen their consulting skills.

A body of literature dealing with general consulting practices is already available to social scientists (Parsons and Meyers 1984; Silva and Slaughter 1984). A specialized approach for applied sociologists has also been initiated (Lazarsfeld and Reitz 1975). Our discipline has made headway in designing applied programs at both the undergraduate (Satariano and Rogers 1979) and the graduate levels (Grusky 1983). The way is now clear for sociology to build consulting skills through applied internship programs, thereby contributing both to social betterment and the development of sophisticated, practice-oriented professionals.

This chapter will present findings on 16 years of experience in training and supervising intern consultants through an M.A. applied sociology program at Kent State University. We shall briefly describe our training model, give an overview of the consulting experience of 75 interns, and focus on four cases illustrating major types of consulting service. The implications of training applied sociologists through consulting intern- ships will conclude our discussion.

AN OVERVIEW OF THE TRAINING PROGRAM

To prepare our students as consultants in the human services, we had to provide both course work and practice-oriented skills beyond their required sociology courses in theory and research methods. All applied students are expected to take the course, Sociology of Human Services, to orient them to the working environment they will later enter as junior consultants. As electives, each student chooses courses relevant to the knowledge and skills needed to pursue their applied interests. In ad- dition, students take Applied Sociology, which focuses on applying so- ciological perspectives to concrete problem-solving assignments for agency programs. Under the supervision of a three-member faculty team, each intern contracts with practitioners for a consulting service that averages eight weeks. A Practicum in Applied Sociology is held in conjunction with the summer internships. Composed of all interns, it is rotated each week to different internship sites to maximize shared prob- lem-solving. In this way, the personal consulting experiences of each intern are expanded beyond a single agency project.

There is a definite range of consulting activities common to applied social scientists (Gallessich 1982). Under the supervision of the major advisor, the intern is guided through: making initial contacts, problem assessment, negotiating contracts, building relationships with organiza- tional staff, gathering and analyzing data, diagnosing organizational problems and needs, developing intervention strategies, evaluating the effectiveness of intervention procedures, and terminating the service in a smooth and timely fashion.

A record of the intern's experiences is presented in a three-chapter monograph of about 100 pages. The first chapter is the "Log" describing daily events and role problems in implementing the project. The second chapter, "The Practitioner's Report," is a revised copy of the final report given to the agency. The "Sociological Perspective" is the final chapter and reveals the major sociological insights tested and gained in the con- sulting process. An appendix includes: (1) the Practitioner's Contract, signed by the intern and the practitioner, stipulating the conditions and purpose of the consultantship; (2) the Applied Sociology Proposal, signed by the faculty committee and the intern, stating the internship purpose, academic credit, conditions, and relevance to sociological training; (3) the Practitioner's Evaluation of the intern's project, signed by the agency supervisor; (4) the Academic Evaluation, signed by the faculty team stating the student has successfully defended the monograph; and (5) Resources Consulted.

CONSULTING EXPERIENCES

Here we would like to update a previous report on our graduates and their consulting experiences (Boros and Adamek 1984). In all, 87 students were graduated from the program between its inception in 1969 and March 1985. The data reported below come from a content analysis of the applied monographs of 75 (86.2 percent) of these students.

Of the 75 students, 28 percent were males and 72 percent were females; 55 percent had prior work experience and were older than the typical first-year graduate student. This facilitated their selecting internship projects. Although we gave them guidance where necessary, project selection was the student's responsibility. This insured that students were working on problems of interest to them, and helped them develop strategies and skills needed to deal with clients as independent, community-based sociologists.

The 75 students chose 61 different agencies as internship sites. Approximately half chose projects requiring 40 or more working days in the field, and half chose projects requiring 20 to 39 days. More than half (51 percent) of the students chose to do their internships in private, nonprofit, nonreligious agencies; 16 percent worked in local government agencies; 12 percent in colleges, high schools, or grammar schools; 8 percent in nonprofit, religious agencies; 7 percent in federal government agencies; 5 percent in state government agencies; and 1 percent in a private business. The major focuses of these agencies' programs were social (19 percent), medical (19 percent), rehabilitative (16 percent), educational (15 percent), and mental health (12 percent) services. A smaller percentage of internship agencies offered employment (5 percent), legal (5 percent), recreational (4 percent), and housing (4 percent) services. One offered funeral services—the intern studied the coping mechanisms and needs of the bereaved. Thus, the types of agencies the students choose seem limited only by their interests and ingenuity, and the willingness of agencies to cooperate.

DIMENSIONS OF CONSULTING ROLES

Although there was considerable overlapping in some cases, the student-consultants played four major roles during their internships. These

Table 10.1
A Typology of the Entry Process

Newcomer's Specification of Role Relationship	Organization's Specification of Role Relationship	
	Clear	*Ambiguous*
Clear	Role Taking	Role Making
Ambiguous	Role Learning	Role Emergence

Source: Adapted from W. Van Horne, "The Sociologist as Organizational Newcomer: Problems of Role Emergence," *Sociological Practice* 1(1976):11. Reprinted with permission.

were researcher (40 percent), program developer (36 percent), evaluator (17 percent), and field educator (7 percent). We shall return to a consideration of these roles below.

We also analyzed the interns' roles according to a schema suggested by Van Horne (1976). Several authors besides Van Horne (Gelfand 1976; Russell 1981; Satariano and Rogers 1979) have noted that since applied sociologists are relative newcomers to problem-solving in an agency setting, the agency staff may be unsure of what to expect from them, or what role to assign them. This may present both opportunities and problems for the student-consultant, which should be considered before the consulting relationship is assumed.

Van Horne (1976) suggests that a fourfold typology may be used to analyze situations of this type (see Table 10.1). If both the organizational newcomer's (in this case, the student-consultant's) specification of the intended consulting role and the agency's specification of it are clear and consonant, a situation of role-taking obtains, and few problems should be encountered. If the consultant's role specifications are ambiguous and the agency's are clear, a situation of role-learning obtains, and the consultant may be co-opted by the agency's perspective. In situations where the consultant's role specifications are clear and the agency's ambiguous, a situation of role-making obtains, and the consultant may have a relatively free hand in defining the role. Where both consultant and agency are somewhat ambiguous, a situation of role-emergence obtains, and the consultant's role is defined through mutual negotiation.

Applying Van Horne's (1976) schema in the content analysis of our interns' monographs, we found that the role-taking pattern predominated, characterizing 80 percent of the internship experiences. That is, in general, whatever role negotiation was necessary generally took place in the preliminary discussions between the student and the practitioner, with expectations being written into the internship contract and subsequently carried out with relatively little disagreement.

The role-emergence pattern was the next most prevalent, occurring in 12 percent of the cases. In seven of nine instances, this involved some type of expansion of the intern's role. In three cases, role expansion came about as the result of the student's initiative. For example, one male student had contracted to do a survey assessing physicians' and ministers' knowledge of local mental health agencies, and their willingness to refer to such agencies. Using one agency as the internship site, he also desired to become a participant in its group process sessions in order to become more familiar with them, and to evaluate them on an informal basis. It was only after some negotiation that the practitioner agreed to this expanded role.

In the other four instances, it was the practitioner who initiated negotiation to expand the student-consultant's role. For example, one student had contracted to design a program to train deaf individuals to enter paraprofessional positions in the human service field. Pleased with the design but unwilling to stop there, the practitioner convinced the student to open negotiations with a local university to implement the training program.

The role-learning situation, where the practitioner's perspectives and definition of the consultant's role prevail, characterized four internships. They conspicuously had one thing in common: All involved small agencies with staffs of one to three persons. In two instances the intern became a jack-of-all-trades, being pressed into service to perform several agency functions not directly related to the internship contract, and in two others the practitioner's perspectives and procedures dominated the consultant's work. In only one instance, however, did a consultant feel that this dominance detracted from the value of the internship experience.

As might be expected, role-making—the situation where the agency is uncertain of the consultant's role, but the student-consultant has a clear idea of what they expect to do—occurred least frequently (in only two instances). In both cases, the agencies involved were rather loosely structured. One was a community health center that sponsored an alcoholism counseling program. Here the intern, an older male with prior experience in human service organizations, was able to persevere in a program evaluator role in spite of initial staff indifference on the one hand, and outright resistance on the other. The second agency was a university office responsible for training residence hall counselors. Again, faced with staff apathy and a narrowly defined research clerk role, the intern took it upon herself to design a training program for resident counselors based upon her research findings. While she found this expanded role personally satisfying, she was frustrated by the knowledge that the staff probably would not implement her program.

ILLUSTRATIVE CASES

Here we would like to consider four cases illustrating the major types of consulting roles the interns played: researcher, program developer, evaluator, and field educator. As will be evident, although one of these roles predominated in each case, internships often involved a combination of two or three roles. These confidential cases were chosen to illustrate some of the successes and failures of the student-consultants, both of which can become valuable learning experiences. Given the variety of our interns' projects, we could not hope to choose "typical" cases for each type of role.

Consultant as Researcher

Our first case involves one of the minority (23 percent) of our students who were regularly employed by the agency that served as their internship site. While this situation may present complications of its own, it obviously facilitates the getting-acquainted phase of the consultant-practitioner relationship. It has also been our experience that a distinct internship project, separate from the employee's normal duties, can be worked out without much difficulty.

The site involved was a juvenile court system serving a largely residential, rural county. The court's professional staff included one judge and five other persons, including our intern, who worked as the court's intake officer, responsible for prehearing social investigations. Approximately 1,300 cases were heard by the court in the year preceding the internship.

The consulting project grew out of a dispute between the staff and the judge over the underlying problem of bringing many of the juveniles before the court, and hence over the major types of case dispositions that should be made, given that rehabilitation and prevention of recidivism were major goals. The intake worker and probation officers felt that many of the cases coming before them were symptoms of drug and alcohol abuse, and that this was the major problem that should be addressed by the court's case disposition. The judge, on the other hand, tended to focus on the presenting complaint (breaking and entering, truancy, and so on), and indicated that he felt his staff was simply succumbing to the faddish view that substance abuse was becoming a major problem among youth. Our intern offered to settle the dispute through applied research.

Contracting for a 30-day internship, our intern agreed to analyze the court's records for a three-month period to determine type of offense, sex and age of offender, recidivist rate, and whether or not the offense could be considered drug-related. She also agreed to compare the three-month period with the same period in the previous year, to assess the court's resources for dealing with chemically dependent children and their families, and to make recommendations regarding an intervention model should it be deemed necessary to deal with substance abuse among youth coming before the court.

Because of her ongoing intake duties, the student researcher had to spread the 30 days of the project over a five-month period. She defined the key variable—whether or not the offense was drug related—according to three criteria: the child must either be under the influence or in possession of a drug or alcohol when the offense was committed; the child must have committed the offense to obtain drugs or alcohol; or the child must have admitted that the offense was committed under one or more of these circumstances.

Content analysis of case records showed that 69 percent of the offenses were drug-related. In addition, the intern was able to profile the offenders by type of offense, sex, age, and recidivism rate, and to indicate that the number of cases had increased by 26 percent over the previous year. This information had never before been compiled by the court.

In her practitioner's report, the intern drew several explicit implications from her findings: (1) drug and alcohol abuse was a leading contributor to the behavior of the majority of juveniles coming to the court's attention; (2) this called for major changes in case management and disposition on the part of the court; (3) court officials need to be trained, through seminars, conferences, and workshops so that they may recognize the symptomology, behavior patterns, and defense mechanisms involved in drug abuse; (4) similarly, the staff need to appreciate and respond to the role of the family in drug/alcohol abuse and rehabilitation; (5) the court needs to be aware of drug and alcohol programs available in the schools, churches, and other social agencies, to utilize these as referral sources where appropriate; and (6) a drug and alcohol studies program for juveniles should be instituted as part of the court's program.

As a result of the intern's research, the court did contract with an outside agency for a drug assessment and education program to which its clients could be referred. Primarily because of a lack of funds, but perhaps also partly because the judge became somewhat defensive when the research results began to undermine his initial assessment of the situation, the staff training program was implemented only to a minimal degree.

Consultant as Program Developer

As we indicated previously, 36 percent of our interns contracted primarily to design, write a grant for, or implement a new program for the practitioner. Our second case is one of this type. The intern contracted for a 30-day internship to write three grant proposals for a four-person, nonprofit agency concerned with facilitating women's careers and career changes. This contract was later recognized to be somewhat unrealistic by both the intern and the practitioner, who renegotiated it to require only two written proposals: one major proposal calling for a renewal of the agency's funding for the coming year under the Comprehensive Employment and Training Act (CETA), and a smaller proposal for audio-visual equipment to be used in the agency's client training program.

Although the internship did not begin officially until the summer, the intern spent considerable effort throughout the preceding spring quarter preparing for it. She attended two workshops (one out of town) designed to acquaint participants with funding sources and proposal preparation. She met with the CETA staff to acquaint herself with their funding priorities, and sent a number of inquiries to federal and private agencies with an interest in women's career development. In addition, she studied the agency's files, particularly past funding proposals, held discussions with agency staff, and observed some of its client sessions to familiarize herself with its overall operation. She also completed much of the background reading pertinent to her major proposal prior to her internship period. The student-consultant was also able to learn a good deal about grant writing since her university assistantship involved working for the university's research office, which was responsible for processing grant proposals.

With this background, the intern was ready to begin writing a draft of the CETA proposal on the first day of her internship, with the proposal deadline being only one month off. Although the current proposal guidelines were not yet available, she recognized the importance of getting something down on paper and submitting it to others for an initial critique. She presented her first draft on the needs and objectives sections of the proposal to agency staff, selected fellow students, and the director of the university's research office for critique. They were able to pinpoint weaknesses in the proposal's data base and overall strategy, which she quickly addressed.

When the current proposal guidelines did arrive, they were found to be much more detailed than the previous year's, again pointing up the need for more data. Trips to the files of the local newspaper, the library, and city hall helped to fill in the needed details.

It was also discovered that some of the guidelines were not quite appropriate for the agency's program, since they presumed specific blue-collar, job-skills programs, while the agency sought to develop general job hunting skills for both blue- and white-collar positions. A conference with CETA personnel suggested the best way to approach this section of the proposal.

The conference with CETA staff also indicated that they were concerned about a lack of publicity on some of their programs, and had questions about program effectiveness. These were seen as having a possible negative impact on CETA's future as far as the state legislature was concerned. The intern added two sections to the proposal, outlining the agency's positive publicity efforts over the past year, and its self-evaluation program (which incidentally was being developed by another of our interns). Expert accounting advice was also sought from one of the agency's board members when it was learned that CETA was also concerned about cost-effectiveness per client served. As a result, several items were trimmed from the budget.

When the new CETA guidelines came in, the intern had outlined them for herself, and set a personal timetable to respond to each section, so that she could focus her energies and avoid spending too much time on one aspect of the proposal. Nevertheless, as many grant writers do, she still underestimated her time needs, and it was only with the donated services of three secretaries that the final proposal was able to be prepared and delivered to the post office with ten minutes to spare!

Thorough preparation, detailed research, consultation with the granting agency, and presubmission critiques by knowledgeable outsiders paid off. Giving the proposal a score of 97 out of 100, CETA funded the agency at $72,000, $6,000 more than was asked for in the grant. Utilizing the same comprehensive approach, the intern was able to write a second successful grant for the agency in the last three weeks of her internship, netting them $2,500 for audio-visual equipment.

Consultant as Evaluator

The student-consultant in this case had a special interest in serving deaf persons. She chose to intern in a large mental hospital that had a special ward for the deaf mentally ill. Prior to serving the internship, she had completed a course in sign language, worked as a volunteer with a deaf consumer group, and visited speech and hearing centers in four nearby cities as well as a mental health program for the deaf in one of the cities. Background reading and informal discussions with professionals serving the deaf further prepared her for her internship.

Her 60-day contract called for her to evaluate the deaf ward's program. In a mutually beneficial arrangement, the intern was also hired by the hospital as a rehabilitative technician for the contract period. This allowed her to adopt a participant observation approach, and to see the hospital from both the patients' and the staff's points of view. She spent much of each day with the patients on the ward, as well as accompanying them to their various therapies (dance, work, art, and so on), where her duties were to assist the therapists in communicating with the patients. She also attended various staff briefings and conferences. Hence, in the course of a typical week, she was exposed to a variety of patients and staff members at various levels. At the same time, because of her student-consultant role, and recognized short tenure with the hospital, she found it relatively easy to play the role of objective outsider.

The intern's previous reading, consultation with professionals, and own experience with the deaf had alerted her to the fact that deaf persons with adjustment problems typically tend to be somewhat egocentric, have difficulty comprehending concepts that lack concrete referents, lack impulse control, and tend to lay the blame for their difficulties on others, so that conscious anxiety and motivation for treatment are minimal. In addition, because of their language and communicative deficiencies, traditional insight therapy, which depends upon abstract concepts, is relatively ineffective.

The student-consultant's report to the practitioner pointed out both the program's strong and weak points. Its strong points included a physical plant that was clean, pleasant, and home-like, and that facilitated social interaction, while permitting privacy, a high staff-to-patient ratio, and a good patient educational program. Its weak points included a behavior modification program that was not uniformly administered by the staff and was ineffective with the more withdrawn patients; differing criteria among the therapists as to what constituted patient progress; a lack of direct input from the therapists when patient progress was discussed at staff meetings; a system of patient evaluation based on the staff's subjective, personal criteria, transmitted orally; a tendency to discuss the progress of those patients who were currently acting out, or whose behavior had recently changed, while ignoring others who were less dramatic and simply marking time; and a lack of knowledge on the patients' part concerning the type of behavior they should be exhibiting in order to be considered well enough to merit discharge.

As a result, the intern recommended that:

1. The staff develop objective measures of patient behavior, and criteria to determine what demonstrates improvement in behavior. For example, maladaptive behaviors could be defined and their incidence charted for each patient, with a decrease in incidence being considered improvement.

2. The staff should determine goals for behavior change in each patient so that staff can focus on the same behavior and react to it in the same way. As a consequence, the staff would continually be reviewing each patient's progress, while simultaneously evaluating its own effectiveness in the treatment process.

3. The staff should make the patients aware of what behaviors they expect to be changed, how they will be rewarded or punished, how their progress will be measured, and where they stand at any particular time. Patients should also be told the rationale behind the various therapies in which they are asked to participate. In this way, patients would be able to become more involved in their own rehabilitation, and to monitor their own behavior.

4. The hospital should undertake follow-up research on the patients it dis-

charges, not only to evaluate its program, but also to provide the staff with positive feedback about its successes, rather than only negative feedback through readmissions.

As a result of her internship, this student was offered a full-time position with the hospital.

Consultant as Field Educator

Five of our interns functioned as field educators. That is, they taught agency staff or clients a relevant body of social science knowledge to help them perform their roles more effectively. The intern in this case had a particular interest in mental health and also in computers. An undergraduate psychology major, he pursued his interest in our graduate program by taking electives in Medical Sociology, Psychiatric Sociology, and Computer Applications in the Social Sciences. In addition, he was involved in volunteer work in a community mental health center for a short time. During his spring quarter, he approached a community mental health center (CMHC) with a proposal that combined his two interests. He offered to write a computer program that would utilize census data to do a social area analysis of the county the CMHC served. His proposal for a 40-day internship was accepted.

Initially primarily a research proposal, this consultantship emerged into one whose main focus shifted to training the staff to utilize the computer program as both a program planning and research tool. The number of agencies affected by the internship also expanded, since much of the data needed to complete the project were in the hands of the local 648 Board, and early in the project the intern learned that the local Health Systems Agency (HSA) was also attempting to do a social area analysis, but by hand. In exchange for access to their data, much of which was already coded for the area of interest, the intern agreed to include a neighboring county in his study and to furnish the HSA with a copy of the final results.

As the student pointed out in the conclusion to the daily log section of his monograph, this project really allowed him to intern at two different sites—the human services, community-based setting of the CMHC, in which the applied sociologist might be likely to find himself; as well as the more traditional university-based computer center which the academic sociologist is more likely to frequent. In the course of the internship, the student-consultant came to know the computer center staff quite well. They took him behind the scenes, and his classroom learning came to life as a result. As our students have generally found to be the case in other agencies, the CMHC staff were also quite generous with their time and facilities, allowing the intern to familiarize himself with day-to-day agency operations, beyond what was necessary to carry out his project.

The intern's final written report to the CMHC staff included a general description of the technique of social area analysis, its rationale, and strong and weak points. He also described the computer program developed and the variables involved, and presented a social area analysis of the agency's area by county, census tract, mental health catchment area, and social neighborhood, with comparable data for the United States and Ohio included. In addition, the intern demonstrated how the program could be used to locate a particular target group such as the elderly. Finally, the intern gave the computer program to the CMHC and made suggestions for its possible future use for program development and research.

During the course of the internship, the student-consultant was particularly careful to discuss the rationale, utility, and mechanics of his program with various staff members, being determined to leave behind a tool that would be used, rather than simply a report that would be filed. Prior to leaving the agency, and before the final report was written, he presented his work at a full staff meeting. He had been able to conduct a dress rehearsal of this presentation before his fellow interns in a practicum class scheduled the previous week. Two months later the intern was invited by the practitioner to explain his computer program and its utility to representatives from ten mental health agencies at a special seminar organized for this purpose.

IMPLICATIONS

As our discussion reveals, the temporary, unpaid intern-consultant role is not an easy one to implement. Nevertheless, these 75 M.A. interns demonstrated their value to both the profession and the community by applying their sociological training to give a quality service.

In analyzing the letters of practitioners evaluating the interns' final project reports, we noted several recurring positive points. The objectivity of the intern as a person uninvolved in agency politics was greatly valued. Enduring ever-increasing budget cuts while being pressured for improved services, practitioners appreciated the interns' contributions, which required minimum supervision by agency staff. Directors also enjoyed the prestige of a university tie-in and the opportunity to express their viewpoint to academicians, as well as participating in the training of professionals and field-testing interns for possible employment. Practitioners respected the high-quality consultants' reports backed by university resources, which fulfilled their original requests for practice-oriented insights.

As sociologists, we saw the value of sociological perspectives put to use in actual work settings of various human service organizations. While assisting the interns, the sociology faculty also gained an appreciation of the unique social contexts in which each agency exists, confirming that objectivity in the ongoing evaluation of human services is essential, a realization of the import of reexamining agency policies in the midst of societal change, and feedback on the practical value of sociological concepts and research tools.

Although interns were sometimes frustrated that recommendations were not followed after their reports were presented to agency personnel, they obtained practical experiences that would later be helpful. Specifically, they had opportunities to (1) practice the role of an applied sociologist in an agency; (2) be held accountable for service, conclusions, and recommendations; (3) realize that human services need sociological perspectives to improve their delivery system; (4) test sociological theories against practical experiences; and (5) experience the professional identity of an applied sociologist working as a consultant under actual field conditions.

The interns also learned to be reflective about the common consulting processes outlined by Gallessich (1982), which we mentioned earlier. They were assisted in doing this by the need to keep a daily log for their monographs, by the applied practicum course in which they shared experiences with fellow interns, and by conferring with their faculty advisors. Practical experience was also gained in responding to shorter time deadlines, writing more concise, action-oriented reports, and responding creatively to more unexpected problems than are usually encountered in a purely academic environment.

In conclusion, we found that consulting sociology interns could adequately resolve their role difficulties in applied settings, contribute to social betterment, advance their practice-oriented skills, and provide their discipline with validating experiences of the practical value of sociological perspectives to human service organizations.

REFERENCES

Boros, A., and R. J. Adamek. 1984. "The Applied Sociology Internship." *Journal of Applied Sociology* 1:71–81.

Freeman, H. E., R. R. Dynes, P. H. Rossi, and W. F. Whyte, eds. 1983. *Applied Sociology.* San Francisco: Jossey-Bass.

Gallessich, J. 1982. *The Profession and Practice of Consultation.* San Francisco: Jossey-Bass.

Gelfand, D. E. 1976. "Sociological Education and Sociological Practice." *Teaching Sociology* 3:148–59.

Grusky, O. 1983. "Graduate and Postdoctoral Education." In *Applied Sociology,* edited by H. E. Freeman, R. R. Dynes, P. H. Rossi, and W. F. Whyte, pp. 348–76. San Francisco: Jossey-Bass.

Janowitz, M. 1971. *Sociological Models and Social Policy*. New York: General Learning Systems.

Komarovsky, M., ed. 1975. *Sociology and Public Policy: The Case of the Presidential Commissions*. New York: Elsevier.

Lazarsfeld, P. F., and J. G. Reitz. 1975. *An Introduction to Applied Sociology*. New York: Elsevier.

Lazarsfeld, P. F., W. Sewell, and H. L. Wilensky, eds. 1967. *The Uses of Sociology*. New York: Basic Books.

Parsons, R. D. and J. Meyers. 1984. *Developing Consulting Skills*. San Francisco: Jossey-Bass.

Russell, T. 1981. "Undergraduate Education in Applied Sociology and Anthropology: Some Issues in Programming." Presented at the North Central Sociological Association Meeting, Cleveland.

Satariano, W. A., and S. J. Rogers. 1979. "Undergraduate Internships: Problems and Prospects." *Teaching Sociology* 6:355–72.

Silva, E. T., and S. A. Slaughter. 1984. *Serving Power: The Making of the Academic Social Science Expert*. Westport, Conn.: Greenwood Press.

Van Horne, W. 1976. "The Sociologist as Organizational Newcomer: Problems of Role Emergence." *Sociological Practice* 1:10–26.

11

With Feet Firmly Planted on Two Shores: The Consulting Work of Sociologists with Preparation in Two Fields

MARY EVANS MELICK

The routes to sociology's highest degree are many and varied. A popular and expedient method is to major in sociology as an undergraduate and to enter a graduate program in the same discipline. Many sociologists, however, have not taken this route, rather they have majored in other fields, often to the level of the professional (such as nurses, morticians, musicians, clergy), before they enroll for an advanced degree in sociology. Often such persons have come to sociology seeking answers to questions that have arisen during the course of working in another field. An example of such a question is why bureaucratic organizations seem so resistant to change. Other sociologists have obtained the Ph.D. degree only to find that their job or interests lead them to undertake study in a different field. For example, sociologists employed in applied settings, such as health care organizations, may find themselves enrolling for coursework or a degree in public health.

The consulting work of sociologists is primarily an applied endeavor. Although consultees often find sociological theory to be of value in explaining observed phenomena, more often they seek the services of sociologists because of their skills in research design, questionnaire construction, data analysis, grant writing, and related skills. Since the consulting work of sociologists is primarily applied, rather than basic or conventional sociology (see Freeman and Rossi 1984), it could be assumed that sociologists with applied experience in a second field might differ from those without such experience in the selection and nature of their consulting work, the ease with which they adapt to certain settings, and their visibility as a possible consultant. None of these areas has been systematically investigated, however, and a computer search of the literature failed to identify articles related to the work of sociologists with preparation in two fields. Little, if anything, is known about the employment choices, the self-perceived identity, the self- and other-perceived advantages and disadvantages of such preparation, or the actual consulting work of sociologists with preparation in two fields.

Relevant to considering the consulting work of sociologists with dual preparation is a distinction made by Glazer (1978) between the disciplinary and professional styles of graduate education. The disciplinary perspective, according to Glazer, emphasizes learning and research for their own sakes independently of their usefulness for practice. In contrast, the professional perspective is concerned with practice effects and the preparation of students for practice. Glazer believes that a greater infusion of the professional perspective into disciplinary study (for example, conventional sociology) is needed if the social sciences are to adapt to a changing world. This melding of the theoretical and practical is probably nowhere more important than in the preparation of sociologists who work in applied settings, either in full-time employment or in consulting roles. In a survey of the employers of sociologists in nonacademic settings, for example, Lyson and Squires (1982) found that the major shortcomings of Ph.D. sociologists were lack of sophistication about the realities of nonacademic life (52.3 percent), limited knowledge of important substantive areas outside sociology (46.2 percent), limited training in research methods (44.6 percent), and inability to communicate with nonacademicians (43.1 percent). In contrast, only 7.7 percent of the employers cited lack of sociological expertise in the Ph.D.s they employed. These findings support Glazer's argument for an infusion of the professional perspective into disciplinary study, particularly when the student intends to seek an applied position.

Because the consulting work of sociologists is often an applied endeavor, sociologists with both a professional perspective, which may have been gained from education in another field, and a disciplinary perspective, gained from advanced study in sociology, may be in an ideal situation to do consulting work. At present, however, it is not possible to confirm or deny assertions of the advantages or disadvantages of dual preparation with data, nor was it possible to undertake a systematic study of the consulting work of sociologists with and without dual preparation before completing this chapter. Instead, beginning with a convenience sample and using a snowball sampling technique to identify sociologists with dual preparation, an exploratory study was undertaken. The discussion that follows is based on the author's personal experience and on the data gathered during the exploratory study. It is hoped that these preliminary data may encourage future systematic studies of the consulting work of sociologists.

THE ADVANTAGES OF DUAL PREPARATION

Preparation in sociology and another discipline, particularly a profession, may be helpful in obtaining consulting work. Respondents indicated that consulting work was usually obtained through professional networks, which often existed before completing the degree in sociology. Discussions and advice about finding consulting work often begin with a description of the steps that can be taken to develop expertise in a field where there are opportunities for consulting or the ways in which the would-be consultant can make one's interests and skills known to possible employers. Wray (Beaudry and Wray, 1982), for example, describes attending a convention of prospective employers, in his case coroners, and discussing what a sociologist does. His opportunity to discuss the role of the sociologist came at a reception or cocktail party. For those sociologists who are insiders in a particular discipline, the networks in one's areas of interest and expertise are generally well established and less effort is needed in the identification of possible employers and in explaining the services one could provide.

In addition to having contacts in a field other than sociology, there may be an advantage in speaking a common language with the contractor. Contractors are sometimes timid about seeking a consultant's services and may be concerned that the consultant will not understand their problem or that they will not be able to explain the problem well. If a consultant can be hired, however, who has a basic understanding of the problem at hand and who shares a common language and traditions with the contractor, there may be a tendency to hire such a consultant over one who does not have this background. This does not mean that many sociologists without dual preparation do not have the background or understanding of the contractor's problem. The contractor may perceive less social distance between the self and the consultant, however, if the consultant shares common socialization and work experiences, a common language and understandings. For example, a consulting position was offered to a sociologist to work with the interdisciplinary staff on a renal dialysis unit to prepare several articles for publication and to develop a grant proposal to evaluate their patient education program. The names of a number of researchers were suggested by the group, but the one selected had preparation in nursing as well as in sociology. The contractors believed that it would take less of their time to work with a consultant who was familiar with publications in their area of practice, had knowledge of appropriate funding sources, and who was also well grounded in research methods.

For the consultant, there is the advantage of spending less time in preparation of initial materials to be delivered to the contractor when there has been fairly intensive preparation in the field of consultation. Recently, for example, a consultant accepted the task of preparing a request for a proposal for the study of nursing practice, including a job analysis and role delineation of the entry-level performance of registered nurses. In addition to the doctoral degree in sociology the consultant was a nurse and had the advantage of knowing the various routes to achieving registration as a nurse, the characteristics of the basic educational programs, and the expectations for performance held by employers. This saved the time that would have had to be expended by most nonnurse consultants in learning the confusing array of educational programs that all lead to the same R.N. license.

Consultants with backgrounds similar to those of the respondents may also have an advantage in securing the cooperation of the respondents. The consultant may be less likely to appear as an outsider and may be viewed as one who would understand the respondent's circumstances because both share common experiences and perceptions provided by their educational programs. A recent example is a survey of nurses' attitudes toward employment in a public mental health setting. The survey instrument was accompanied by a letter from the researcher who signed the letter as an R.N., Ph.D. It is not known to what extent this influenced the response rate, but the rate of 98 percent is far in excess of most surveys of staff attitudes. Prior research indicates that response rate may be favorably influenced by the similarity in demographic characteristics of interviewer and interviewee. Benny and Hughes (1956), for example, comment that interviewing seems to be most productive when the parties to the interview are equals, at least for the purposes of the interview. They suggest that inequalities that may exist between parties should be muted for the duration of the interview. Perceived similarities may likewise influence the response rate to written survey instruments.

Another advantage of a dual background is that so many consulting options are available. The options available to generically prepared sociologists are available to those with dual preparation, while additional options in the second discipline may be more readily available to these consultants. One of the respondents from the snowball sample noted that her dual background was an advantage in obtaining consulting work since sociology provided the methods and theory while nursing provided the context for the consulting work. This would be particularly true when the consulting work requires intensive involvement in settings with limited access to outsiders or extensive interaction with clients.

The research literature in sociology, as well as in other social sciences, is replete with discussions of the necessity of maintaining objectivity. As Beaudry and Wray (1982) note, however, there are times when the sociologist-consultant is not a disinterested spectator. This occurs when the sociologist is involved in a particular role within the system under study. In these situations the sociologist can make informed judgments about the ratio of costs to benefits of the proposed solutions and the fit of proposed solutions with the goals and norms of the system. In such cases, the sociologist may assume an advocacy role, which the authors note may be a satisfying role for the sociologist-consultant. As an insider, the sociologist with preparation in two fields may have more opportunities to function as an advocate. In such cases, the sociologist should be aware of functioning as an advocate and should ensure that the advocacy position is well supported with data and other documentation.

THE DISADVANTAGES OF DUAL PREPARATION

Although none of the snowball respondents indicated that dual preparation hindered their acquisition of or functioning in consultant roles, several disadvantages could be postulated. First among these is the perception by possible contractors that the dual-prepared sociologist is not a "real" sociologist. Sociologists with backgrounds in nursing, for example, are often referred to as nurse-sociologists rather than as sociologists, as if this were a particular type, like experimental psychologists, rather than as nurses and sociologists. The impact of this type of labeling on the contractor and consultant has not been systematically studied.

A second possible disadvantage of dual preparation is the concern about consultant bias. Would an employer, for example, be comfortable in hiring a consultant prepared in music and sociology to survey musicians about their level of job satisfaction or would the employer expect such a consultant to be critical of the employer while identifying with the musician employees?

The maintenance of objectivity and the development of rapport are particularly important in doing fieldwork, as Hunt (1984) reminds us. Rapport, the trust that exists between the researcher and the subjects or clients, is necessary to facilitate acquiring of valid and reliable data. If the sociologist is too detached, "under-rapport" may exist and subjects could be hostile and uncooperative. If the sociologist becomes too involved with the subjects and identifies with the group under study, "over-rapport" may develop and may impede the research by undermining objectivity. It seems reasonable to assume that dual-prepared sociologists might be more at risk of developing over-rapport rather than under-rapport when working in their second field. Closely related to the concern about over-rapport is the possibility that the dual-prepared sociologists may unconsciously interpret a respondent's actions or responses according to the consultant's understanding or definition of the situation. This understanding may have existed prior to the consulting work and may be the result of being an insider. The imposition of one's own views and meanings is always a risk in doing field study, and sociologist consultants must carefully ensure the collection of the respondent's interpretations of the situation.

Another possible disadvantage of dual preparation in working as a consultant in the area of the second discipline is that the consultant may be viewed as a threat. This is probably nowhere more likely than in nursing. Over the last 20 years considerable pressure has been exerted, primarily from within the profession, for nurses to acquire a baccalaureate degree in order to be considered professional nurses. Sociological consultants with nursing backgrounds plus advanced education may be viewed with hostility by nurses without such advanced education, particularly if the consulting work involves activities that would accentuate the educational and income differences between the consultant and those with less preparation.

WEIGHING ADVANTAGES AND DISADVANTAGES

On balance, weighing the advantages and disadvantages, dual preparation is probably more an advantage than a disadvantage. This is true in terms of the sheer volume of consulting work alone. One of the snowball sample respondents, who is a nurse and a sociologist, indicated that she is involved in consulting work with two different groups. One consulting firm is composed of an economist and two other sociologists with special interest in research methods and data analysis. The respondent's dual background is viewed as an advantage in aiding the firm to secure work in the areas of health and mental health. During preliminary negotiations regarding work in health-related fields this sociologist functions as the lead person for the consulting group. In addition, the respondent is a member of a partnership with a pharmacologist, and their consulting work is primarily in the form of providing continuing education programs on drug therapy to health care professionals. Membership in these groups results in considerable variety and volume in the types of consulting work available.

In theory at least, some of the concerns of the employers of sociologists (see Lyson and Squires 1982) could be addressed by hiring sociologists with dual preparation. Because of their preparation in a second field, often an applied field or profession, dual-prepared sociologists could be expected to recognize and perhaps more successfully negotiate the realities of nonacademic life. In addition they have expertise in a substantive area outside of sociology and should be able to communicate with nonacademics, at least those working in the area of their preparation.

The grounding in a practice-oriented field, in particular, should decrease the initial reality shock that may be experienced by new sociology Ph.D. recipients when they are hired by nonacademic organizations or when they begin to do consulting work in applied settings. Reality shock as defined by Kramer (1974) is the startling discovery and resulting reaction that school-bred values conflict with those in the work world. In some cases the perceived disparity in values is so strong that the individual cannot adjust to or remain in the situation. Clinical or field experience in an applied program, for example, is likely to provide students with perceptions of and experiences in dealing with bureaucratic organizations that other sociologists may not acquire until they take their first professional position. Students from applied programs may experience less reality shock in adjusting to a first professional position or in doing consulting work in applied settings because they bring with them a prior understanding of such realities as paperwork, the privileges of rank, and the functioning of the informal organization.

When a person has been trained in two different fields there is always the risk of values conflict and loss of objectivity. Values conflicts can arise in individuals trained in clinical fields when they enter sociology. The applied field may have stressed individual responsibility and accountability for life circumstances, attention to feelings and emotions, and a focus on the individual, while sociology's emphasis is more likely to be on structural determinants of life situations, objective study of social actors and society, and focus on groups and on society. These conflicts can arise in doing consulting work as well as in other professional activities. This is not to imply that values conflicts must occur if an individual has training in two disciplines, but only to indicate that such conflicts may occur and that value consensus and conflict are areas that are apparently unstudied in sociologists with dual preparation. The problem of values conflict was raised recently at a disaster conference attended by administrators, health professionals, and researchers, including sociologists. When the author of one of the papers was identified as a sociologist, a conference participant remarked that sociologists were the people who went into postdisaster communities asking questions, but who were unwilling to hand the respondent a tissue. Another participant jumped to the rescue of the sociologist, claiming that this was not true of this sociologist-author because she is also a nurse and would certainly hand the respondent a tissue. The values conflict alluded to here is values related to the role of the unbiased observer-interviewer versus those of the supportive helper in a situation of human calamity. At present we do not know the frequency with which such values conflicts arise, or how they are managed by dual-trained sociologists. We also do not know the factors associated with precipitating and successfully managing such conflicts—for example, what effect the extent of the socialization in both fields, the identification with a particular role model, and seeing the self as a sociologist or as something else might have on the conflict.

Sociologists with preparation in two fields must strive to maintain objectivity in doing consulting work particularly when they are working with individuals in positions they once held or those in supervisory positions for previously held job titles. In such situations the consultant must exercise considerable care in determining the respondent's perception of the situation, rather than imposing one's own values, perceptions, and emotions. For example, one of the respondents in the snowball sample is a sociologist and a nurse with considerable experience in operating a hospice. Much of her consulting work is in the area of hospice care. If she were hired to study other hospices, she would need to listen as objectively as possible to the respondents and to verify her understanding of their responses. Any sociologist does this to ensure that they have secured the respondent's perception of the situation. However, for a sociologist and former hospice director who is now interviewing a hospice director, it is especially important to be certain that the respondent has been heard and understood and that one's prior perceptions and experiences in that position do result in a biased response being recorded.

CHOOSING THE FIELD OF EMPLOYMENT

In collecting data by way of the snowball sample survey of sociologists with dual preparation, an interesting phenomenon of movement between the fields of expertise became apparent. All respondents had their basic preparation in another field (nursing or divinity) before enrolling for doctoral study in sociology. After receiving the doctorate, about half of the respondents worked as sociologists. Those who did not work as a sociologist had been affiliated with a school of nursing as a faculty member before and during doctoral study and went back to full-time nursing faculty employment following conferral of the Ph.D. These respondents identified themselves as nurses or as nurse-sociologists. Other respondents worked as sociologists in faculty positions, consultants, or as full-time data managers. After a number of years (ten for one respondent) these sociologists left full-time sociological work and went back into their original field, one as a pastor and the other as the director of a hospice unit and then as a faculty member in a school of nursing. It is not at all clear how these sociologists perceived themselves and the factors that influenced them to choose full-time employment in sociology or their second field. It appears that the same factors facilitating their consulting work—that is, professional networks—may contribute to expanded opportunities and long-term pressures to consider employment in the second field. The consulting work in the second field itself offers continued exposure to the field and may result in job offers. Sociologists with dual preparation may be more inclined to reenter the original field because of the perspectives they have gained as a result of advanced study or work in the field of sociology. The study or work experience in sociology may result in advancement in the second field and may also contribute to the belief that the individual is more able to function as a change agent than before entering sociology. One of the respondents noted that she could rise higher and faster in nursing than in sociology because nursing had fewer people with doctoral degrees. These comments are tentative, based on the exploratory study, and should be subjected to systematic investigation.

It would be particularly interesting to study the factors contributing to the professional identity of sociologists trained in two fields. Several of the respondents identified themselves as nurses, despite having a Ph.D. in sociology, as nurse-sociologists, or as pastors. One respondent noted that she had been advised by her mentor that she must totally reject her former identity as a nurse in order to be a successful sociologist. She was advised to seek employment only in the field of sociology and to write her resume minimizing her life experiences before studying sociology. This sociologist was delighted to find consulting work that permitted her to use both her nursing and sociological knowledge.

It would be interesting to investigate the role of prior experience, predoctoral study attitudes, mentors' attitudes, and the job market on decisions to enter sociology, to continue in the original field, or to try to integrate both the original field and sociology. Consulting work offers the dual-prepared sociologist one means of integrating both fields of study.

REFERENCES

Beaudry, James A., and Steve Wray. 1982. "Consulting in the Public Sector: From Research to Legislative Action." *Wisconsin Sociologist* 19 (Fall): 87–95.

Benny, Mark, and Everett C. Hughes. 1956. "Of Sociology and the Interview." *American Journal of Sociology* 62 (July): 137–42.

Freeman, Howard E., and Peter H. Rossi. 1984. "Furthering the Applied Side of Sociology." *American Sociological Review* 49 (August): 571–80.

Glazer, Nathan. 1978. "Graduate Training Needs Professional Perspective." *Footnotes* 6 (October): 1 and 12.

Hunt, Jennifer. 1984. "The Development of Rapport Through Negotiation of Gender in Field Work Among Police." *Human Organization* 43 (Winter): 283–96.

Kramer, Marlene. 1974. *Reality Shock: Why Nurses Leave Nursing.* St. Louis: C. V. Mosby.

Lyson, Thomas, and Gregory D. Squires. 1982. "Sociologists in Non-Academic Settings: A Survey of Employers." *Society for the Study of Social Problems Newsletter* Spring: 16–18.

PART IV

Establishing a Consulting Practice

According to some experts, consulting in the United States is $32 billion industry and still growing. A few years ago *Forbes* magazine indicated that the demand for management consultants had increased by 200 percent since 1973.

Unfortunately, there are few sociologists who have taken advantage of the growing need for specialized services and they have not entered the consulting profession in great numbers. Much of this can be attributed to the discipline's neglect of its applied side and the desire by mainstream sociologists to maintain their "purist posture" (See Freeman et al. 1983).

According to Freeman et al. (p. xxiii), one very significant consequence of this attitude for the discipline is that "a growing number of persons with training in other social sciences and in the professions—public administration, health services, social planning, and management—are engaged in work that from a craft-union perspective, should be undertaken by sociologists."

Essentially sociology has not very effectively defended its "space." Even with sociology's lack of visibility and the extent to which sociology is not highly valued on the broader scene, there have been sociologists who have effectively established a consulting practice. Unfortunately for the discipline, many of these sociologists no longer identify themselves as such.

Sociologists who want to establish a consulting practice have an obstacle to overcome that other professionals—such as psychologists, economists, M.B.A.s—do not have. Sociologists must be able to convince others of their skills since potential clients probably have very little idea about what sociologists are or what they can do. No doubt, all consultants must be able to market their skills, but sociologists have an extra burden to carry.

There are other basic features to establishing a consulting practice: ethics and understanding the consultant-client relationship; getting leads and turning prospects into clients; setting fees; assessing performance; and managing a business.

This list is by no means exhaustive, but it provides a basis for understanding the "nitty-gritty" of establishing a consulting practice.

The chapters in this part of the book examine some of the many facets of setting up a consultant practice. Jay Williams and Donald Jones, in Chapter 12, provide some insight into the role relationship between research consultants and agency practitioners. They argue that the working relationship between research consultants and practitioners has been and continues to be one characterized by conflict rather than consensus. The authors, a research consultant and a public agency practitioner, use their experiences to describe how the working relationship between research consultants and public-sector practitioners is representative of consultant-practitioner conflict and consensus issues in general. The reasons for this consultant-practitioner conflict are reviewed and strategies are suggested for how consensus and cooperation may be achieved.

In Chapter 13, Bernie Jones reflects on the dozen years he spent running Social Change Systems, Inc., "a nonprofit corporation for social research, education, and action programs." The chapter traces how he started consulting and the various specialities he eventually developed as he worked with designers, planners, nonprofit organizations, and various kinds of agencies. At least as challenging as being a sociologist was being a businessperson, a role for which nothing in his background prepared him. Much that was learned was after-the-fact. Major issues Jones faced were cash flow, figuring out how to avoid selling himself too cheaply, maintaining his integrity with profit-oriented clients, and collecting fees. The satisfactions that kept him in the consulting business for a dozen years are outlined, as are the lessons derived from that experience.

In chapter 14, Jack Hutslar introduces the would-be consultant to the world of making a living based on what you know and what you can do. He primarily addresses academicians who are interested in professional consulting and discusses how to identify a market for and then sell services (skills) and products (?) in the open marketplace. He offers some suggestions regarding the theoretical material that sociologists may find useful in their work. Hutslar also discusses a number of personal and practical business tips. The chapter concludes with a brief section on Sources of Assistance for the new consultant.

REFERENCES

Byrne, John A. 1983. "Are All These Consultants Really Necessary?" *Forbes* October 10:136–144.

Freeman, Howard E., Russel R. Dynes, Peter H. Rossi, and William Foote Whyte eds. 1983. *Applied Sociology.* San Francisco: Jossey-Bass.

12

Researchers and Practitioners: Conflict or Consensus

JAY R. WILLIAMS AND DONALD E. JONES

The causes of conflict between research consultants and practitioners originate from their orientation to differing research styles. The researchers' academic training prepares them to do basic research while practitioners are generally in need of applied research. We have observed and experienced this conflict in a variety of specific consultant and practitioner settings. However, we believe that the conflict/consensus issues explored here aptly reflect researcher/practitioner relationships in general.

Practitioners here are defined as those persons who are in public (state and local government) agencies, and as such are responsible for developing and implementing public policy. Although consultants also work with corporations and federal agencies, our experience leads us to conclude that the public agency practitioners present a more significant though common set of problems for the research consultant. Therefore, the focus of this discussion will be on the conflict and consensus issues between practitioners in the public sector and research consultants. It is our view that these issues are representative of the general consultant/practitioner relationship. The final judgment of whether these issues are truly generalizable to all consultant/practitioner relationships will be left to your experience.

The practitioner uses consultants in three basic ways: for training, for research, and for diagnosis/problem-solving. The training consultant brings specific training skills and knowledge to the practitioner who is interested in being schooled in the information the consultant has to impart. The research consultant offers information to the practitioner through the use of research skills, including problem definition, data gathering, and analysis or data interpretation. The diagnostic consultant combines the skills of the training consultant and the research consultant by trouble-shooting in agencies to identify problems and to suggest (and frequently help implement) remedies. However, the research consultant has, in our opinion, the greatest potential for conflict with the practitioner.

Consultants, regardless of type, usually come from four major sources: the university, contract research organizations, consulting firms, and those who are self-employed consultants. Research consultants operating from any of these bases are viewed by the practitioner as sharing a common set of characteristics. The practitioner sees them as university-trained, Ph.D.-level professionals who see the world from a different perspective than they do. Even those practitioners who are highly educated themselves frequently find that the day-to-day pressures of running a public agency have caused them to view the world (especially their working world) from a different perspective than their academic background would suggest.

ORIGINS OF THE CONFLICT

The basis of the conflict between research consultants and practitioners can be traced to differences in research styles as described by Kidder (1981, 83):

Basic research is conducted to add to our store of knowledge, test hypotheses, build theories, and perhaps find some practical application in the future. But even with no foreseeable practical application, basic research is carried on for its own sake. Applied research, as its name suggests, is carried on for practical reasons—to produce findings that are applicable, practical, immediately useful.

Why then, despite their need for applied research, have practitioners typically turned to the basic or academic researcher for help? Some of the reasons for this are:

1. Practitioners have a lack of knowledge and/or confidence to do the research themselves.

2. Practitioners believe that the researcher's prestigious credentials (Ph.D.) will give needed credibility to their programs.

3. Practitioners feel the need for an impartial outside judgment so that the results of the research will not be challenged on the grounds of vested interest.

4. The pool of consultants specializing in applied research is small and difficult to identify (few consultants really specialize in applied research; of those who do, even fewer understand the "practical" or day-to-day needs of the practitioner and are able to address them to the practitioner's satisfaction).

Thus, in the past, practitioners had to pay their money and take their chances with researchers disinclined by preference and training to take on the practitioner's research problem. Few researchers chose to be involved in applied research and those that did were often spurred on by the desire or need for money. This money spur was sometimes personal and sometimes dictated by university concerns. Longmire (1983, 341) provides an example of the latter point:

In this dilemma, . . . researchers find themselves being pressured or "seduced" to conduct research simply because there are readily available funds. The interests of the researchers are secondary, and some other person (e.g., University Provost, Department Chair, Division Head) applies pressure to "go for the grant" whether you are interested in the topic or not.

The practitioner then often needed to rely on consultants who were reluctant and disinterested parties. Furthermore, the research consultants were not especially well trained to address the applied research issues of the practitioner. However, about 15 years ago, a type of research that had direct utility for the practitioner began to emerge and have credibility among academics. It was called evaluation research.

Evaluation research is a special form of applied research, designed to evaluate programs, usually ameliorative social programs such as remedial education, welfare reforms, innovative teaching methods, health care delivery systems, job training programs, and the like. The results of evaluation research are not meant merely to add to our store of knowledge or develop theories. They are used, often immediately, to decide whether programs should stop or go, whether budgets should expand or contract, whether personnel should be hired or fired— all based on whether the program accomplished what was intended (Kidder 1981, 83).

Partially in response to funds for program evaluation from the Law Enforcement Assistance Administration in the early 1970s, evaluation research began to grow as a methodology and as an acceptable application of academic research talents. Despite the increasing sophistication and experience of researchers in applied research through the evaluation methodology, many evaluations conducted by academicians were addressed to academic audiences with a greater concern for theoretical issues than for practical problem solving (National Institute of Justice, 1979, 365–68). Although more researchers were willing and better prepared to assist the practitioner, the product still often fell short of the practitioner's needs.

Because of an increased need for program evaluations, spawned by federal monies, and in response to fewer career options in the academic marketplace during the decade of the 1970s, persons trained in research were seeking out, and being recruited for, nonacademic positions. This in turn gave rise to an interest by some universities for developing a curriculum in applied research. Unfortunately, many of these programs have been staffed with academics who may have little or no applied research experience. In the future, however, as more and more of the graduates from these applied programs choose nonacademic careers, the pool of potential faculty (who have experience in applied settings) for these applied research programs will grow. The anticipated result of this will be applied research programs in major universities that better reflect the needs of the nonacademic, applied marketplace, in both their curriculum and the experience of the teaching staff.

Despite the recent developments in evaluation and applied research programs, the dilemma of the practitioner continues essentially unabated. This apparent move to consensus and mutual understanding between the research and practitioner communities is still marked by a significant hiatus between them. The contributing factors to this hiatus are discussed and some remedies for consensus are suggested.

THE RESEARCHER/PRACTITIONER HIATUS

There are two research approaches that differ, primarily, in degree of difficulty. One is research done "to" an agency and the other is research done "for" an agency. Research done to an agency involves a researcher, funded by a source external to the agency, in pursuit of a research question generated by the researcher or by the external funding agency. The agency that the research is being done to is primarily a data source. On the other hand, research done for an agency typically involves a concern of the agency as the focal point of the research. The agency provides the funding, formulates the issues to be researched, and has a vested interest in the outcome of research.

In doing research to an agency, the research consultant is independent and the task is reasonably straightforward (although data collection may have its complications). In doing research for an agency, the research task is far more complicated. The researcher is less independent and must constantly struggle against being co-opted by the agency for which the research is being done. Since this latter approach is fraught with the greater number of problems for the researcher, it will be the focal point for the following discussion. The issues discussed are relevant for both approaches but appear to be more central to research done for agencies.

Basic Assumption and Prejudices

When the consultant and the practitioner deal with one another, they do so with a basic set of prejudicial assumptions that often keep them from getting work done. Given these prejudices, it is a tribute to both sides that they continue to try to do business with one another. While one would hope that no researcher or practitioner would hold all or even most of these notions dear, some of these prejudices will drive most researcher/practitioner interactions.

The research consultant is viewed by the practitioner as an intellectual who is in pursuit of the trivial, who is slow moving, who lacks common sense, and is not in or of the real world. Bierstedt (1965) notes that the Germans have a proverb, presumably directed at academics, which says, *Je gelehrter desto verkehrter* (the more learned they are the crazier they are). In writing about psychologists in a nonacademic setting, Takooshian (1983, 7) notes how the world sees psychologists, which in this case is interchangeable with consulting researchers, to the extent they are viewed as academics.

At the point of receiving their Ph.D., many social psychologists have spent their entire career in school—from kindergarten to D(octorate)-Day—and working in a nonacademic setting takes some adaptation. This challenge is compounded by the often intense "ambivalence" that members of the "real world" harbor towards psychologists ranging from "psychophilia" to "psychophobia."

Some employers are admiring psychophiles, who see us psychologists as powerful scientist-mindreaders, who can shape human behavior and accomplish miracles. Such an employer may have unrealistic expectations that may lead to easy disappointment with a new psychologist, thus creating adaptation problems.

At the other extreme are the psychophobe employers, who see us psychologists as overeducated, ineffectual putzes who entered our field due to our personal problems, and are not much good at what we do. In 1981, former treasury secretary William Simon said in defense of the much-criticized Director William Casey, "we have made public service so unattractive that if we don't watch out, we'll soon be run by academics and neuters!" Many practitioners harbor this attitude towards academics in general and psychologists in particular.

The consulting researcher returns the compliment by viewing practitioners as being shallow thinkers, moving too quickly, oversimplifying, being too political, being too involved in everyday details to see the big picture, and relying too much on common sense or gut feelings. Because of these characteristics, the consultant might describe these persons as taking the "ready, fire, aim" approach to their work (the practitioner would surely counter that the researcher uses the SWAG method—Scientific Wild Ass Guess).

These characteristics are basically molded by the training and work requirements of both the researcher and practitioner. In their own environments these characteristics work most of the time and are accepted coin of the realm. In each other's environments, they become exaggerated traits that are viewed with derision. With these expectations and rigidities of behavior on both sides, conflict is inevitable but not necessary.

Doing Business

Following is a typical example of how the consulting researcher and the practitioner do business.

	Practitioner	Researcher
PROBLEM DEFINITION	I have this problem. I need research for it.	The research can't be done. The problem is too complex. I have no way to introduce the necessary controls for the research.
	I have this solution. Do research to demonstrate that it's the correct solution.	I don't do that sort of thing, it's too political (you aren't going to use my good professional reputation for that).
TIME SCHEDULE	I need the results in six to eight weeks.	This will take five years to do correctly.
RESOURCES	I have very little money to support the research. I can get you $5,000.	My bare bones estimate for this effort is $85,000—that's just the field work. I'll try to bootleg the data preparation, analysis, and report writing.
DATA AVAILABILITY	Don't go digging in my files or talk to my people. You can't have that information; it's politically sensitive.	If I don't have good data, it will be garbage-in/garbage-out, at best.
RESULTS	What do all of these numbers mean?	Well, as you can see by the regresion coefficients . . .
	That's true, but you can't say that!	I call them like I see them.
	You don't understand.	Ah, but I do understand.

	Practitioner	Researcher
RESULTS CONCLUSIONS	But other research reports the opposite. This is confusing—what am I to believe?	Yes, isn't it exciting? I think we're on to something here!
IMPLEMENTATION	O.K., but now what do I do? What do you recommend?	A need for further research is clearly indicated.

With this kind of experience, it is small wonder that both the practitioner and the researcher feel that their views of the other are confirmed, and it is a great wonder that they continue to do business at all. Fortunately, there are remedies for consensus.

REMEDIES FOR CONSENSUS: CLOSING THE GAP

The burden of changing the relationship from conflict to consensus must be equally shared by both research consultants and practitioners. Undeniably, the practitioner must get the job done—with or without the consultant's help. Researchers, on the other hand, may have ample outlets for their talents and skills without having to perform a consultant role. Introspective members of each group will realize, however, that when circumstances call for them to work together, the combination of their needs and skills can be mutually beneficial if they accept and use some common ground rules for closing the gap between them.

The remedies suggested here for building consensus between the research consultant and the practitioner are balanced to address the perspectives of each. The researcher must at once serve and educate the practitioner, and accept the legitimacy of the practitioner's role in the fabric of public policy implementation. The practitioner must at once provide a policy framework within which the research consultant is to work, and accept the researcher as a contributor to the knowledge base for decision making.

The following list is not intended to be exhaustive. It does, however, touch on the critical activities that serve to facilitate a productive working relationship between practitioners and research consultants. As Zetterberg (1962, 182) points out, "applied social science is most likely to be used when there is a habit of cooperation between scientist and executive."

Research Consultant

- Become familiar with the work of practitioners and the problems their work addresses and encounters.

Practitioner

- Become familiar with the researchers' methodologies and the reasons that their academic preparation drives them to be dispassionate and objective observers.

Research Consultant

- Have the practitioner participate in formulating the research questions and design (lead them through the necessary steps). Because they generally have a sense of data availability and quality, practitioners can be of great help to researchers in defining the problem and clarifying the nature of the problem to be researched. Although it may strain their patience, researchers must encourage this participation as an aid to the practitioner's willingness to take ownership of the research and its results.

- Researchers should approach data sources in a nonthreatening way, remembering that the thrust of applied research is to provide useful information to the practitioner. Strict observance of all rules (guaranteeing anonymity or confidentiality, for example), negotiated before the project begins, is paramount.

- Consultants must understand that practitioners and their agencies rarely (if ever) have information already captured and stored in a form useful to the study at hand. Rather than being critical of the practitioner's routine data collection methods, researchers should approach that problem with a view toward expanding the practitioner's knowledge of information management.

- If the consultant's efforts are directed at developing a new

Practitioner

- Practitioners cannot simply turn the problem over to the research consultant. Unless practitioners are willing to contribute to the research design, they may never really understand the significance of the research and its results. That understanding may mean the difference between taking ownership of the consultant's work (even if the conclusions conflict with the practitioner's intuitive notion of what is right), or dismissing the effort as another fruitless "academic exercise."

- Practitioners must provide adequate entree to the research consultant, insuring that persons to be interviewed and files to be examined are, in fact, available as promised. Most important, practitioners must make it known to persons within their influence that the consultant is working under the practitioner's authority and that cooperation is necessary and expected in order to achieve a useful result.

- Practitioners should realize that the research consultant's information needs are probably beyond the scope of the agency's routine information management methods. To meet those needs, agency resources may have to be devoted to manipulating data bases or developing new programming capabilities. From this experience, practitioners should learn that information management should be oriented toward facilitating evaluation.

- Practitioners should not have a casual or hostile attitude about

Research Consultant

program, consider a pilot (trial) program rather than full implementation. Choose those who support the program to pilot it—this insures commitment and biases for the most positive outcome possible (which highlights problem areas). If the program is less successful than anticipated, no "face" is lost because the participants know it is a "trial" program. Willing participants, because of their commitment, provide a higher quality of data than do reluctant participants. Various adjustments can be made during the pilot effort to fine tune the program for future implementation. A pilot program becomes known on its merit and is more easily given wider implementation compared to those programs that are expected to be like politically driven agency or system program—a lot of hype, a lot of work, and little results.

- Triangulate the data collected as much as possible. Researchers should have multiple data sources to insure that at least some data will be available if some sources fail, to insure that there is corroboration of information collected, and to insure that they are exposed to different perspectives of the issue or program being researched.

- Share preliminary findings with the practitioner for interpretation and clarification.

Practitioner

pilot implementation. They must realize that as much can be learned from failure as from success. When the consultant points out problems and indicates the appropriate adjustments that can be made, the practitioner needs to be open to making the changes for program improvement. Practitioners who make the overly simplistic statement, "We tried that and it did not work," clearly indicate that they have little or no understanding of the problem.

- Insure that the researcher gets full benefit of all possible data sources. Practitioners should not be defensive about the consultant's need for corroboration or when the validity of a data set is challenged ("don't you trust me?").

- Check the preliminary findings against the policy framework within which the research consultant is to work. Practitioners should insure, at this point, that they understand the findings, that the work is proceeding in a direction that will benefit the agency, and that both data and conclusions are accurate.

- Share the final draft with the practitioner. Encourage constructive criticism from the practitioner's viewpoint (are the research findings in context? realistic? acceptable?). Negotiate changes with the practitioner. On points where, in good conscience, change cannot be allowed, allow the practitioner a section of the report for rebuttal. Most of all, insure that any descriptions of the agency or how it does business are completely accurate.

- Consider discussion of the final draft report as an opportunity to completely understand the results of the work, and to avoid unpleasant surprises at publication. Negotiate changes with the consultant. Rather than being defensive about deficiencies in service delivery that the report may identify, practitioners should be grateful for early notification so that corrective procedures can be instituted. Consider how the tone of the report will be received within the agency, and suggest ways that will result in the greatest positive impact.

- Do not have great expectations for immediate or dramatic results. A good effort will invariably have positive results, in ways sometimes least expected. Agencies, particularly large ones, move slowly and, sometimes, in mysterious ways.

- Practitioners should be careful to understand that it will take time for the results of the consultant's work to be understood throughout the agency. If a report is forthcoming that indicates some kind of change is needed, by the practitioner or within the agency, that change should be accomplished in a methodical and well-planned manner, with clear objectives in mind.

- Above all, consultants should take time, throughout the project, to put the work aside and get to know the practitioner's agency. Many misunderstandings and prejudices can be eliminated by an honest effort to "live with" the practitioner and his problems for a while.

- Above all, practitioners should provide their consultants with opportunities to experience the day-to-day concerns of "doing business" within the agency. While care should be taken not to co-opt consultants and spoil their objectivity, practitioners should continually monitor the consultant's level of understanding of how the agency really works.

CONCLUSION

The relationship between research consultants and practitioners has been, and continues to be, one of conflict. However, this is not a necessary condition. Although past experiences, and the basic assumptions that each makes about the other are largely negative, there is great potential for cooperation and consensus. As the educational level of practitioners continues to rise (it is no longer uncommon to find doctorate-level persons managing public agencies), a portion of the problem should dissipate. While this happens two ways (Ph.D.s going to work for public agencies rather than for universities, and practitioners completing doctoral requirements while in-service), these groups will probably never achieve academic parity (nor should they). Their willingness to learn to communicate effectively will set the tone for the success of future working relationships.

The practitioner has challenging and interesting problems to be addressed. The researcher, as a consultant, has specific skills to address these problems systematically and to suggest strategies to the practitioner for effectively dealing with the problems. The future will place increasing demands on each to be responsive to the needs and skills of the other. Both the researcher and the practitioner will have to work hard to dispel the myths they believe about each other, and to alter the truths that they know or have experienced first hand. The consultant will have to creatively construct research designs that are responsive to the needs of the practitioner and that maintain the integrity of the research effort. Conversely, the practitioner will have to be candid with the researcher about the nature of his or her agency and its research needs, and undertake only that research that will maintain the integrity of the agency's mission. Hence, building consensus out of conflict will be challenging and trying; but, for those who dare, it promises to be highly rewarding.

REFERENCES AND SUGGESTED READINGS

Bierstedt, Robert. 1965. "Social Science and Public Service." In *Applied Sociology*, edited by Alvin W. Gouldner and S. M. Miller, pp. 412–20. New York: The Free Press.

Freeman, Howard E., and Peter H. Rossi. 1984. "Furthering the Applied Side of Sociology." *American Sociological Review* 49 (August): 571–80.

Freeman, Howard E., Russell R. Dynes, Peter H. Rossi, and William Foote Whyte, eds. 1983. *Applied Sociology*. San Francisco: Jossey-Bass.

Gardner, Burleigh B. 1965. "The Consultant to Business—His Role and His Problems." In *Applied Sociology*, edited by Alvin W. Gouldner and S. M. Miller, pp. 79–85. New York: The Free Press.

Gelfand, Donald E. 1975. "The Challenge of Applied Sociology." *The American Sociologist* 10 (February): 13–18.

Giles-Sims, Jean, and Barry Tuchfeld. 1983. "Role of Theory in Applied Sociology." In *Applied Sociology*, edited by Howard E. Freeman, Russell R. Dynes, Peter H. Rossi, and William Foote Whyte, pp. 32–50. San Francisco: Jossey-Bass.

Gouldner, Alvin W. and S. M. Miller, eds. 1965. *Applied Sociology*. New York: The Free Press.

Hakel, Milton D., Melvin Sorcher, Michael Beer, and Joseph L. Moses. 1982. *Making It Happen: Designing Research With Implementation In Mind*. Beverly Hills, Calif.: Sage.

Kidder, Louise H. 1981. *Research Methods in Social Relations*, 4th ed. New York: Holt, Rinehart and Winston.

Lazarsfeld, Paul, and Jeffrey G. Reitz. 1975. *An Introduction to Applied Sociology*. New York: Elsevier.

Longmire, Dennis R. 1983. "Ethical Dilemmas in the Research Setting." *Criminology* 21 (August): 333–48.

Morrissey, Joseph P., and Henry J. Steadman. 1977. "Practice and Perish?: Some Overlooked Career Contingencies for Sociologists in Nonacademic Settings." *The American Sociologist* 12 (November): 154–62.

National Institute of Justice. 1980. *How Well Does It Work?: Review of Criminal Justice Evaluation, 1978*. Washington, D.C.: U.S. Government Printing Office.

Olsen, Marvin E. 1981. "Epilogue: The Future of Applied Sociology." In *Handbook of Applied Sociology*, edited by Marvin E. Olsen and Michael Micklin, pp. 561–81. New York: Praeger.

Olsen, Marvin E., and Michael Micklin, eds. 1981. *Handbook of Applied Sociology*. New York: Praeger.

Pettigrew, Andrew M. 1982. "Towards a Political Theory of Organizational Intervention." In *Making It Happen*, edited by Milton D. Hakel, Melvin Sorcher, Michael Beer, and Joseph L. Moses, pp. 41–60. Beverly Hills, Calif.: Sage.

Rock, Vincent P. 1965. "The Policy-Maker and the Social Sciences." In *Applied Sociology*, edited by Alvin W. Gouldner and S. M. Miller, pp. 358–66. New York: The Free Press.

Rodman, Hyman, and Ralph L. Kolodny. 1965. "Organizational Strains in the Researcher-Practitioner Relationship." In *Applied Sociology*, edited by Alvin W. Gouldner and S. M. Miller, pp. 93–113. New York: The Free Press.

Struening, Elmer L., and Marcia Guttentag, eds. 1975. *Handbook of Evaluation Research*. Beverly Hills, Calif.: Sage.

Takooshian, Harold. 1983. "Entering Nonacademic Social Psychology." *SASP Newsletter* 9 (February): 6–9.

Twain, David. 1975. "Developing and Implementing a Research Strategy." In *Handbook of Evaluation Research*, edited by Elmer L. Struening and Marcia Guttentag, pp. 27–52. Beverly Hills, Calif.: Sage.

Zetterberg, Hans L. 1962. *Social Theory and Social Practice*. New York: Bedminister Press.

13

Operating a Nonprofit Consulting Corporation in the Business Environment

BERNIE JONES

GETTING STARTED

In completing the application for admission to graduate school, I wrote, if memory serves me correctly, some vague career goal statement about wanting to combine teaching, research, and action. That was in 1965. Little did I know that a few years later I would be hanging out my shingle as Social Change Systems, Inc., "a nonprofit corporation for social research, education, and action programs." For the next dozen years, I ran—and sometimes *was*—Social Change Systems, a nonprofit corporation trying to make it in the marketplace environment. I learned many lessons during those years, unfortunately not always in time. This chapter is my retrospective analysis of the challeges I faced along the way.

The first consulting opportunity came when an architect-planner I had met on a university project asked me and a colleague to do a community survey for him, to provide a basis for a comprehensive plan for a suburban community. For a variety of bureaucratic reasons, we couldn't do the survey through the university, so we did it on our own. When that project was finished, our client had another contract for a comprehensive plan. At the same time, my community service unit at the university, where I was also working on my doctorate, ran out of research funds, so I took on the second survey project and started to define myself as a "consultant." A few months later I borrowed the Articles of Incorporation from the Denver Welfare Rights Organization with which I was doing volunteer work, changed the name and a few words, took $10 down to the Secretary of State's office and, low and behold, Social Change Systems, Inc., (SCS) a legal creature, was born!

My political ideology and my close acquaintances said to me that I didn't want to be a profit-oriented corporation, so I incorporated SCS as a nonprofit corporation. My goal wasn't to make money but to use research as a vehicle for social change and the empowerment of people through demystifying and democratizing research.

BEING A SOCIOLOGIST

Clients started coming my way—not exactly in droves—but in sufficient numbers to warrant my continuing that consultant life-style. Eventually, I started to carve out areas where most of my work occurred. One of my mainstays was program evaluation as the War on Poverty, the Model Cities program, and other community service and community change programs became aware of the need to document their accomplishments. Another SCS focus was environment sociology. The War on Poverty and other programs had raised everyone's consciousness about citizen participation, and designers and planners doing public or quasi-public projects saw the need to subcontract with someone who could orchestrate and obtain that participation, either through surveys, public meetings, or other methods. A third focus of my work was in organizational development and training, usually with nonprofit agencies, educational or church organizations, or public agencies. Fourth in the growing SCS repertoire was social impact assessment, especially after the 1973 oil embargo when the western United States came into sharper focus as a storehouse of untapped energy resources.

On most projects, SCS was directly contracted to those kinds of clients I've mentioned; quite frequently, we were subcontractors to another contractor, such as a design or planning firm. It became, in fact, a source of pride when a tasty RFP (request for proposals) was out and two or three different firms would ask us to be written into their proposal.

On occasion, SCS did gratis work, such as helping a neighborhood organization get off the ground, or conducted self-initiated projects, such as a postoccupancy study of various kinds of senior housing. Utilization of student interns from various colleges made some of this work possible.

One of the curious things that happened as I responded to various and sundry requests was that I found myself getting into fields of sociology or forms of practice rather early, before a subspecialty really emerged. For instance, I was doing evaluation research, work with the design/planning professions, and social impact assessment in the late 1960s, essentially before those fields developed with their own professional organizations, journals, and annual conventions. This is not something about which I am boasting, because my efforts weren't deliberately planned but were responses to potential clients.

Such experiences began to instill in me greater confidence about my skills as a sociologist. What I found I could bring to a project were group process skills, basic survey methodology, conceptual skills for modeling phenomena as one way of figuring out what to do about them, and an ability to size up a situation quickly and propose a sequence of appropriate actions. On that last skill, I remember once being asked what it means to be a consultant, and responding, "It's being able to stand in front of a group of people and say, 'Now there are three things going on here,' and as I said number one, I was *making up* number two and number three!"

Another characteristic I developed that served me well included the willingness to work in interdisciplinary groups of professionals, not all of whom either understood or appreciated the role of the sociologist. I also had to achieve a balance between the rigors of good research methods on one hand and the demands or the constraints of the project on the other hand. I recall on one occasion telling a client I certainly could get good student and faculty input to the design of a new community college within two weeks. Constraints came in the forms of time, budget, or client unwillingness to allow the data collecting that really needed to be done.

BEING A BUSINESSPERSON

Being the sociologist in the job description of "consulting sociologist" is one thing: to a reasonable degree, my education prepared me for that. Being the consultant, however, meant being a businessperson, and *nothing* in my entire background had prepared me for that. Sociology curricula in the 1960s and early 1970s didn't include courses on applied sociology, clinical sociology, consulting, or anything like them. Not that curricula included courses on environmental sociology, program evaluation, or social impact assessment either, but trained as a sociologist, I could easily "slide" into those specialty content areas.

When I opened up Social Change Systems, I knew nothing of what running a business required, including bookkeeping and accounting, taxation, marketing, and so on. I learned what had to be learned in various ways. Sometimes, in the corporation's early days, I learned of government filing regulations only after I missed some deadline and had been fined. Some things I learned from other businesses, such as how to construct a fee schedule that adequately covered salary and overhead. Yet other things I learned from experts, such as accountants, whose skills I purchased once and then copied.

I eventually got my act together sufficiently to have a consistent rate structure, contract forms or letters of agreement, proposal and budget formats, and regularly kept books. As for marketing, I developed a variety of approaches including using former clients to help me establish new contacts, attending many public events where one could press the flesh and flash one's card, testifying in public, doing a regular column of political commentary in a neighborhood newspaper, and mailing brochures to potential clients. Sometimes, having seen an item in the newspaper about someone doing an interesting project, I would call that person and offer my services.

One of my best sources for contracts became the university bureau in which I had previously worked: they would either contract with me to do studies for them or refer to me others who were seeking consultants.

Another technique I utilized for client-building was to distribute to potential clients selective reports or summaries of reports I had prepared, in the hope that it would suggest some study to them or at least alert them to the existence of SCS. As I became aware of RFPs that were out where SCS could team up with another firm, such as a design firm, I would call some firms and propose joint-venture responses to the RFP.

Throughout SCS's entire history, the major business challenge facing me was cash flow, stemming from inadequate, better yet nonexistent, capitalization. Only on rare occasions could SCS get ahead enough to be able to do some extra marketing. Adequate capitalization might have meant being able to have someone more versed in business than myself, to take trips as part of marketing, and to have permanent staff instead of many temporary staff as contracts required. Without adequate capitalization, one finds oneself taking out personal loans to pay staff, rent, and such.

Being a businessperson oftimes got in the way of being a sociologist. As a sociologist, for instance, I might want to play with a computer printout of survey data forever to milk it for all that's there; as a businessperson, I knew that at some point such extensive time devoted to playing with the data amounted to giving away my services. Actually, it was after I closed down Social Change Systems that a friend, also a one-time consultant, drew on the back of a napkin a little triangle, with the sides labeled "time," "cost," and "quality." His rule of thumb was to let the client dictate any two of the three conditions as long as he, the consultant, got to specify the third. If a client wanted a high-*quality* job and *right away*, my friend would say, "Ok, but that's going to *cost* you." The client wanting a *cheap* product *right away* was reminded that the *quality* wouldn't be very great. Someone seeking a high-*quality* product but unwilling to *pay* for it was told that task would be relegated to a lower *priority* in time (while better paying projects were completed). For a dozen years, I realized, I had pretty much let clients dictate all three conditions.

As a nonprofit corporation, SCS had a social mission, as mentioned earlier, namely, to use research as a way to bring about social change. That mission I tried to fulfill as SCS dealt with a variety of profit-oriented and nonprofit clients. Each type of client system presented its own set of challenges.

Working for the profit-making entity at times meant having to struggle to maintain my integrity—as a sociologist and as a person—against the pressures of "bottom line" concerns. One project, for instance, entailed helping a large multinational company select the best place for employee housing on a power plant construction project. After all the data from our research and that of other consultants were in and pointed to one area as the optimal site, the company selected another, less-preferable site where they already had an option on the land. Our research on social and environmental factors was made subservient to financial considerations.

Doing work for nonprofit clients presented a different set of frustrations. Basically the biggest problem was that they were always poor, as poor as SCS, and didn't have the money to do the job properly. Too often I would say the work *could* be done within their limited, fixed budget and then end up taking a loss. A second problem with nonprofit clients was having to deal with different layers or loci of decision makers, something that would slow down a project or produce contradictory expectations and wants.

With both kinds of clients, getting paid was at times a problem, even after the work had been completed satisfactorily. The nonprofit client didn't have the money on hand while the profit-making company tried to hang onto it as long as possible. This was especially a problem in cases where SCS was a subcontractor or a sub-subcontractor and the payments had to flow down through one or two firms before they got to SCS.

One might query why I continued to operate Social Change Systems as a nonprofit corporation, considering some of the disadvantageous positions in which that put me. The overarching reason was a political one, namely, my not wanting to be a capitalist, not even a small one. However, there were other considerations as well. Having defined for SCS a social mission and having chosen to work mainly with other nonprofit or public entities, I believe SCS's nonprofit status lent some credibility to our work: Prospective clients could see we weren't just trying to make a buck on them. That nonprofit status also enabled SCS to pursue self-initiated and gratis or pro bono projects without the worry of a bottom-line consideration on the part of stockholders or partners. Finally, not having an additional figure for profit built into our budgets kept our costs and hence our fees down below what other consultants might have charged. In fact, it was always a principle (as well as a result of low revenues) to keep SCS's overhead down by being modest in our physical surroundings and other aspects of the operation.

CONCLUSIONS

At this point in this retrospective chapter, what I would like to do is focus on two kinds of conclusions: the sources of satisfaction that kept me involved in consulting work for a dozen years, and the lessons to be derived from my experiences.

Satisfactions

One of the things that I came to realize I enjoyed about consulting work was the involvement in several, usually different, kinds of projects at one time. I might be engaged in a program evaluation, a community survey, some training, and something else during the same period of time. This keeps one fresh, alert, and constantly challenged. I particularly enjoyed those occasions where, in a meeting with clients, I could fruitfully apply some idea, piece of information, or method I had just picked up or developed the day before on another project.

The fact that the projects SCS took on placed me in different settings, with different kinds of clients and different kinds of tasks, was a second source of frequent excitement. To continue the example from the above paragraph: That program evaluation might have me meeting with social service providers in the city, while the community survey was going on in a small mountain town, and the training was for low-income inner city residents.

Third, as suggested earlier, the nature of the requests from clients often had me on the cutting edge of sociology. Though it was at times scary, it was also exhilarating, having to devise some seat-of-the-pants method for some task or problem I had never faced before. One striking example was when I was the successful proposer for the organizational development work a social service agency wanted done. I had outlined a fancy multistep work plan that drew on some systems analysis concepts from an engineer friend, and I ignored the fact that I knew very little about social agency dynamics or adoption (the agency's major function). I was able to organize a three-step process of evaluating the agency as it then stood ("what is"), engaging its leadership in goal setting ("what should be"), and then facilitating a process for agency redesign ("what could be"). I continually had to invent diverse and interesting small group processes to keep the agency's Research and Development Committee actively involved and on a track toward final decisions over an almost 12-month period.

The varied contracts SCS entered into often entailed interdisciplinary work, a fourth source of satisfaction. Not only might I be working with planners or architects on a given design or planning project, but engineers, economists, lenders, and others would also be regular actors on the project. Explaining and then legitimizing the sociologist's role was at times a real challenge since lay people don't pretend to know about the engineer's domain, but everybody believes they're experts on human behavior and social life. Therefore, who needs a sociologist?

Yet another payoff for me—number five—was the invaluable set of experiences I had that I could bring to the classroom (as I generally was teaching part time at one area institution or another).

Still other sources of satisfaction included training others in the work; seeing bright, fresh-off-the-press copies of final reports over which I and my associates had toiled; and, of course, receiving the news that SCS had been the successful proposer on an exciting and lucrative project.

Lessons

The first lesson I would derive from the SCS experience concerning initially hanging out one's shingle has to do with money. One shouldn't try to enter consulting work without *some* minimal level of working capital—to cover the start-up costs (office, phone, stationery, calling cards, and such) *and* for the rainy days that regularly punctuate the calendar in the early months of one's consulting career. I know some people "back into" consulting by virtue of being asked to do a specific project that looks very lucrative. That's well and good, but what happens when that ends and the second contract isn't immediately forthcoming?

A second and related point about money is that even if one chooses to operate in a nonprofit fashion as I did, one still has to run the operations in a businesslike way, attending to cash flow, writing paychecks, and keeping the wolf from the door.

Therefore, I would advise would-be consultants to familiarize themselves with small business history (which reveals a staggering rate of early failures) and practices. If one lacks business skills, one would be advised to team up with someone who has them. Perhaps an even better route to follow is to work in a larger consulting firm for a while in order to learn about doing business, build up contacts, and establish a track record of quality work.

Once a person has entered the consulting business, a number of other issues crop up and I have some observations about those as well. First, keeping one's overhead moderate at the start is quite advisable. In the early stages, it's far more important to have simple things like stationery, calling cards, and brochures than an office, which is costlier. Chances are most deals will be made elsewhere than *your* office, and at least at the start most of one's work can be done at home. SCS's home for its first couple of years was my own apartment.

Second, in preparing proposals, it's vitally important to be realistic and tough with yourself when estimating how long it will take to get the job done. Invariably, something goes wrong that delays the project. Anticipate that and build in time for that rather than innocently embracing the most optimistic assumptions. Remember my friend's time-cost-quality triangle and don't give yourself away.

Third, when it comes to preparing contracts, it's quite advisable to seek legal consultation, especially concerning payment schedules. Spending a hundred dollars or two at the front end can save many headaches and maybe dollars later. You might find you need to do that only once or twice before you learn the best approach yourself.

As one gets on in the consulting business, opportunities or requests to do gratis work will come one's way. For SCS, that form of work was an important, principled part of how we functioned. Fourth, even if your consulting business doesn't define for itself such a social mission, doing occasional free work is advisable for the experience and exposure it gives one: "resume-building" as it were.

Finally, and this is the most valuable lesson I can share: Don't go into the consulting game if you're not able to deal with insecurity, ambiguity, and uncertainty.

14

Gitt'n Down: Entrepreneurialship out of the Womb

JACK HUTSLAR

The purpose of this chapter is to give people some insight into independent business, consulting, and entrepreneurial roles. It will enable readers to determine if they want to and are capable of making a living based on what they can do or what they can sell. In my view, there is little similarity between working for a company or a university and working for yourself.

The major topics in this chapter include the attitude of the business community, how to identify your salable products and skills, examples of theoretical material that you may find useful in professional consulting, concerns about running a small business, personal tips, and business tips. Conclusions, sources of assistance, and a bibliography complete the chapter.

DO YOU KNOW YOURSELF AND THE COMMUNITY IN WHICH YOU WANT TO DO BUSINESS?

Why go into business for yourself? This is a question you should answer. Working for others is all right but it can become dull, unrewarding, and sometimes unhealthy. You might be swayed into starting your own business just because self-employment is a popular trend. Other contemporary fads that might influence your personal decision making include fitness, personal computers, wellness, music videos, dieting, financial independence, stress reduction, employee assistance programs, and uncounted distributorships and franchises. So, before you jump, realize that going into business for yourself is "hot."

People who go into business for themselves must settle on the products and services they can sell and to whom they will be offered. Starting a new business in a new field (such as consulting sociologist) is difficult. Major business problems were identified with what Ray Considine, motivational speaker, referred to in *The Great Brain Robbery* (1977) as the "curse of assumption." These statements pinpoint the obstacles that new business people will encounter:

- I don't know who you are.
- I don't know your company.
- I don't know your company's product.
- I don't know what your company stands for.
- I don't know your company's customers.
- I don't know your company's record.
- I don't know your company's reputation.
- Now, what was it you wanted to sell me?

This attitude by prospective clients should be a powerful incentive for new entrepreneurs to identify their products, services, and clients carefully before starting in business. As you can see, it is far easier to sell common products and services to the masses than sell unique consulting services to an elite clientele. For example, you can go to most well-to-do neighborhoods in any community and make $25,000 per year mowing grass during the growing season. On the other hand, you may work many 60-hour weeks with major problems and headaches and never get a consulting business into a comparable financial position.

The message is clear: Identify your products and skills; then determine if people are buying or will buy them. For instance, look in the telephone directory. See if there are businesses similar to what you wish to establish. If so, take it as a good sign. If not, then know that you will have to break down psychological barriers before you make any sales. That is difficult and it takes time. Look before you leap. This starts by knowing yourself and your business community.

Know yourself! This is a good admonition that applies to all people, but particularly to those who are considering self-employment. Start your own self-study project by making unqualified lists. List all of your interests. List your skills on another page. List what you would like to do. You can take a stab at your biases and limitations too but this is a continual challenge. Use the Yellow Pages of the telephone book when your lists appear inadequate.

Now collect your lists and review them, one at a time. Cross off those interests, skills, and jobs that are less appealing. Reduce your lists even more. Now see if you have created a new product or service or if you have found an existing line of work to your liking.

An alternative to this is to go to work for someone whose business you want to learn. If you can come up with the cash, you can buy a franchise, follow their directions, work hard, and make a good living. A number of people have built successful companies by copying other businesses. In fact, this is one of the cornerstones of Theory Z management.

If you are unsure about the potential of your business venture, retain full-time employment while testing career options. Then, cut the cord and throw your time and energies into self-employment. This is a ticklish decision. Working full time for others is both a cushion as well as an obstacle. It provides financial and emotional security but it prevents you from expanding your business so you can really capitalize on your talents.

The remainder of this chapter addresses reality outside university walls. It starts with three examples of what practicing sociologists might consider doing. Then, more specific business and personal information is provided on how to market (find prospects) and sell your products (plans, books, tapes, videos, courses) and services (skills) in a business rather than an educational environment.

WHAT CONSULTANTS SELL

Pure sociologists must look very carefully at what they have to sell in the marketplace. It may be difficult to trade in socialization or symbolic interactionism as psychologists sell stress management, physicians sell diets, or management science leaders sell computer programs and seminars. The constructs of pure sociology, it seems to me, must be sold to business and community leaders. Then your theories can be applied organizationwide to benefit the people of intact social units like schools, churches, corporations, and governmental units.

If you do not know or do not like what you have to offer, look around. See what professionals are capitalizing on in the marketplace. Your degree is reasonable proof that you know how to learn. So, learn what professionals in the 1980s have learned: wellness, stress, videos, and going into business for yourself. Even being a Republican is hot. Notice that there is nothing here that would cause people to look up sociologists in the Yellow Pages. Sociology is not a household word in the business community.

Therefore, to "practice" sociology, I suggest that you identify a common field (that is, sports and recreation, education, business, religion, law, medicine, media) in which to apply your professional education. Do not try to conquer the world. This is a major point and it may send you back to your lists. There you may be able to identify a central life interest that you can sink your teeth into profitably. It may revolve around management and the family business, children and sports, fitness or wellness, aging relatives, religion, marriage and divorce, alcohol and drug abuse, or social welfare.

Careerwise, if you are not where you want to be at this time based on your list of interests, develop a step-by-step self-help plan to get yourself there. Spend no more than three years at any given stage: one to learn it thoroughly, one to do it well, and one to innovate and prepare to move on. Monitor your performance so you will know when you are on track, have reached your level of incompetence, or have lost interest in your objectives.

This will sound a bit harsh for scholars but you must have something people will buy. In the sections that follow are three examples of theoretical material that can be used in both personal and business management consulting: process consulting, self-help, and quality of life testing.

Process Consultation

This is a method to bring about change in organizations. In business or education, for instance, the technique prescribes that management and labor join together to identify problems, develop solutions, and implement change. The consultant's role is that of teacher, facilitator, mediator, and process leader. A consultant strives to teach owners and managers how to analyze and resolve their own problems (Schein 1969; Hutslar 1984). For consulting sociologists, they will apply the appropriate social theories to produce these changes.

Self-Help

This is a standard way for people to change individual behavior. People want either to stop something (smoking, eating, child abuse) or start something (running, making more business calls). The self-help model can be used with individual clients, systemwide for all employees, or in personal planning. Here is the outline of a self-help model I use.

1. Identify something you wish to evaluate or want to change.
2. Specify the event in observable and measurable terms in the form of a task, condition, and criterion level.
3. Decide that you definitely want to change.
4. Identify just one thing you want to change.
5. Record to obtain a baseline incidence level.
6. Set a target or criterion level for yourself.
7. Start the change process and record your performance.
8. Compare these results to your baseline data.

9. Evaluate and reward yourself when you meet the target on time.

10. Repeat on another task.

Try it on something easy the first time. As a professional business-person, you must stay on top of your field. You must also know how to run a business profitably. Therefore, you may want to set personal goals to read 20 professional journals a month, write two articles a year, and scan three business magazines monthly. For personal stress management, you will want to develop a plan to reach 11–15 miles of running each week. In family affairs, you will want to spend a minimum of 30 minutes each day with your children and at least the same amount of high-quality time with your spouse. Teach your clients to use this method of change where applicable.

Quality of Life

Quality of life testing can be associated with any type of intervention and change. It complements fitness and wellness consulting. My interest in this area and a questionnaire that I developed grew out of my dissertation (Hutslar 1975). It is based on research in sociology and clinical psychology (Campbell, Converse, and Rodgers 1976; Blau 1977). The focus tends to be on the major social domains in our life (work, marriage, recreation, health, religion, life satisfaction) and how we evaluate each area personally. The assumption is that people in specific fields have predictable needs and can become predictably dissatisfied with some aspect of life. Problem areas may be successfully addressed with a standard evaluative instrument. The Jack Hutslar "True Life Adventure" Test (see "Sources of Assistance" section at the end of this chapter) is a simple questionnaire that assesses satisfaction in the major domains that influence the lives of people.

These management consulting, self-help, and quality of life "tools" are examples of what sociologists might do. They represent a ready methodological base that can be modified and expanded upon to provide clients with a variety of services. They are useful concepts because they can be used in both individual and corporate consulting.

THE BUSINESS SIDE OF CONSULTING

How to run a small business can be divided into at least five categories, more if you adhere to strict administrative science theory. Traditionalists focus their attention on plan, organize, staff, direct, and control. In the remainder of this chapter I am going to deal with the people and material side of business, marketing, plus some tips that you can take or leave.

You can study formal management theory when you are ready to seek more information.

The People Side of Business

Self

The first requirement to go into business for yourself is desire or motivation. If you are the type of person who needs to be pushed, go to work for someone else. They will care for you. On the other hand, you must be a self-starter in your own business. If you do not do it, "it ain't gonna git done and you ain't gonna eat."

People

Your people are your associates, staff, and clients plus your suppliers and manufacturers. They include also a banker, an attorney, and an accountant, all for business or legal reasons. It is also useful and therapeutic to have a friend or personal advisor with whom you can share your deepest thoughts, fears, and secrets.

The greatest single factor in business excellence is how well you are able to work with and lead people. Social theory shows repeatedly that you accomplish the most with people, both in quantity and quality, when they are involved in their work. Most research shows that good business, management, and leadership follow the democratic style. I described this in my book on how to develop and conduct safe, effective, high-quality sports programs for school-age children (Hutslar 1985).

One of the great challenges of life, particularly when your business and your money are on the line, is to have faith in a theory you promote that also effects you personally. In a society that preaches democratic ideals but tends to act in an authoritarian manner, you may have to live or die personally and professionally by your theoretical contructs.

Location

The type of business dictates the office needs. An operation that relies on walk-in trade (such as book store, gift shop) must be located in a high-traffic area. Doctors, counselors, psychologists, and consultants must locate in professional settings to fulfill expectations. However, many people can operate quite well from a home/office when they mow lawns, write and publish, or do certain types of consulting work. There are specific tax advantages when you put your office in your home.

The Material Side of Business

Budget

When you go into business for yourself, start with enough capital so that you do not have to make a profit for 12 months. Your fixed yearly expenses generally include rent, utilities, license fees, insurance, and taxes. Expenses that vary include product inventory, supplies, equipment, furnishings, labor, advertising and marketing, travel, legal and business fees, and labor. Do not take personal expenses from business income until all the bills are paid.

There are a number of budget systems but they all boil down to two factors: IN and OUT. IN must exceed OUT. In business, unlike education, decision making ultimately reduces profit and cash flow. When OUT exceeds IN, get busy or get out.

Product or Service

Your product or service determines the form your business takes. It establishes your location, your marketing, the talent you need, the clients you will have, and your fees or pricing structure.

Businesses can be organized as sole proprietorships, partnerships, and profit or nonprofit corporations. Personal liability may be high in certain advising, consulting, and action-oriented businesses. You can protect your personal finances by incorporating. However, in doing this you lose tax advantages where personal and professional expenses overlap in sole proprietorships and partnerships. Many professionals now form nonprofit corporations to gain business, grant, and tax advantages. Licenses and memberships vary depending on the type of business form you select and what you sell. See the "Sources of Assistance" section at the end of this chapter for more information.

Pricing products and services is interesting. It hinges on what people will pay and what others charge for similar items. There is no general rule on pricing services except that you should charge enough to maximize profits. A fee of $20.00 per hour and $200.00 per day is out of sight for poor people and ridiculously low for upwardly mobile professionals and corporate clients. In fact, some people will neither listen to you nor use your services when your prices are too low. A service is worth as much as people will pay for it. When you get too busy, raise your prices.

Product pricing does not float as freely as does service or talent pricing. Products like books and videos are usually offered at three or more times production costs. This allows you to sell your product to dealers for resale and still make a good profit.

Proposals

Develop a standard written business proposal. It should be a specific explanation of your service, costs, and how you will deliver it, including handout material, to your client. Put it on a word processor. Then plug individualized information for each potential client into the blanks. There is insufficient space to go into this in more detail here. Ask the advertising sales department of your local newspaper for samples of the proposals they use.

MARKETING YOUR BUSINESS TO POTENTIAL CLIENTS

Marketing merits special attention for two reasons. First, it helps you identify how you are going to "hawk" your business to your clients. Second, marketing is another hot buzzword of the 1980s.

Let us first make a few basic distinctions. Public relations or publicity involves creating a favorable image for yourself and your company. Advertising is informing and selling your products and services to people. Marketing is identifying where and how specific products and services can be sold best. It is a type of research and, as such, might become one of your service lines. The topics in this section are personal contact, advertising, and networking.

Personal Contact

One of the best ways to drum up business in the marketplace is through personal contact. People like to see what they are buying, whether a product or a person. Get on the telephone, make appointments, and sell your products and services in person with a slick presentation.

Extend this to your friends and acquaintances, as is done in many of the franchise operations. Ask them to buy your service. Ask them for referrals. Your acquaintances can help you get your foot in the door and overcome the "I don't know who you are" obstacles. Eventually, though, you must stand on your own.

As you meet with customers, be mannerly and leave them in good graces whether or not you make a sale. You will make return calls on these same people, so do not burn your bridges. Remember that sales calls will lead to referrals *and* build your image in the community.

Advertising

Most of us are familiar with advertising and the media. It is cost effective for large businesses but many new operations are unable to operate at this financial level. Through market research, you can locate your customers and develop advertising material that is best suited to your business and budget.

There are two forms of advertising that are hot. The first is direct mail advertising, which means to target or match advertising material through the postal system with customers who *will* purchase your product. A version of this is to publish a newsletter, sell it or give it away, and mail it to your clients at bulk rates in quantities over 200. The cost to publish a small "letter" is minimal. It can be just a "clipping service" for your clients, but it will produce results.

Second, many professionals now offer workshops and seminars to recruit new clients. Generally they run for 60 to 90 minutes and feature the seminar leader's services or products. The latter include the speaker's book or workbook, longer seminars, films, tapes, belief system, or other types of beauty, nutritional, pleasure, money management, real estate, or profit-making enterprises.

For the most part, workshop leaders must be able to sell popular products or services with mass appeal or sign up people "on the spot." However, this illustrates also what many professionals now do to find new clients. This is called prospecting and professionals in many fields now work at this type of marketing as they have seldom done in the past. It makes mowing grass look pretty good by comparison.

There are other ways to advertise your products and services. It costs very little to issue public service announcements, called PSAs, to the media. Learn to write these to promote your activities. Consider also writing a free column for the weekly tabloids in your community. Local conferences and mall exhibitions are other inexpensive ways to introduce yourself to the public.

At the other extreme, you might recruit an investor with big bucks and go heavily into mass marketing. Venture capitalists will generally want a high return on their investment. A less-expensive option is to do video marketing through independent television stations. It is effective with certain products and services.

Networking

This is a strategy whereby you join forces with other people, businesses, or groups in a symbiotic relationships. When two people work together as associates, they are able to feed work to each other, share the work, and use their collective resources efficiently. When individuals form networks with organizations, they can offer their services in exchange for access to the group's members.

Whatever your approach to advertising and marketing, plan to reach your customers in two or more ways simultaneously. So, study and learn from the media and the direct mail advertising you receive.

Most businesspeople advertise. Select your target and hit them right between the eyes with exactly what you know they will purchase. Successful marketing and advertising lead to profitable businesses.

SOME PERSONAL TIPS THAT YOU CAN TAKE OR LEAVE

The ethics in business and sales range from absolute honesty, to do what you can live with, to anything to make a dime. When going into business for yourself, particularly when you consider yourself a permanent member of the community, be scrupulously honest. Never lie and cheat. Say what you can do and do what you say. Be straightforward with your clients and ask them to do likewise.

Be neat and clean. Wear the appropriate clothing and keep your weight under control. Avoid smoking and drinking while you are with clients. When you work closely with people, brush your teeth frequently so that you will have pleasant breath.

Meet people, attend community functions, and become known. It will pay dividends in unexpected ways.

Be positive. Be upbeat. Be happy to see friends and clients. Greet them with genuinely positive actions. It will help establish your image in the community, and it will improve your outlook on life, particularly when you are in the start-up phase.

Develop your position on matters that concern you and acknowledge the position of others. Avoid personal anger or hatred. Stay calm when others lose theirs. You will not be able to please everyone but you can treat everyone with dignity.

You can win the favor of some people for no reason other than they like you. Then there are some who will never call on you because of their personal biases and perceptual blinders. For instance, I have worked with teachers who did not like certain students. Their faults were usually unattractiveness, swarthy skin, and unacceptable accents.

My point in offering these personal tips is to know that people respond favorably to attractive people. Know yourself and how people respond to you. Act as though you are on stage. Give your audiences your best performances. Keep "other" actions back stage. After all, you establish and control the image that you want your clients to see. Know what image you want to convey to your customers. Mary Parker Follett made a comparable observation about business in her 1904 Law of the Situation. She said: "If you don't know what business you are in, conceptualize what business it would be useful for you to think you are in." Get the idea! (Naisbitt 1982, p. 88).

SOME BUSINESS TIPS THAT WILL HELP YOU BECOME SUCCESSFUL

Let me offer a few tips that may help you make a profit. It is my belief that persistence has a lot to do with how you feel about what you are doing and success. Ray Considine (1977) was more specific about persistence when he developed his "FOURmula for success." In his self-help plan for success, he directed entrepreneurs to:

1. Make four phone calls a day
2. Send four notes or letters a day
3. Ask for four referrals from clients and friends a day
4. Ask for the order four times a day

Considine said that his FOURmula for success in business was what Joe Girard called "doing ordinary things an extraordinary number of times."

Bill McKenzie (1983), another motivator of businesspeople, mentioned two points worth emphasizing here. He told entrepreneurs: "Sell, don't tell." In other words, do not give away what you want clients to buy.

He recommended also that you find a hero and find a foe. In both instances, he directed us to take the best of what these people have to offer and knock the business socks off our competitors.

If you do not have a business slogan, develop one that expresses your philosophy. It will help you stay on track. A beer commercial writer stated: "We do a good job at a fair price." That says it just fine. Other slogans that may give you something to build on are:

1. The mail must get through.
2. The customer is always right. (A fellow who ran a hang gliding school disagreed with me on this one.)
3. Quality is our most important product.
4. It's not whether you win or lose that counts but how much you get to play. (This is one of mine.)

CONCLUSIONS

Self-employment is stimulating and addicting. Most people never work harder than when they work for themselves. Plan well, start with sufficient capital, work with your clients and advisors, and believe in yourself. Stay on top of your profession and your market. Capitalize on what is hot. This will help you become a successful businessperson.

Take care of yourself physically, socially, and psychologically, because all work and no play will make you sick, not to mention dull. Do not put yourself in the hospital with stress problems. Set limits, make time for yourself and your family, and get regular cardiovascular exercise by walking, running, hiking, or playing tennis. Balance your work, social life (marriage, family, friends), and leisure activities. Enjoy your work but keep it all in balance to have a satisfying life.

SOURCES OF ASSISTANCE

Considine, Ray. 1977. *The Great Brain Robbery*. 521 South Madison Avenue, Pasadena CA 91101. 224 pp. $12.00.
Home Office (The magazine for people who work at home). Time Inc., Time & Life Building, Rockefeller Center, New York NY 10020.
Hutslar, Jack. 4985 Oak Garden Drive, Kernersville NC 27284. Telephone 919 784-4926. Personal, business, and sport management consultant. Send $1.00 for the "True Life Adventure" test.
Metcalf, Wendell O. 1973. *Starting and Managing a Small Business of Your Own*, 3rd ed. Washington, D.C.: Small Business Administration. 95 pp. Available in a packet of information from the Small Business Administration.
Peters, Thomas, J., and Robert H. Waterman, Jr. 1982. *In Search of Excellence: Lessons from America's Best-run Corporations*. New York: Harper and Row, 360 pp.
The Pitfalls of Managing a Small Business. 1977. Small Business Handbook. New York: Dun & Bradstreet, Inc., 20 pp. $1.50.
Retired Executives Volunteer Service (REVS). A business consulting service offered to anyone without charge. In some places it operates as the *Service Corps of Retired Executives (SCORE)*. Call your local Chamber of Commerce for specific information.
Small Business Administration. Offers books and materials plus small business loans at reduced interest rates. Call your local Chamber of Commerce for the mailing address and telephone number of an office near you.

REFERENCES

Blau, Theodore H. 1977. "Quality of Life, Social Indicators, and Criteria of Change." *Professional Psychology*, November: 464–73.
Campbell, Angus, Philip E. Converse, and Willard L. Rodgers. 1976. *The Quality of American Life*. New York: Russell Sage Foundation.
Considine, Ray. 1977. *The Great Brain Robbery*. 521 South Madison Avenue. Pasadena CA 91101.
Hutslar, Jack. 1985. *Beyond X's and O's: What Generic Parents, Volunteer Coaches and Teachers Can Learn about Generic Kids and All of the Sports They Play*. Welcome N.C.: Wooten Printing Company.
———. 1984. "Using Organizational Development Techniques to Improve Teaching." In *Ideas II*, edited by Ronald P. Carlson, pp. 30–34. Reston Va: NASPE.
———. 1975. "Social Factors Influencing Superior Male Bowling." Ph.D. dissertation, The Ohio State University.

McKenzie, Bill. 1983. Presentation at Recreation Management '83. April 17, 1983, Philadelphia, Pennsylvania.

Naisbitt, John. 1982. *Megatrends: Ten New Directions Transforming Our Lives.* New York: Warner Books.

Schein, Edgar. 1969. *Process Consultation: Its Role in Organization Development.* Reading, Mass.: Addison-Wesley.

PART V

Sociologists in Practice

In previous parts of this book it has been argued that sociology must be relevant, have policy implications, and be "workable" (Boros 1984). According to Boros, to determine what is workable it is necessary to use the pragmatic criterion for testing the validity of our principles. Indeed, sociological knowledge does not have the same public acceptance as do the sciences with strong pragmatic accomplishments, such as physics, chemistry, and biology. Sociology has not been as successful in using pragmatic tests to help determine the acceptance or rejection of sociological theories.

This is beginning to change, however; there are more consulting and applied sociologists who are putting their sociological knowledge and skills to test. They are out in the field and who could better provide feedback on the workability of sociological perspectives in solving social and political problems? Indeed, applied sociologists and those in the consulting role have become more accepted within the discipline and more professional in their outlook. Given this, there are now better opportunities for these sociologists to provide feedback to colleagues on the workability of sociological principles in real-life settings. Thus, the outcomes of the consulting work of sociologists can be seen as critical in the development of the field. However, these outcomes are not useful unless they are communicated and then further used to refine both sociological knowledge and methods.

Part V of this book provides concrete examples of sociologists in practice. Each of the chapters in this part describes specific consulting experiences of sociologists that, in turn, provide useful feedback concerning the workability of sociology.

In Chapter 15, Penelope Canan describes her experience, as part of a multidisciplinary team, in conducting a Social Impact Assessment for the City and County of Honolulu, Hawaii. Her consulting team had the task of reviewing an earlier consultant's Social Impact Management System for guiding land use decisions and then devising an alternative to the existing procedure. She pointed out that interpersonal and political aspects of the experience were influential in determining the final outcome of her project.

Alexander Boros, in Chapter 16, describes a seven-year project that involved improving the welfare of deaf people in Cleveland, Ohio. A history of how and why the project began is given, and the service-oriented projects that were implemented throughout the duration of this consulting activity are described. Boros further identifies 15 guidelines followed by the consultants in giving assistance to the deaf-community leaders. He emphasized that these guidelines and illustrations can be useful in consulting with nondeaf groups as well. The major finding of this project was how much ordinary deaf people could accomplish in bringing about change for the betterment of deaf people with only little assistance from professionals.

Jean Thoresen, in Chapter 17, describes her approach as a consultant to the issue of homosexuality among adolescents. She argues that consulting about deviant behavior among adolescents, usually at the request of adults in authority, raises some special issues of both ethics and practice for the consultant. A consultant may be called in because those in authority wish to "stop" behavior. The appropriateness of this goal is discussed within the context of the distinction between behavior and identity. Suggestions are offered for working with both the adults in authority and gay teenagers. The possible effect of the consultant's own sexual orientation is considered. The necessity of designing techniques that take account of unintended and potentially embarrassing stereotypes or prejudices on the part of participants, and that are designed to protect the sensitivities of participants, is emphasized. For practice use, examples of consciousness-raising, projectives, and role plays specifically for working with camp personnel on the issue of lesbianism are presented. In addition, some ideas on presenting oneself as a consultant in an appropriate and effective way are briefly shared.

REFERENCE

Boros, Alexander. 1984. "Sociology: The Workable Myth." Founders Address, Second Annual Conference of Society for Applied Sociology, Covington, Kentucky, October 13.

15

Consulting for City Government on the Heels of Another Consultant

PENELOPE CANAN

Given the bureaucratic policy of relying on external expertise for non-routine tasks—and sociological research is seldom a built-in routine government operation—government agencies often find that when work produced by consultants is unacceptable, they must rely on a new group of consultants to "mop up" the original project. Internal blame-shifting and external "face-saving" regarding the failure to produce a usable product are not unusual; neither is modifying the definition of the work task desired. For the "mop up" consultants, the situation is a bit tricky: They must gain the confidence of the insiders with little knowledge of how agency dynamics were affected by the previous consultants; they must not discredit their discipline with petty *ad hominem* criticism; and yet their work must be performed within a context that is heavy with the baggage of history.

This chapter is about a sociologist in such a role, that of consultant to the public sector, on the heels of a previous consulting contract. The task for our consulting group—a sociologist, an economist, and an urban planner—was to design a Social Impact Management System for the Hawaiian island of Oahu. Part of the request was to review the work of the previous consultant, X.

The chapter is organized into five sections: the history of the contract; the logic of creating design guidelines to permit an "objective" evaluation of various alternatives, including X's proposal; a brief summary of the decision process we suggested; a discussion of how our recommendation contrasts with earlier conceptions of Social Impact Assessment; and, finally, the interpersonal and political aspects of this experience that might be instructive to the sociologist as consultant.

THE HISTORY

During the 1960s the pace of land development in the state of Hawaii was hectic, especially on the island of Oahu where the City and County of Honolulu are located. Hotels, condominiums, and single-family houses sprang up rapidly, traffic congestion became problematic, the cost of living increased, and cherished agricultural, recreational, and scenic areas were bulldozed. The extent and pace of development led citizens to question the wisdom of unbridled land use intensification at the expense of the quality of life. On Oahu, where 80 percent of the population lives, the 1973 City Charter Commission responded to public complaints by recommending that "city policies affecting transportation, housing, population and the physical environment are all to be seen and solved as social policies, not developed as solutions to functional problems apart from their social context."[1]

The revised City Charter of 1973 mandated the creation of a General Plan and specific Development Plans that treat the "fair distribution of social benefits" as a matter of paramount importance. In 1977 the Department of General Planning (DGP) began preparing Development Plans for the island of Oahu. As the elected governing body of the City and County, the City Council decided that the resolution of major development issues, such as those raised by the preparation of the Development Plans, should involve a systematic investigation of their social implications.

By the late 1970s the enterprise known as Social Impact Assessment (SIA), so named to parallel the Environmental Impact Assessment required federally by the National Environmental Protection Act of 1969, had led to the creation of SIA consulting firms. The City selected one such firm, X,

to develop an overall social impact management process that will (a) help the City Council understand, predict and act upon social consequences resulting from current and future Development Plan activities, and (b) prevent the occurrence of new issues that are detrimental to the residents as a result of preparing and implementing the Development Plans.

X proposed a Social Impact Management System (SIMS) that relied on 12 City-funded Social Impact Representatives geographically distributed across the island who would advise land developers of locally based social issues important to "human resource units." In addition to following existing land use regulations,[2] X proposed that the City require developers to address local social issues as a condition of receiving a Social Impact Permit. The developer was required to analyze how a proposed project would aggravate or ameliorate neighborhood issues.

Developers would determine these effects by interacting with "social networks," using X's eight idealized steps to "keep the individual and neighborhood in harmony with the environment." The result would be a series of independently negotiated agreements that would form the basis of the Social Impact Permit application.

After four years of researching neighborhood issues (at a cost of about $400,000), DGP still had not devised a way to implement the X SIMS. In 1982 another agency of the City, the Department of Land Utilization (DLU), was charged with reviewing X's recommended SIMS and devising an organizational structure and implementation procedure. DLU chose our ad hoc consulting team of an economist, an urban planner, and a sociologist to perform these tasks.[3]

DEFINING THE PROBLEM, CREATING GUIDELINES, AND REVIEWING VARIOUS APPROACHES

Initial interviews with government officials, land developers, and active citizens taught us that the problem was not that social impacts do not surface—eventually they do. Rather the problem was that they surface *too late* for compromises or mitigating measures to be achieved. Thus, designing a SIMS was redefined as a task of combining three concerns: timeliness, the ability to flush out social controversy, and a process that would engender meaningful discussion, compromise, and mitigation. Our design objective for evaluating alternative approaches became "to provide to affected parties . . . sufficient socio-economic information regarding a proposed project so they can respond sufficiently early and with enough leverage to affect cost-effective design improvements and needed mitigating measures.

Guidelines

We chose to present guidelines for constructing a workable SIMS partly to provide an explicit professional base for our report, given the sensitive nature of the required review of X's proposal. These guidelines were derived largely from recent literature on social impact assessment, community planning, and citizen participation, as well as from the experiences of many practitioners. We used the guidelines to examine the current City permit process, to evaluate various approaches to a SIMS, including X's, and to design our recommendation.

The SIMS guidelines were to:

- Standardize the basic features of a SIMS process so that it is *consistent* and procedurally *predictable* for all participants;

- Design a SIMS so that it enhances current decision-making procedures rather than create an entirely new process;

- Make a SIMS as *nonburdensome* as possible in terms of its monetary and time costs for all participants;

- Use objective information that is already *available* or easily obtainable from existing sources;

- Establish *safeguards* to ensure that no single party either dominates the SIMS process or is unfairly disadvantaged by it;

- Ensure that all parties *benefit* from the SIMS by having their interests recognized and their concerns dealt with in an equitable way;

- Make a SIMS process *inclusive* of all potentially affected parties, including concerned citizens, community groups and organizations, and government agencies;

- Involve all relevant parties in the SIMS process as *early* as possible, so that there is time to respond to their concerns before the project plan is finalized;

- Include in a SIMS both *objective* data on likely socioeconomic effects of the proposed project, and *subjective* evaluations by affected parties about the likely social impacts of the project on them;

- Limit the scope of a SIMS to project-specific effects and impacts, and keep the process focused on *relevant* issues and problems;

- Communicate all information concerning the potential objective effects of a project and its possible subjective impacts in language that is clearly *understandable* by all involved parties; *and*

- Maintain *flexibility* in the application of a SIMS process to differences in the issues, concerns, complexity, participants, and changing information associated with individual projects.

Subsequent Preparatory Steps

Having defined the contract task, reviewed the research literature, and developed design guidelines, we then researched the existing decision-making process in detail. We distilled numerous decision-making processes into a general process in order to identify potential intervention points. (See Figure 15.1).

For the purposes of identifying socioeconomic impacts early—in time to develop mitigation measures—the best intervention points occur before the application has been accepted by the lead agency and the decision-making period has begun. We found that although the public was legally involved through "public notice of land use change application," the range of publics actually notified was inadequate and notification came too late to accomplish the goal of early identification of social concerns (see Arnstein 1969; Heberlein 1976; Forester 1982). In brief

Figure 15.1
Current Land Use Decision-Making Process of the City and County of Honolulu

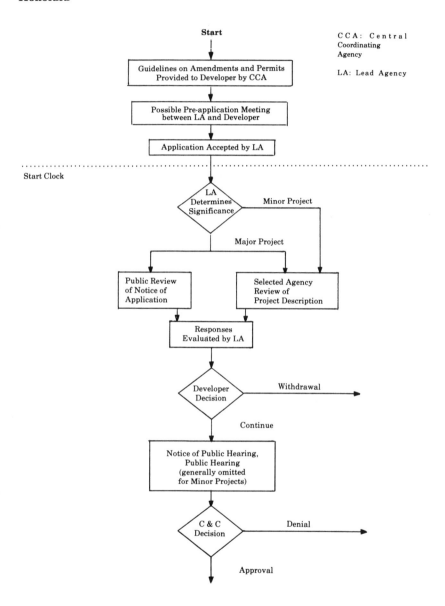

Source: Decision Analysts Hawaii, Inc., A Proposed Social Impact Management System for the City and County of Honolulu, January 1983.

Table 15.1
Indicators of Community Controversy

Population Relocation/Displacement. Forced displacement or relocation of any group of people may result in hardship, stress, or controversy. In particular, the resulting "loss of community" may be especially traumatic for long-time residents, the elderly, and the poor.

Low Compatibility of Clientele Groups with Existing Groups. Such incompatibility may produce life-style conflicts as a result of noticeable differences in socioeconomic status, ethnicity, nationality, life-style, cultural/religious beliefs, or recreational activities.

Low Compatibility with Community Issues. Unresolved community issues may generate immediate neighborhood opposition even though the proposed project will not directly affect these issues.

Obnoxious Noise or Smell. Obnoxious noise or smell from construction or operation that interfere with living or working conditions may produce immediate community opposition to the project.

Increased Traffic Flow. Frustration with traffic congestion may bring immediate opposition from people who use the affected roads.

Threat to Cherished Areas. Loss of beach access, open space, recreation facilities, or social gathering places can lead to community opposition.

Rate of Change. A project that will induce rapid change will be especially disruptive to a community that has recently experienced a rapid rate of change or that cherishes a slow pace of living.

Recent Controversy. A community that is already stressed from a recent controversy is likely to oppose any new project that appears even slightly controversial.

Insufficient Public Resources. A community may be stressed by a lack of adequate infrastructure facilities or public services to cope with the proposed project.

Source: Compiled by the author.

we decided that improvements in developer-community interaction were needed before the official application period started and that enhancements in the public notification step could provide an opportunity to validate preapplication activities.

Next we chose those land use actions to which the SIMS should apply.[4] We also presented a list of project effects likely to create community controversy that should "trigger" a formal SIMS process (see Table 15.1).

Reviewing Alternative Approaches

The X SIMS required thoroughly documenting local community concerns and issues through ethnographic research, the inclusion of Neighborhood Policies and Objectives in the Development Plans, and the creation of five-year scenarios for each Development Plan area. This research and policy formulation would supply 12 Social Impact Representatives (SIRs) with the information they needed to guide developers in addressing local social concerns toward the goal of three-year agreements with community groups.

The X SIMS had three disadvantages. First, a key player in X's SIMS was the SIR, hired by the City to work within island districts and advise developers. The lack of accountability and inherent role conflict, however, were troublesome barriers to the effective functioning of SIRs. Second, reliance on the input of neighborhood residents, owners, and workers excluded both community- and islandwide interest groups and assumed that the government would represent nonpopulated geographic areas. Third, the serial and independent nature of negotiated agreements was problematic because in Hawaii local leaders do not have the authority to bind the community for the three-year period recommended by X; furthermore, informal groups formed in opposition to a proposal often lack a history of leadership or continuity.

Other Approaches to SIMS

Besides the X recommendation, we examined other general—as opposed to fully specified—processes. They dealt primarily with the public interaction component of a SIMS and varied along four basic dimensions: undefined versus fully specified process; voluntary versus mandatory implementation; expert versus community input about impacts; and private versus public responsibility for the SIMS.

OUR RECOMMENDED PROCESS

We recommended that project proponents complete a three-page "Socio-Economic Effects Description" (SED) for the City before applying for development permits and amendments to those land use ordinances mentioned earlier. The SED form, based in part on typical real estate appraisal practices, requires description of the location and physical features of the project, the character of the existing neighborhood, changes the project is expected to cause in the neighborhood, the adequacy of facilities and services in the area, and the parties most likely affected.[5]

The City review of the SED form would suggest whether the project represents a major change in development direction or if there were a significant possibility of its becoming controversial. For "major," "significant," or "controversial" community projects (Table 15.1), developers would be encouraged (with assistance from the City) to interact with community groups to determine trade-offs among affected parties. (See Arnstein 1969 for a ladder of citizen participation ranging from ritualistic cooptation to ownership and local control.)

Developer-Community Interaction Programs

The purpose of all developer-designed interaction activities is to contact affected parties early enough so that aspects of projects that have negative social impacts can be modified. Flexibility and creativity were encouraged: the developer would be free to tailor a community interaction program for a particular project, the community(ies) that will be affected, and its own experience/skills in community relations. Nevertheless, three general program levels can be distinguished that match broad degrees of community concern.

Practically, these program levels should be seen as forming a nested continuum such that the level of community concern discovered at one level may suggest another level of more extensive community interaction activities.[6] The City would assist the developer in evaluating the likely level of community concern, but the responsibility rests with the developer. We believed a spirit of creativity, flexibility, and responsibility would be superior to a mandated, rigid routine that could be carried out ritualistically without achieving the goal of developer-partnership.

Incentives to Perform: Carrot and Stick

The SIMS we designed was based on incorporating both positive and negative incentives for developers to consult with community groups voluntarily. We wanted to improve the developer's chances for smooth and profitable developments through cost-effective participative planning. This was the carrot. We also needed a "penalty" for ignoring community concerns. That "stick" lay in increasing the leverage of opposition groups if they had been prematurely dismissed by the developer.

The results of all developer-public interactions would become part of the formal permit/amendment application. The incentives to developers to initiate, voluntarily, responsible community interaction activities are both positive and negative. If done properly, the developer is more likely to find an acceptable design and to get a clear reading of community support early in the process. If not performed or performed improperly, seemingly minor issues are more likely to develop into roadblocks for the project at the public hearings. Documenting efforts to involve a wide range of the affected publics provides the developer with insurance that uncooperative groups cannot wait until the eleventh hour to voice major opposition.

The SIMS provides a greater incentive to the developer by increasing the likelihood of the negative consequence of failing to interact meaningfully with affected parties. This is done by enhancing the public notification process through an information packet mailed to all potentially affected parties.[7]

CONTRAST WITH EARLIER CONCEPTIONS OF SOCIAL IMPACT ASSESSMENT

Our procedurally driven approach represents a departure from earlier conceptions of Social Impact Assessment. The discussion that follows outlines such a departure, showing how our rethinking of SIA was instrumental in creating guidelines for constructing a workable SIMS.

When social impact assessment was first promoted as a distinct area of professional practice in the 1970s, the logical sequence of exploring the social interplay between project and community could be summarized as a straightforward application of the logic of problem solving.[8]

As Armour points out (1984), since then pressure for change in SIA procedural principles and methodology has come from within the field and from the planning and decision-making context within which practitioners operate. She advocates turning from a straightforward professional assessment and verification of social impacts (that is, applying scientific means to prove cause and effect) to dealing responsively with those groups likely to be affected by the proposed project. Our design guidelines reflect concern with procedural issues that call into question the openness of the planning and decision-making process, the timing of information dissemination, the timing of decisions, and the role of the parties involved.

The design guidelines incorporate a basic distinction between social effects and social impacts. Social effects are the estimated "objective" socioeconomic consequences of a proposal; for example, the influx of 500 construction workers, the addition of 200 new families to a neighborhood, or the replacement of farm land by a shopping center. Development projects have social impacts *to the extent that affected parties subjectively define the objective effects as important and assign a positive or negative evaluation to them.* This means that subjective definitions of "objective" consequences depend on location within the social structure. So, for example, a general increase in purchasing power associated with higher wage levels may be beneficial to working-age people but problematic for those on fixed incomes. Likewise, transportation changes may improve the trade of nearby merchants at the expense of displacing or relocating residents.

Sociological understanding that communities are not homogeneous units, but social arrangements of diverse groups with varying interests, values, and resources, leads to an appreciation that the various publics affected by a proposal must be involved in defining the impacts from their position in the social structure. This means that assessments based solely on expert opinion are flawed at the outset (see Olsen et al. 1985).

The guidelines also reflect a movement away from the early presumed functionalist focus on community stability to an interest in the distributional or equity effects of a proposed project (Gale 1984). Recognizing the potential for conflict over land as a valuable resource points to designing a system in which the role of the physical environment is appreciated and conflict is legitimized and constructive.[9]

INTERPERSONAL AND POLITICAL ASPECTS OF THE SIMS CONTRACT

Interpersonal Aspects of the SIMS Contract

Interpersonal relationships play a large role in the success of consulting contracts. We found that this was true within our own consulting group, in our dealings with the client, DLU, and in our relations with people who would become participants in a SIMS.

Besides combining three perspectives (sociology, economics, and urban planning), our consulting group varied in occupational roles (academic, private firm, and free-lance consultant). At the outset we agreed among ourselves to be true to our individual expertise and training, to produce recommendations that were truly multidisciplinary, to interpret our insights in a practical, usable, and acceptable way, and to communicate the reasons for our recommendations.

We spent many hours sharing disciplinary views among ourselves so that we could integrate them in application to the "real world." In turn we discovered that the urban planner was more familiar with mechanisms and procedures of governmental regulation; that the economist was more conversant with efficiency and profitability orientations of the private sector; and that the sociologist was more concerned with equity and community viability. Since each of these perspectives was critical to the SIMS, the collaboration functioned well. In hindsight, more attention to political reality might have added to the chances of our recommendation's acceptability.

To grasp the practicalities of land use regulation, we sought information from people already involved in land use decisions to make sure that we were grounded in an understanding of the existing system. Frequent meetings with DLU and interviews with community representatives and developers provided actual experiences that refined our thinking, supplied test cases, and taught us the language of practitioners so that we could communicate our recommendations effectively. In the process of these familiarization activities, we earned the trust of people who might otherwise have rejected our recommendations had they been presented as *faits accomplis* or imposed by "outsiders."

The person within DLU charged with responsibility for the contract, the deputy director, played a key role in the development of our SIMS.

He was frequently part of our thinking sessions and he arranged access to other officials and resources. His untimely death was a great loss, both to us as friends and as consultants. Besides disrupting deadlines and interrupting progress, his death meant the loss of someone who had shared in our collective thinking, whose ego was involved in the outcome, and who acted as champion of the notion of SIMS. No one assumed his critical role; instead, SIMS was overshadowed by pressures on his successor to carry out the more routine duties of the position. Thus a major lesson for us was the importance of leadership of the contracting client and the need for broader-based ownership of the concept of SIMS.

Political Aspects of the SIMS Contract

By definition, consulting for government implies politics. This case involved the political agenda of the City administration, turnover in the City Council, and the political backing of the previous consultant, X.

Typically, consultants unknowingly inherit more than the tasks outlined in the contract. We were aware that designing an implementable SIMS required knowledge of the political relations among community groups, the City government, and developers. Indeed, we had set out to discover these political realities and to base our recommendations on understanding them. Yet political relations within the government itself turned out to be more important than we anticipated, an oversight that might have been avoided had we been more politically astute.

For example, the staff at DGP had been responsible for the four years of X's work and had little to gain—perhaps something to lose—should DLU's consultants' (our) recommendations be adopted. Furthermore, during our contract the City Council was up for reelection. A major sweep of the Council brought in new members who had been marginal to the events leading up to the notion of a SIMS. SIMS was seen as part of the political agenda of the "old guard" and new Council members arrived with fresh ideas; by this time, SIMS had the reputation of being worked and reworked to death.

Interestingly the Council members that were replaced had been identified with progrowth politics. We speculate that their backing of SIMS research may have been in a "no-action" stance designed to placate antigrowth coalitions (see O'Riordon 1976).

Finally, the lengthy contractual period with the previous consultant had created an impression of SIMS as an exercise in report writing and difficult to implement as a bureaucratic process.

CONCLUSION

We presented our SIMS recommendation to the City at a routine meeting late in 1982; soon thereafter we submitted the technical report

(Decision Analysts Hawaii 1983). The document sits on shelves through-out local government offices; no official action has been taken to date.

A final lesson—a personal one having to do with professional integrity and ego involvement—may be worth sharing. We learned that regardless of the quality of the work, political realities may preclude final accep-tance. Since consultants typically work within the public policy arena, professionals must seek validation and input among their own colleagues. Sound advice to policy makers depends on solid grounding in the profes-sions. Thus, consultants have an obligation to their clients, as well as to themselves, to be actively involved in professional organizations as in-valuable sources of peer review and new developments in their fields.

NOTES

1. The recommendation cited in City and County of Honolulu (1973) uses the phrase "functional problems" in the sense of physical structure planning, not to be confused with the sociological connotation found in the structural/functionalist perspective.

2. According to the *Atlas of Hawaii* (University of Hawaii, Department of Geography, 1973: 139),

Hawaii was the first state to adopt a general plan and a land use law. This law, passed in 1961, established the State Land Use Commission whose task it is to classify and regulate the use of all lands in the State. Particular attention is given to encouraging orderly and efficient development of land for urban use, with least possible encroachment on prime agricultural land, and giving maximum economy and efficiency in public services and utilities. Land uses within urban districts are administered solely by the counties.

3. For this contract the author, at the time a sociologist serving on the faculty of the Department of Urban and Regional Planning at the University of Hawaii, teamed up with Bruce Plasch, Ph.D. (economics), president of Decision Analysts Hawaii, Inc., and David W. Rae, M.U.R.P. Our subcontractors were Dr. Marvin E. Olsen, currently chairman, Department of Sociology, Michigan State Uni-versity; Mr. David Matteson (M.U.R.P., M.P.H.), currently Director, Conflict Management Program, Neighborhood Justice Center (Honolulu); and Mr. Jef-frey M. Melrose (M.U.R.P.), currently a planner with Amfac (Honolulu). I am indebted to these contributors to the SIMS, and to Reid T. Reynolds, Ph.D., Demographer for the State of Colorado (Department of Local Affairs) for his editorial review of earlier drafts of this manuscript.

4. Our criteria for selecting land use actions to include in the SIMS were that they impact land use *policy and direction*, be discretionary in nature, and include socioeconomic information in the decision-making process. Thus in Honolulu, the SIMS would apply to Development Plan amendments (including major Cap-itol Improvement Projects), General Plan Amendments, Plan Review Use, Zone Changes, Cluster Development, Conditional Use Permits, and Planned Developments.

5. A SED Documentation, limited to 30 pages, would also be required to clarify and document sources for the information contained in the SED where the

proposal was likely to become controversial. (The Indicators of Community Controversy presented in Table 15.1 are relevant to this determination.)

6. *Level A Community Interaction Programs*: Level A "Minimal Potential Community Concern" applies to situations in which little or no community concern is anticipated, that is, where the project is small, unobtrusive in nature, and compatible with existing conditions. The main objectives of Level A activities are to generate and verify community support for the proposed project. Suggestions are to hold small meetings with the interested publics, provide newspaper and radio announcements, and establish telephone "hotlines" for people to call in questions.

Level B Community Interaction Activities: The main objectives of programs for Level B, "Medium Potential for Community Concern," are to identify crucial social consequences, major social issues, and the involved stakeholders in those issues to promote creative problem solving.

Level B programs may take several different forms, depending on the particular situation and the anticipated community concern. We recommended, as examples, Random Sample Impact Assessment Surveys—of the small "mini-survey" type described by Finsterbusch (1981)—to tap the opinions of a wider range of the public than usually attends public hearings; Community Leader Evaluations in which formal and informal leaders are involved in intensive two-way discussions about significant social impacts and ways of preventing or mitigating them; and Cooperative Scenario Development (see Vlachos 1981) in which the developer presents alternative futures that outline expected desirable and undesirable social effects to affected parties—preferably in a series of small meetings—to elicit their responses and suggestions for outcomes and modifications.

Level C Community Interaction Activities: Level C applies when there is a "High Potential for Community Concern." Because the relevant impacts and stakeholders are likely to be known from Level A or Level B results, the main objectives are to seek workable alternatives—perhaps by encouraging conflict mediation—and to resolve the community concerns in an acceptable way to most, if not all, persons involved.

7. The mailing would be directed to affected residents (not merely property owners) within the immediate area; all affected groups and organizations listed in the SED; and any other group identified by the City or the developer.

The direct mail packet would contain a summary of the socioeconomic effects of the project prepared in narrative, readable language (known as the SED Summary, also prepared by the developer and reviewed by the City); an evaluation form to return to the lead agency that elicits views on the proposal, desired change(s), and specific concerns/comments; a listing of the public agencies that are involved by the proposed action; and an announcement of the likely timing and location of the public hearing for the project.

8. In the standard social impact assessment vocabulary, this logic has been presented in steps known as scoping, profiling, projecting, assessing, and evaluating.

9. Sociology is not particularly known for its interest in the physical environment (see Dunlap and Catton 1979). "Environment" within mainstream sociology has meant social and cultural influences upon behavior, particularly in contrast

to "heredity" (Swift 1965). Precursors of environmental sociology—for example, Landis (1949), Mukerjee (1930, 1932), Sorokin (1942), Sumner (in Keller 1913), and Cottrell (1955)—were largely ignored. More recently the general oversight is being corrected amplifying Duncan's (1959) simplified version of ecosystems that emphasized aspects of human life not shared by other species. Besides the emergence of environmental sociology in which the physical environment is seen as a factor that may influence, and in turn be influenced by, human behavior (Schnaiberg, 1972, Catton and Dunlap 1978), sociologists espousing a political economic perspective approach land and its regulation as a legitimate topic for critical analysis (for example, Guterbock 1980; Molotch 1976).

REFERENCES

Armour, Audrey. 1984. "Teaching SIA in Times of Transition." *Impact Assessment Bulletin*, Special Issue: Teaching and Learning Impact Assessment, edited by Sally Lerner, 3 (2): 219–26.

Arnstein, Sherry R. 1969. "A Ladder of Citizen Participation." *American Institute Planners Journal*, July:216–24.

Catton, W. R. Jr., and R. E. Dunlap. 1978. "Environmental Sociology: A New Paradigm." *American Sociologist* 13:41–49.

City and County of Honolulu. 1973. *Revised Charter of the City and County of Honolulu.*

Cottrell, F. 1955. *Energy and Society: The Relation Between Energy, Social Change and Economic Development.* New York: McGraw-Hill.

Decision Analysts Hawaii. 1983. *A Proposed Social Impact Management System for the City & County of Honolulu.* Honolulu.

Duncan, O. D. 1959. "Human Ecology and Population Studies." In *The Study of Population*, edited by P. M. Hauser and O. D. Duncan, pp. 678–716. Chicago: University of Chicago Press.

Dunlap, R. E., and W. R. Catton, Jr. 1979. "Environmental Sociology." *Annual Review of Sociology* 5:243–73.

Finsterbusch, Kurt. 1981. "The Use of Mini Surveys for Social Impact Assessment." In Kurt Finsterbusch and Charles Wolf, *The Methodology of Social Impact Assessment*, 2nd ed., pp. 261–66. New York: Hutchinson, Ross.

Forester, J. 1982. "Planning in the Face of Power." *APA Journal*, Winter:68–80.

Gale, Richard P. 1984. "The Evolution of Social Impact Assessment: Post-Functionalist View." *Impact Assessment Bulletin*, Special Issue: Teaching and Learning Impact Assessment, edited by Sally Lerner, 3 (2): 27–36.

Guterbock, Thomas. 1980. "Sociology and the Land-Use Problem." *Urban Affairs Quarterly* 5 (March): 243–67.

Heberlein, Thomas. 1976. "Some Observations on Alternative Mechanisms for Public Involvement: The Hearing, Public Opinion Poll, The Workshop and the Quasi-Experiment." *Natural Resources Journal* 16 (January): 197–212.

Keller, A. G., ed. 1913. *Earth-Hunger and Other Essays.* New Haven, Conn.: Yale University Press.

Landis, P. H. 1949. *Man in Environment: An Introduction to Sociology.* New York: Crowell.

Molotch, Harvey. 1976. "The City as Growth Machine: Towards a Political Economy of Place." *American Journal of Sociology* 82 (2): 309–22.

Mukerjee, R. 1930. The Regional Balance of Man." *American Journal of Sociology* 36:455–60.

———1932. "The Ecological Outlook in Sociology." *American Journal of Sociology* 38:349–55.

Olsen, Marvin E., Penelope Canan, and Michael Hennessy. 1985. "A Value Based Community Assessment Process: Integrating Quality of Life and Social Impact Studies." *Sociological Methods & Research* 13 (February): 325–61.

O'Riordan, T. 1976. "Policy Making and Environmental Management: Some Thoughts on Processes and Research Issues." In *Natural Resources for a Democratic Society: Public Participation in Decision-Making*, edited by A. E. Utton, W. R. D. Sewell, and T. O'Riordon, pp. 55–72. Boulder, Colo.: Westview Press.

Schnaiberg, A. 1972. "Environmental Sociology and the Division of Labor." Unpublished manuscript, Department of Sociology, Northwestern University, Evanston, Illinois.

Sorokin, P. A. 1942. *Man and Society in Calamity*. New York: Dutton.

Swift, D. F. 1965. "Educational Psychology, Sociology and the Environment: A Controversy at Cross Purposes." *British Journal of Sociology* 16:334–50.

University of Hawaii, Department of Geography. 1973. *Atlas of Hawaii*. Honolulu: University of Hawaii Press.

Vlachos, Evan. 1981. "The Use of Scenarios for Social Impact Assessment." In Kurt Finsterbusch and Charles Wolf, *The Methodology of Social Impact Assessment*, 2nd ed. pp. 162–74. New York: Hutchinson, Ross.

16

Consulting with a Grass-Roots Community Group

ALEXANDER BOROS

THE NEED FOR SPONSORED SELF-HELP

In the 1960s, tragic neighborhood riots emerged from angry citizens, frustrated in obtaining social justice from legitimate centers of power (Gechwender 1968). Since then, the causes and consequences of powerlessness among the urban poor have come under analysis by social scientists (Piven and Cloward 1979; Moore 1972). The solutions proposed have varied from a major reconstruction of the social fabric of primary communities (Etzioni 1983) to intense self-renewal at the individual level for improved community mutuality (Gardner 1981).

One possible approach at community activation is the model of the Chicago Area Project used successfully by sociologists in the 1930s to identify local community residents and train them as community organizers (Carey 1975). The idea of assisting people to pursue social justice within our legal framework through the exercise of their own resources for their self-interests has been revitalized (Wyckoff 1980; Delgado 1986). I will demonstrate how such self-help consultations by an academic-based sociologist proved effective with one grass-roots group of the deaf that has implications for other minorities as well.

In the following sections, I will discuss the growing importance of advocacy by local deaf leaders in the face of rapid social changes that are causing personal and social disorganization in the lives of deaf persons (Nash and Nash 1981). I will then present both the methodology and the consulting guidelines that I used in working with a deaf action planning group as we carried out 16 action research projects to improve the welfare of deaf people in Cleveland, Ohio. Finally, this total effort will be evaluated for its relevance to the future of deaf Americans and applied sociologists.

Local Deaf Community Projects: Mixed Results

Unintentionally, the importance of developing organized self-help activities among all disabled people has been recognized as a necessary alternative to rehabilitation services with dwindling financial backing (Thursz 1969). This takes on even greater importance in the 1980s as we witness an erosion in federal and state dollars for support of what in the 1960s and 1970s we had come to expect as basic entitlements of deaf people for vocational rehabilitation as well as social and adult educational services. The specific case of deafness affords other important reasons as well. Even in the best of times, too often agency services have been unresponsive to the unique communication and education problems of deaf clients (Boyd and Boros 1975). In short, genuine rehabilitation will occur only when the deaf community is master of its own fate (Vernon 1971) and commands respect from agencies that are critical to its welfare.

Although there are several outstanding deaf community projects that continue to serve as examples of what effective local deaf leadership can accomplish, they are not representative of the typical deaf community (Crammette and Schreiber 1961). There are a number of issues that historically divided and weakened the deaf community. First, deaf people in the United States are reluctant to accept special treatment from the majority. This sense of independence was illustrated when the National Association of the Deaf opposed the special income tax exemption for deaf persons, which was already being received by blind persons (Schein 1968). Second, deaf people disagree over the role of hearing people in helping them improve the operations of their social action organizations. They may reject the perpetuation of paternalism that started in deaf schools; they may distrust the motives of hearing persons who are outsiders to their community of peers; and they may doubt how long these persons will maintain their interest in the problems of deaf people. After all, deaf people know no matter what happens they remain within the deaf community through identification with the deaf world, shared experiences that come of being deaf, and participation in the deaf community's activities (Higgins 1980). Third, there is ambivalence toward the well-educated deaf person who is postlingually deaf and has acquired intelligible speech, often becoming a spokesperson and leader in deaf organizations that interact with hearing people (Higgins 1980). As useful as they are, such sophisticated deaf leaders may command respect but may not lead in the sense of having a loyal followership.

When all these various problems are present simultaneously within the deaf community, it is difficult to obtain a concerted effort behind any one social action plan. The despair of one such deaf community will be described next. Existing in the industrial city of Cleveland, its problems were immense.

The Cleveland Situation

In the 1960s, the deaf population of the greater Cleveland area was the largest in the state of Ohio. The deaf community here had many special-interest organizations, sports groups, a large deaf social club with a bar, and four deaf religious congregations. They also had the usual competition for members to keep their individual organizations going. A few deaf leaders, who were able to communicate with hearing persons, were burdened with frequent requests for help in problem-solving by less verbal members of the deaf community. There were many discussions in the Deaf Club regarding how much to expect from the government in the form of help in establishing a true Deaf Community Center that would be a meeting place for social activities and adult education. The role of hearing persons in helping deaf people was often debated. There was much dissatisfaction with the deaf education program, the Bureau of Vocational Rehabilitation, and the Ohio Employment Services.

In the 1960s, Cleveland was generally unresponsive to the unique needs of deaf people. Deaf people complained that deaf schools did not allow the use of sign language in educating their deaf children. The Cleveland office of the Bureau of Vocational Rehabilitation, a vital agency to deaf people, did not have one counselor who could use sign language. The other major human service agencies did not use interpreters when dealing with deaf clients. Deaf people in courts did not have the use of interpreters. To a deaf person, it almost seemed to be hopeless.

The frustration that can be felt within a deaf community was brought to my attention in 1970 when a group of Cleveland deaf leaders asked me to assist them. They were worn out and overwhelmed by seemingly insurmountable problems left unresolved by unresponsive agencies in their community. I did not know it at the time, but I agreed to help them on a journey to improve social services to deaf people that lasted seven years.

FORMING AN ACTION PLANNING GROUP

Action Research Design

Since I knew next to nothing about deafness and these angry deaf leaders were ignorant about the complexity and operation of human services, I decided to follow the action research design made famous by Kurt Lewin (1948) and combine our skills into a working partnership. According to Lewin, action research involves the role of groups and their internal dynamics in bringing about both personal and organizational improvement. The social scientist, as a source of professional knowledge, participates with the group in bringing about social change through planning, group action, and fact finding about the result of the action. Much of Lewin's action research involved working through intergroup conflicts and discrimination encountered by a minority group. The situation and intervention techniques appeared to be appropriate to the problems of deaf Clevelanders.

My adoption of Lewin's model was simple. I was to form an Action Planning Group composed of myself, a few graduate students from sociology, interested interpreters, and a group of deaf persons elected through a publicized open meeting of deaf community members. Together we would plan projects that were agreed upon at this and other such open meetings. The professional staff would assist with the training of the group members in advocacy work aimed at those agencies that were unresponsive to the needs of deaf people. Graduate students would research the action phase that would be implemented by deaf leaders from a plan agreed upon by the entire Action Planning Group. When each project was finished, another one would be planned, acted upon, and evaluated. In this way, deaf leaders would experience sponsored self-help, while the social scientists installed fact-finding procedures and became the social eyes, right in the midst of social action bodies operating within the deaf community itself. The entire effort over seven years was conducted by volunteers.

The major workshops and conferences were carefully recorded and printed as monographs, to be distributed to each deaf leader of the Action Planning Group. Other copies were purchased by libraries and organizations around the country. In this way, the findings of a collaborate attempt between a team of applied sociologists and deaf leaders to bring about improvement in the welfare of deaf people could be disseminated to others wanting to engage in similar courses of action.

The Original Cast

I had my first formal contact with the deaf community of Cleveland at an open meeting in their club, which had been advertised to all local deaf groups. There were 200 people present to hear me speak about various alternatives to the several problems they had already identified for me. Afterward, they elected 13 deaf persons to be part of the Action Planning Group; I later joined as a consultant. Different students, interpreters, and workers for a number of deaf church congregations assisted and had input in the activities of the Action Planning Group.

Most of these 13 elected leaders continued as members of the Action Planning Group for the seven years of projects. What is important to note is that only one of the elected was a traditional leader within the deaf community. The others were all new to leadership posts. Yet they were keenly interested in correcting injustices they believed existed for deaf people. They were never in the limelight before. The next section presents the guidelines I followed in assisting this dedicated group of novice leaders to accomplish social change for the betterment of deaf Clevelanders.

GUIDELINES FOR CONSULTING

Although there were excellent materials on general community organization work with indigenous leaders (Cox et al. 1970), these books and articles did not consider the special considerations of a deaf minority living in a large industrial city. Consequently, I began to consult with my team of deaf leaders, largely on a trial-and-error basis, guided only by my general professional background as an applied sociologist involved in previous advocacy projects. Over the ensuing seven years, a number of practical guidelines began to evolve:

1. *Start with a Basic Orientation to the Deaf Community.* Consult the literature written by deaf people, talk to deaf people, and actually visit activities within the deaf community groups to obtain glimpses of the day-by-day world of deaf people. In the beginning, an interpreter is essential. Endeavor to become a proficient signer, setting aside time for formal training. Through interacting with deaf people, make efforts to appreciate the achievements of deaf people in adapting to the handicapping conditions they continuously face. As soon as it is possible, discover the critical problems facing deaf people from their point of view.

2. *Clarify Your Own Consulting Orientation.* Although the first step is obvious, the second one is not. Confusion and disappointment could develop if the consultant's activities do not measure up to the expectations held by the deaf leaders. At the onset, take a thorough inventory of the resources you are able to make available to help them. Determine if there is any conflict of interest between professional agency responsibilities and deaf community work. Make a realistic estimate of the duration of your commitment to the group and honor it.

3. *Earn Their Respect.* Do not expect to obtain instant rapport with deaf people simply because you are prepared to donate your skills and time. Obtain an entry point into the deaf community that does not threaten their self-respect. The initial meeting should be on their terms if possible.

4. *Provide a Service Orientation to Deaf Community Goals.* Serving the deaf group is of prime importance and should never be neglected. Rapport with the deaf community should never be exploited for personal gain, personal research, and professional articles. In order to clarify the problems that are to be solved, propose a public meeting of concerned deaf persons and encourage them to rank their problems in terms of importance and immediacy. If they do not offer the idea by themselves, recommend an election of an advisory board of deaf people to guide the larger group in working through their problems. With the installation of a citizen board, the professional gives advice only when they require it. This point was basic to Lewin's action research model (1948).

5. *Establish Regular Public Meetings.* Meet regularly (for example, monthly) at a convenient place where other deaf people from the community can observe the proceedings of board meetings. A chance to observe planning activities by nonboard members affords others to participate with ideas and be supportive later on during the actual implementation of the projects. Also, openness at public meetings can take the sting out of petty gossip by deaf persons who otherwise would believe that they have been purposefully excluded by the deaf "elites." With open meetings, we were never a mystery to anyone, nor were our intentions misjudged. The consultant must be credulous (Gallessich 1982).

6. *Arrive at Manageable Goals.* One of the most essential advantages of the consultant is to help frustrated, confused deaf members clarify and objectify their group goals and arrive at realistic, reachable objectives. It is important for them to distinguish the goals that are short-range, intermediate, and long-range. Help organize the group into a committee structure in order to divide projects into manageable work units among many members. A newly formed advocacy group can not survive too many serious setbacks. Therefore, it is vital that criteria for success be realistic.

7. *Subordinate Hearing Members under Deaf Leadership.* As early as it is possible, require deaf members of the board to assume full responsibilities for their group decisions. To get them started, the professional staff led many of the early planning activities of the first project because it involved a grant proposal to the Ohio Rehabilitation Service Commission. No deaf board member had the necessary grant-writing skills. However, soon after this early project, the board wrote by-laws that gave voting privileges only to deaf members. It became clear thereafter that the hearing consultants could offer their ideas and even recommendations, but only deaf members could vote and cast the final decision on plans.

8. *Teach Self-Sufficiency.* To avoid perpetuating paternalism, teach deaf members how to plan, manage, execute, and evaluate their own activities. Encourage as much risk-taking in decision making as the board members can handle. The amount and kind of instruction will be de-

pendent upon how much extra guidance the group needs. In any case, provide them with feedback after each major undertaking as a group. If the group is moving into new and difficult ventures, offer them positive reinforcement.

9. *Establish a Permanent Organization.* Usually when it becomes necessary for a citizen's advocacy group to form, their problems of community living are at crisis levels. Deep-rooted social ills do not miraculously improve with one ameliorative project by a disgruntled group of consumers, no matter how just their cause or how well they are organized. Instead, it becomes necessary to plan numerous short-term projects as part of a protracted comprehensive plan for remedial social change. A permanent, incorporated organization helps to guarantee continuity in personnel and maintenance of effort. Help the board create by-laws and obtain incorporation for the handling of donated monies, property, and grant funds. Suggest dues-paying membership as one source of income and a stake in the deliberations of the board. In order to be responsive to membership, the group should have an annual meeting with an election of the necessary officers. The Cleveland deaf leaders incorporated themselves as Northeast Ohio Deaf Development Organization (NODDO) after their first project. Thereafter, the deaf leaders and soon everyone else called this Cleveland Action Planning Group by its nickname, derived from its own initials NODDO (pronounced as no-dough).

10. *Execute Projects from Available Resources.* To prevent getting bogged down in a relentless search for funding, choose projects that are within the means of your group. For instance, utilize skills, equipment, supplies, and space (for example, churches, college auditoriums). Although NODDO did write unsuccessful grant proposals, their projects were successfully completed through the donation of space and volunteer labor. Sale of monographs written about their ventures accounted for only a minor source of income. Independency is vital (Warren and Warren 1977).

11. *Do Not Interfere in the Social Dynamics of the Deaf Community.* The deaf community is a complex world with an intricate set of separate organizations caught in an even finer web of gossip. It is essential that the consultant refrain from taking sides in the many disputes that may arise between deaf organizations. Trust the leadership of your own group to know what to do in times of these conflicts (Craven and Wellman 1973).

12. *Expand the Membership.* The Action Planning Group (that is, the board) of any organization requires the support and resources of a large committed membership in order to implement its projects. In 1977, my last year as a consultant with NODDO, it had 138 members, two-thirds of whom were deaf and one-third were hearing. Dues should be set low enough not to discourage membership. In negotiating with agencies, the

influence of an advocacy group is always enhanced if their membership rolls are high (Heumann 1983).

13. *Have an Annual Review of Group Gouls.* At least once a year, conduct a business meeting with the entire membership. Review projects and activities of the last year. New priorities for group projects should be established for the following year. A proportion of the board should be reelected each year in order to introduce fresh views and insights from new leaders, while providing continuity to the organization.

14. *Publicize Successes.* It is vital for sustained growth that the deaf advocacy group receive a certain amount of respect for actual accomplishments from both the deaf and hearing communities. Favorable publicity is one of the rewards for months of dedication and labor. The work of the organization should be communicated regularly to the deaf community via a newsletter or special presentations at the meetings of other deaf groups for local acceptance (Biddle and Biddle 1965).

15. *Provide In-Service Training for Deaf Leaders.* Throughout all phases of organizing and implementing group projects, the consultant should be prepared to offer leadership training to board members. Besides guiding the leaders through diverse problem-solving activities, the consultant might also conduct periodic leadership workshops for all board members (Parsons and Meyers 1984).

Some of the outcomes of applying these 15 guidelines to assist NODDO in their 16 major projects are presented in the next section.

THE RESULTS: ACHIEVEMENTS OF NODDO

The following projects will be discussed briefly in the order of their implementation by NODDO. They represent a natural order of deaf community problem-solving, with the consultant playing only a minor role.

1. *Grant Proposal for a Comprehensive Service Center for the Deaf (1971).* Deaf Leaders incorporated themselves as Northeast Ohio Deaf Development Organization. After several months, NODDO submitted a grant proposal to the Ohio Rehabilitation Service Commission for a Comprehensive Service Center for Deaf Clevelanders. Because there was hesitancy in funding an indigenous deaf group, the contract was awarded to an established agency. However, as a result of the stimulation and advocacy of this small group of deaf leaders, a specific service utilizing sign language interpreters was finally a reality.

2. *A Confrontation Workshop with Local Agencies (1972).* NODDO spent several months to put on an encounter workshop between representatives of different community agencies and deaf challengers. The all-day debate included consumer critiques and rebuttals that were influential

in producing subsequent changes in agency policies (Boros and Lavin 1973).

3. *The Deaf Expo (1973)*. NODDO spent nine months organizing a gigantic three-day Ohio Deaf Expo in a large exhibition hall of a prestigious downtown Cleveland department store. The achievements of deaf Ohioans were organized around several booths: Job Opportunities, Religious Groups, Aids for the Deaf Person, Books about Deaf People, Cultural Programs, Business Opportunities, Education, Organizations of Deaf People, Agencies Serving Deaf People, and Deaf Development. Presentations at the well-attended Expo included speeches by the Cleveland mayor, a U.S. congressman, an Ohio State representative, and the superintendent of the Maryland School for the Deaf (Boros and Hawkes 1974).

4. *The Indigenous Deaf Leadership Symposium (1974)*. NODDO and Kent State University sociology graduate students cooperated to create a leadership symposium for all leaders in the deaf community of Cleveland. The all-day meeting centered on leadership development topics presented by graduate students to deaf members within a workshop format (Boros 1974).

5. *A Conference on Television for Deaf People (1974)*. NODDO arranged a conference with representatives from local TV stations and the deaf community, which resulted in more captioning and interpreted public announcements on Cleveland television broadcasts.

6. *A Deaf Development Newsletter (1975)*. In order to communicate regularly with increasing numbers of members and friends of NODDO, a newsletter was established.

7. *Mock Trial with an All-Deaf Jury (1975)*. In order to publicize the difficulties deaf people have in courtrooms, NODDO organized an all-day mock trial with a deaf plaintiff, an all-deaf jury, actual trial lawyers, and a common pleas judge in the mock courtroom of the law school at Case Western Reserve University.

8. *A Workshop on the Deaf Alcoholic (1975)*. NODDO sponsored a workshop on alcoholism among deaf people, which drew participants from five states and Canada, representing 37 different human service agencies (Boros and Sanders 1977).

9. *College Training for Deaf Leaders (1976)*. NODDO helped to organize their own one-year certificate human service counseling program from Cuyahoga Community College. Eight NODDO board members graduated from that accredited program, doing internships at various human service agencies in Cleveland that had deaf clients.

10. *An Indigenous Deaf Development Center (1976)*. In cooperation with their community college teachers, NODDO counselors conducted free outreach services to deaf Clevelanders from temporary facilities loaned by sympathetic agencies.

11. *Sponsoring Programs for Deaf Alcoholics (1976).* NODDO was instrumental in establishing an Alcoholics Anonymous chapter for deaf alcoholics and a free pilot outreach program for deaf alcoholics in Northeast Ohio, staffed by a clinical sociologist and an interpreter.

12. *A Workshop on Problem-solving within the Deaf Family (1976).* NODDO organized an intense workshop on difficulties faced by hearing parents of deaf children.

13. *Cosponsorship of National Theater for the Deaf Performance (1976).* NODDO cosponsored with the Cleveland Chapter of the National Association of the Deaf the first National Theater for the Deaf performance ever seen in Ohio.

14. *Workshop on New Horizons in Deaf Education (1977).* Responding to a local demand for a full discussion on the role of deaf education in the family and vocational life of deaf people, NODDO presented a statewide conference on the use of total communication with deaf children.

15. *Grant Proposal for Deaf Community Center (1977).* After seven years of working on 14 projects, NODDO returned to its original plan for a Deaf Community Center, which would promote advocacy work and outreach services. They submitted a grant proposal to fund the center, but it was turned down again.

16. *An Interpreters' Training Program (1978).* A number of NODDO leaders and hearing friends submitted a grant proposal to the Cleveland Foundation for an interpreters training program to be conducted through Cleveland State University. It was funded.

POSTSCRIPT ON NODDO

On its own without any support of sociology consultants, NODDO organized in 1978 one more major conference after its Interpreters' Training Project. This last public effort involved a disability awareness conference, done in cooperation with the Handicapped Students' Office of Case Western Reserve University. From this point on, changing social dynamics within the deaf community made the independent advocacy role of NODDO unnecessary. After months of planning, NODDO and all other Cleveland deaf groups formed the Joint Council of Deaf Organizations in 1979.

NODDO, made up of deaf leaders only, remains intact. At present, NODDO advocates the various causes of deaf people through their affiliation with the Council. The Council was created entirely by deaf leaders without any help from professional consultants. Advocacy is now where it belongs, entirely in the hands of those persons who are adversely affected by unresponsive agencies.

THE CONSULTATIONS EVALUATED

The NODDO Action Planning Group was but one force of change operating in Cleveland between 1970 and 1977. It is therefore difficult to make conclusions about the influence of this small advocacy group operating in the Greater Cleveland Area with a population of 2 million people. Seven years of major, conspicuous public projects by NODDO cannot be without a telling effect, however. Recognizing the limitations and the importance of evaluation, I will assess the impact of NODDO upon the deaf community as well as upon the team of university consultants. Somewhat more difficult, I will also estimate the value of professional consultation upon the successes of NODDO.

Social Betterment of Deaf People

Mass media coverage for most of the NODDO's 16 projects, some of which were televised, produced a deaf awareness for both the general and deaf communities. An inspired Cleveland deaf community became more change-oriented as various deaf organizations adopted NODDO's service orientation in their own activities (Boros 1979). The Deaf Expo especially increased deaf pride as deaf children and hearing parents observed deaf leaders manage all the activities of a stupendous three-day event (Boros and Boyd 1976).

NODDO also stimulated more responsive services from agencies that were unintentive in 1970. By 1981, several worthwhile programs for the hearing impaired were in place and offered interpretive services. There is a fine program for work evaluation and adjustment for deaf clients with a regular funding base. A Community Service for Deaf People now provides interpreters for any deaf person seeking help from any human service agency. There also are five Bureau of Vocational Rehabilitation counselors who use sign language when giving services to deaf clients. AID (Addiction Intervention with the Deaf) is a project that advocates for deaf alcoholics who need service from alcoholism agencies and developed from the original NODDO pilot project and conference on alcoholism (Boros 1981). Cuyahoga County Community College, which offered a one-year training program for NODDO leaders with the use of interpreters, now regularly employs interpreters for students in mainstreamed classrooms. There is an interpreter training program as part of the regular curriculum at Cleveland State University. There is an increase in the use of interpreters by agencies, hospitals, courts, and the police since 1970. Nearby University of Akron now has an associate degree program in sign language interpreting.

Besides an improved responsiveness of agencies to deaf clients, other benefits accrued. New deaf leaders emerged under NODDO's management. These leaders went on to become representatives on agency boards, delegates to national conventions, and teachers of sign language. A few of the original leaders made considerable advances in their employment, owing in part perhaps to their experiences gained as active members of this organization. Four monographs and four journal articles inspired other deaf persons around the country to leadership through the reading of the NODDO story. The national impact of the NODDO story is yet undetermined.

As a model to other deaf communities, NODDO failed in some of its objectives. It never did succeed in building a Deaf Community Center for social activities; nor was NODDO able to attract the low verbal deaf persons to their functions. Hearing parents of deaf children never became active with NODDO's advocacy for total communication in public schools. Despite a few young board members, NODDO was unable to replace retiring members with young deaf leaders. Perhaps it was a generation-gap problem not fully understood by all parties involved. At any rate, NODDO's shortcomings are challenges for any other similarly dedicated deaf advocacy group to overcome in another place at another time.

Contribution to the Professions

It would be a gross oversight if the effect of NODDO upon the consultants was not properly reported. The advocacy projects provided a unique training ground for graduate students from different disciplines. Hundreds of students had an opportunity to leave their confining classrooms to participate with deaf people seeking ways to improve life for deaf Clevelanders. Ten students were inspired by NODDO to develop a career with deaf people. Of these ten, one became a president of the American Deafness and Rehabilitation Association, one organized the first national conference of the deaf and blind Americans, and one went on to be a state coordinator of deaf programs. Since none of these students were from specific academic programs on deafness, their achievements bear a direct relationship to the impact of their NODDO involvements and experiences gained from their consulting roles.

As the principal consultant over the entire seven-year period, I gained more than just a glimpse of the inner workings of a deaf community and more than an adequate field test of my applied sociology skills. I found advocacy work with deaf leaders to be a multidimensional development that touched all aspects of their lives. Without realizing it, I found myself participating in a primary group of close friends where the concern for each other's welfare was both honest and mutual. I experienced their problems as a friend—not as an agent of an institution. In this way, I never knew the manipulation, the anxiety-ridden demand,

and the complaints that often occur between client and professional counselor. Perhaps the greatest gift was to have my faith confirmed in the ever-present potential of ordinary people accomplishing extraordinary deeds.

The Value of the Outside Consultants

There are several advantages to the deaf community's acceptance of volunteer professionals as outside consultants. Their highly developed skills are needed in communicating with representatives of schools, agencies, and government officials when deaf leaders prove to be ineffective. Consultants can make an objective analysis of problem formulation by deaf leaders when years of frustration and anger may have clouded the issues. Consultants are more apt to have studied the literature on similar problem-solving attempts and offer workable answers. Operating in different social circles, they might also be able to tap different resources that could be used by deaf leaders.

In the case of NODDO, the consultations were invaluable and absolutely necessary for its sophisticated functioning. Deaf leaders required the most assistance during the early stages of the development of their organization. They always enjoyed the reassurance of experienced professionals who had already done similar projects. Although I do not believe NODDO could have been as effective in implementing the 16 projects without consultants, neither do I believe that those achievements could have been accomplished without the deaf leaders. In the final analysis, it was the mutual contributions of deaf leaders and consultants that made NODDO an effective Action Planning Group.

Wider Relevance

Both academia and social organizations are being pressured to be more relevant to disgruntled minorities. Providing voluntary consultations to grass-roots organizations can be a valuable extension of the research experiences of both teachers and students. Agencies could also benefit from improved reciprocal relationships with community members by employing "detached workers" (Litwak 1970) who follow the guidelines discussed in this chapter. As with NODDO, these professional consultations could benefit other struggling groups such as urban relocated reservation Indians (Ablen 1964), inner-city black residents (Warren 1975), citizens facing urban renewal displacement in their neighborhoods (Fellman 1968; Davis 1965), and citizens evaluating mental health services (Bradley et al. 1984). In providing free consultations to such grass-roots groups, professionals can participate in the understanding and excitement of the "other side" (Becker 1967), while community people can gain an insight and respect for professionals as caring individuals.

REFERENCES

Ablen, J. 1964. Relocated Indians in the San Francisco Bay Area: Social Interaction and Indian Identity." *Human Organization* 23:296–304.

Becker, H. 1967. "Whose Side Are We On?" *Social Problems* 14:239–47.

Biddle, W., and L. J. Biddle. 1965. *The Community Development Process: The Rediscovery of Local Initiative.* New York: Holt, Rinehart and Winston.

Boros, A. 1979. "Deaf Leaders Inspire Cleveland." *The Broadcaster* 1:10–14.

Boros, A., ed. 1974. *Demonstrations in Indigenous Deaf Development.* Kent, Ohio: Kent State University.

Boros, A. 1981. "Alcoholism Intervention for the Deaf." *Alcohol Health and Research World* 5:26–30.

Boros, A., and D. Boyd. 1976. "Serendipity and the Deaf Expo." In *VII World Congress of the World Federation of the Deaf*, edited by F. and E. Crammatee, pp. 61–63. Silver Spring, Md.: National Association of the Deaf.

Boros, A., and J. Hawkes, ed. 1974. *The Deaf Create an Expo.* Cleveland: Northeast Ohio Deaf Development Organization.

Boros, A., and B. Lavin, eds. 1973. *Encounters in Deaf Development.* Cleveland: Northeast Ohio Deaf Development Organization.

Boros, A., and E. Sanders, eds. 1977. *Dimensions in the Treatment of Deaf Alcoholics.* Kent, Ohio: Kent State University.

Boyd, D., and A. Boros. 1975. "Bridging the Gap with Deaf Paraprofessionals." *Journal of Rehabilitation of the Deaf* 8:9–14.

Bradley, V. J. et al., eds. 1984. *Citizen Evaluation in Practice: A Casebook on Citizen Evaluation of Mental Health and Other Services*, Rockville, Md.: National Institute of Mental Health.

Carey, J. T. 1975. *Sociology and Public Affairs: The Chicago School.* Beverly Hills, Calif.: Sage Publications.

Cox, F., J. L. Erlich, J. Rothman, and J. E. Tropman. 1970. *Strategies of Community Organizations.* Itasca, Ill.: F. E. Peacock.

Crammette, A. B., and L. E. Schreiber, eds. 1961. *Proceedings of the Workshop on Community Development Through Organizations of and for the Deaf.* Washington, D.C.: Gallaudet College.

Craven, P., and B. Wellman. 1973. "Informal Interpersonal Relations and Social Networks." *Sociological Inquiry* 43:57–88.

Davis, F. J. 1965. "The Effect of Freeway Displacement on Racial Housing Segregation in a Northern City." *Phylon* 26:209–15.

Delgado, G. 1986. *Organizing the Movement.* Philadelphia: Temple University Press.

Etzioni, A. 1983. *An Immodest Agenda.* New York: McGraw-Hill.

Fellman, G. 1968. "Planning Implications of Neighborhoods' Resistance to Proposed Housing and Highways." *Digest of Urban and Regional Research* 15:61–69.

Gallessich, J. 1982. *The Profession and Practice of Consultation.* San Francisco: Jossey-Bass.

Gardner, J. W. 1981. *Self-Renewal: The Individual and the Innovative Society.* New York: Norton.

Gechwender, J. A. 1968. "Civil Rights Protest and Riots: A Disappearing Distinction." *Social Science Quarterly* 49:474–84.

Heumann, L. F. 1983. "The Grassroots Response to Government Housing Intervention." *In Handbook of Social Intervention,* edited by Edward Seidman. Beverly Hills, Calif.: Sage.

Higgins, P. C. 1980. *Outsiders in a Hearing World.* Beverly Hills, Calif.: Sage.

Lewin, K. 1948. *Resolving Social Conflicts.* New York: Harper and Row.

Litwak, E. 1970. "An Approach to Linkage in 'Grass Roots' Community Organization." In *Strategies of Community Organizations—A Book of Readings,* edited by F. Cox et al. Itasca, Ill.: F. E. Peacock.

Moore, B. 1972. *The Causes of Human Misery.* Boston: Beacon Press.

Nash, J. E., and A. Nash. 1981. *Deafness in Society.* Lexington, Mass.: Lexington Books.

Parsons, R. D. and J. Meyers. 1984. *Developing Consultation Skills.* San Francisco: Jossey-Bass.

Piven, F. F., and R. A. Cloward. 1979. *Poor People's Movements: Why They Succeed: How They Fail.* New York: Vintage.

Schein, J. D. 1968. *The Deaf Community: Studies in the Social Psychology of Deafness.* Washington, D.C.: Gallaudet College Press.

Thursz, D. 1969. *Consumer Involvement in Rehabilitation.* Washington, D.C.: HEW Social and Rehabilitation.

Vernon, M. 1971. "Crises of the Deaf." *Journal of Rehabilitation of the Deaf,* 5:31–33.

Warren, D. T. 1975. *Black Neighborhoods: The Dynamics of Community Power.* Ann Arbor: University of Michigan Press.

Warren, R. B., and D. I. Warren. 1977. *The Neighborhood Organizer's Handbook.* Notre Dame, Ind.: University of Notre Dame Press.

Wyckoff, H. 1980. *Solving Problems Together.* New York: Grove Press.

17

Deviant Behavior among Adolescents: Ethics and Practice Concerning the Issue of Homosexuality

JEAN H. THORESEN

The role of the consultant can be a difficult and complex one. This is perhaps especially true when the behavior about which one consults presents its own difficulties. Deviant behavior, by definition, is behavior that is problematic to at least some members, usually powerful ones, of a society. When deviant behavior involves adolescents, the situation becomes more complex. Consulting about deviant behavior among adolescents offers a significant challenge to the consultant and raises a number of interesting and important issues. The example of deviant behavior with which I am concerned is homosexuality, specifically, lesbianism.

In this chapter I will discuss some initial concerns that need to be addressed: ethical dilemmas, varying perceptions about gay behavior and gay people, and some specific aspects of dealing with gay adolescents. Then I will present techniques a consultant could use in working with clients.

HOMOSEXUALITY AND LESBIANISM

Recently some people, among them some sociologists, have questioned the designation of homosexuality and lesbianism as "deviant" behavior. However, I am referring to homosexuality and lesbianism as "deviant" behavior in this context not because of personal beliefs, or disciplinary or theoretical categorizations, but because when I am called upon as a consultant with regard to gay teenagers, it is invariably because *somebody* thinks the behavior is deviant.

It is only within the last generation that homosexuality has come to be viewed as nonpathological behavior. The nomenclature changes that removed homosexuality from the category of mental illness, according to the American Psychiatric Association and the American Psychological Association, did not occur until the mid-1970s. Some professionals, and many lay people, still seem unconvinced as to the appropriateness of this redefinition. For them, and therefore for the homosexual people who must deal with them, there is still a "problem." The consultant is often called in when this "problem" emerges, or can no longer be ignored.

The consulting work that I have done involving deviant behavior among adolescents has largely centered on the issue of lesbianism among members of college athletic teams and in residential summer camp settings. I have become involved in this work because I have done considerable research on lesbians and gay men, and because I have strong interests in both athletics and camping. I will discuss some of the issues that have arisen when I have been involved in both formal and informal consulting. Informal consulting is, for me, the more usual. First of all, I do not have a consulting "business," though I have designed a brochure to present ideas on how I might be helpful to camp owners, directors, or staff. Second, I am part of a university faculty and am sometimes "consulted" because I teach a course on "Homosexuality and Lesbianism." First I will consider some of the ethical and conceptual issues that arise in dealing with gay behavior as a consultant both with clients and with gay adolescents; then I will describe some of the techniques I use in my work.

INITIAL CONSIDERATIONS: ETHICS

There are several ethical dimensions to this work. The first involves the fact that people who may seek out a consultant may have a goal in mind that is inconsistent both with my viewpoint on homosexuality and, more importantly, with what sociological and other research shows us about homosexual behavior and gay people. People who seek help with this issue, such as athletic coaches, Phys Ed department staff, camp owners and directors, or people involved in staff training of camp counselors, are often negative, or, at best, ambivalent, about the issue of homosexuality, and most often are negative about the presence of homosexuals and/or overt homosexual behavior in the settings for which they find themselves responsible. Very often, their goal is to "stop" the behavior.

My goal, on the other hand, is to promote understanding of both homosexual behavior and lesbians and gay men as individuals, so that productive performance and effective work can be done by all concerned. I do not regard homosexuality as "deviant" behavior; I consider it an alternative life-style, neither more nor less desirable in itself and in general than heterosexual behavior. This is often the starting point for my discussions with coaches, staff people, and others with whom I may be consulting. This raises the first ethical issue in a very specific way: sometimes this is not the approach for which these people had hoped.

To whom do I owe responsibility, and why? If people call on me hoping that I will help them find a way to "stop" behavior, how can I justify substituting my goal, or what may appear to be "merely" my goal, and an inconsistent one at that, for theirs? I believe I can do this for two reasons.

First, most people are very ignorant about gay behavior and gay people. It is my position, and my experience, that when this ignorance is dispelled, goals of "stopping" gay behavior have been replaced by other goals, more comprehensive and more thoughtful. These new goals often include helping gay people to be themselves. Second, I believe I can do this because I define my responsibilities as a consulting sociologist as including responsibilities to lesbians and gay men. I believe that this is appropriate because they are the persons most at risk and liable to be "damaged" by the ignorance of straight people in authority to whom they may be subject, and, if they are adolescents, the inequality of the power dynamic means that they are the vulnerable ones. Because of the level of ignorance, I believe that gay people do not often get treated in ways that are consistent with their dignity and integrity as individuals unless a concerted effort is made by someone such as a consultant to offset the lack of information, or the existence of misinformation, that is apt to exist among straight people in authority—usually the same people who are in a position to have called in a consultant in the first place.

A second ethical concern involves the issue of "recruitment." The most negative attitudes toward gay adolescents that I have encountered have surfaced with regard to this issue. Indeed, when I have been called in to help with issues around gay behavior among adolescents, the primary worry expressed by the adults who wish assistance is that gay kids will "recruit" other kids, by which they seem to mean that an already-gay kid will "turn" another, presumed-to-be-straight, kid gay. What they are often not prepared or willing to hear is that it is the presumed-to-be-straight kid, who often is not, who approaches the already-gay kid for information, for friendship, and for support.

I have tried to make this point to coaches and camp directors who are concerned with recruiting, in both senses of the word; they are most concerned about the issue of the "image" of their program or camp. They do have a point. We are not yet in a position where many parents are going to be delighted that their gay daughter now has an opportunity to meet and socialize with gay friends. However, I try to encourage people in these positions of authority to think about the consequences of denying friends and role models to teenagers. There are also parents who do want their children exposed to a variety of alternative patterns in life, on principle, for the sake of learning tolerance and acceptance. There are parents of gays who hope that their children will find good gay friends, and not be so alone. Even if that is not the case, there is a responsibility to the adolescent. If I know a person is scared and alone, and alone partially because she is scared, and scared partially because she is alone, do I have the right to try to keep her apart from others who might provide her with a circle of friends and support? As a consultant, I try to get the adults in authority to reverse that logic: I think we have an interest in helping adolescents gain access to peer groups and sources of support.

Another ethical issue involves balancing the various concerned parties in issues of deviant behavior among adolescents. In the situation of the residential summer camp, for instance, the sociometry of interested parties can become quite intricate. Minimally, we have the camper and a staff person, who has somehow become aware of an issue of gay behavior or identity. Often that means there is at least one other camper involved, too. But there are also other campers in the cabin. There is the cabin counselor, if she is not the staff person who originally became aware of the issue. There may be a unit head. There are other staff, and the camp owner or director. There are the parents. There is, more broadly, "society" out there, often in the form of an accrediting agency such as the local Girl Scout Council or the American Camping Association. What weight should each of these parties be accorded? Should camp directors espouse a philosophy in accordance with society's norms, or try for something better? Should a parent's wish to segregate a child from another camper who is gay be respected? Should a camp director require that gay staff not disclose their sexual orientation under any circumstances while at camp?

These questions have parallels in the world of college athletics. Should two teammates who are lovers be prevented from rooming together on a team trip? Should players on a team be prohibited from sexual interaction with each other during the athletic season, if heterosexual teammates are not prohibited from dating their boyfriends? All of these questions are ones that have arisen in formal consultation or informal discussion with camping and athletic department personnel within my own experience.

These ethical issues, and the moral dilemmas of choice resulting from them, are often based on varying, and varyingly accurate, perceptions about homosexuality, lesbianism, and gay people. The next section of this chapter discusses some of these perceptions.

INITIAL CONSIDERATIONS: PERCEPTIONS

In beginning to work with clients, I first suggest that normative definitions of deviance are both complex and unstable within contemporary
society—a basic, culturally relativistic point of view. Further, I suggest
that, specifically in regard to adolescents, we may be dealing with the
normative equivalent of a "status offense"—behavior that, if engaged in
by adults, would normally result in little or no comment, and almost
assuredly no response by those in authority. Most adult lesbians and gay
men today are not bothered either by legal authorities or by other people
with whom they come into contact in the course of daily life. Usually
they are left relatively alone to go about their business. This does not
seem to be the experience, however, of gay adolescents. This is the point
I try to raise immediately: If the behavior in question were occurring
among adults, what would your response be? If the answer is, essentially,
"nothing," then I gently try to question why the response is otherwise
simply because of the age of those involved. Usually the reply has something to do with not wanting adolescents to "grow up gay." At this point
I try to distinguish carefully between identity and behavior. They are,
quite simply, not the same thing at all. Perhaps the analog might be to
the concepts of prejudice and discrimination. As we know, they are not
the same. Prejudice is a way of thinking, discrimination a way of behav-
ing—but the two are not the same. Nor are identity and behavior. If a
priest is celibate for a lifetime, does his sexual orientation become less
heterosexual? If a teenager has not yet engaged in sexual intercourse,
is she not heterosexual or homosexual? If a gay male refrains from sexual
behavior because of fear of contracting AIDS, does that make him
straight? No. Identity is not behavior.

The best evidence we have about sexual identity seems to suggest that
it is quite well-established during or before the ages when adult authority
figures tend to become most concerned about gay behavior—the teenage
years—and that identity is a fairly stable element of self, not much amenable to change, by the individual, or by someone else. This position is
not one unanimously accepted by people doing research about homosexuality, nor is it one to which I have come with a great deal of comfort;
I know of too many cases of lesbians, particularly, who have "come out,"
to their own great surprise, in their twenties, thirties, forties, or even
later. But the preponderance of recent research does suggest that if
teenagers think and feel they are gay, they probably are, and that they
cannot be "changed."

It does not make sense to me that behavior that probably results from
reasonable attempts to explore an identity that is already fairly well-
established ought to present a difficulty of the magnitude it is often
accorded by adults in authority. There is an underlying assumption,

either that the behavior is indicative of a life-style that in and of itself is offensive, objectionable, and/or illegitimate, which as I have already said is a position I try to call into question, or that the behavior is being viewed as "experimental" in the sense that, if it is prevented, the life-style itself will be prevented.

Most adolescents who engage in a significant amount of gay behavior are gay. They are not experimenting, and the idea that they are, or that they can be "prevented" from "becoming" gay, is neither supported in the literature nor respectful of them as persons. This is what I think separates the issue of sexual orientation from something like substance use/abuse. That is *behavior*, not an *identity*. A person may be labeled an "addict," but that is usually not an identity deeply located within the person from an early age, as is the aspect of identity we call sexual orientation or preference. If an identity of "addict" emerges, it is almost assuredly a consequence of a labeling process, and is therefore secondary deviance. There are thousands of gay teenagers who know they are gay, even though no one else does, but they have not been labeled. Indeed, they have often gone to great lengths to deny or disguise their identities out of fear of labeling—but they are gay, and it is not a consequence of labeling or the self-fulfilling prophecy. There may be individuals who do come to a choice of gay behavior through that route, too, but I am concerned here with kids who know they are gay, all by themselves. Addiction is a behavior that can, and arguably should, cease, usually for the individual's own good. Sexual orientation is not simply a behavior, and there is no good reason to assume that it can or should cease, on other than the most personal political, moral, or religious grounds. There is no evidence that a homosexual orientation is "bad" for a person, nor that it is "wrong," except in a subjective sense. It is also, needless to point out, a "victimless crime" in the jurisdictions in which it is still classified as illegal behavior.

Therefore, it seems to me that the consultant's role is to assist in dispelling ignorance about what being a homosexual person is all about, and to assist in a rapprochement between the gay adolescent and the adult authority who is concerned about the "problem." In talking with such adults—coaches, for example—I have generally found that they simply have not been exposed to much accurate information about homosexuality within their formal training, so the first step is "bibliotherapy," in which I suggest a number of sources of information about gay people and the issues they encounter in a homophobic society, and some of the things they fear if their homosexuality becomes known. Sources such as Don Clark's *Loving Someone Gay* (1977), Charles Silverstein's *A Family Matter* (1978), Ginny Vida's *Our Right To Love* (1978), or, more technically, both *Homosexualities* (Bell and Weinberg 1978) and *Sexual Preference* (Bell, Weinberg, and Hammersmith 1981) from the Alfred C. Kinsey

Institute for Sex Research at Indiana University have been helpful. I then try to talk with them about their conceptions of homosexuality and homosexuals, and to conduct some "corrective" conversations when unsupported or unjustified stereotypes emerge in these discussions.

WORKING WITH GAY ADOLESCENTS

The next step comes in working with the kids themselves. Gay adolescents are often not the most effective proponents of their own sexual orientation and life-style; they have been raised in a homophobic society. Denied access to adequate role models, subjected to inaccurate stereotypes, and forced to live a hidden existence that has denied them the opportunity to discuss their life-styles and identity with their peers, they often do not "do gay" very well. The socialization is incomplete and inadequate. The wonder is, as has been said in another context, not that they do it badly, but that they manage to do it at all.

I try to work with gay adolescents to undo the negative images of gay people and gay life with which society has provided them, to help them explore their ideas about their identity, to confront the issue of being gay in this society, to ask questions for which they need answers, and to develop constructive and productive strategies for living their lives. Bibliotherapy works here, too. *Annie On My Mind*, by Nancy Garden (1982), is an example of a good novel for teenagers about gay kids who are making it, not without difficulty, but making it. The American Library Association can provide helpful lists of young-adult books that are useful. In the realm of nonfiction, I find *Young, Gay & Proud* (Sasha 1980) very helpful. There are also books that provide small-group exercises for use with gay support groups or consciousness-raising groups. A good source is *Positively Gay*, edited by Betty Berzon and Robert Leighton (1979).

The gay adolescent has reason to suspect the motives and agenda of someone such as a consultant who is called in by an adult when a "problem" arises. As a consultant, I have a responsibility to assure the gay adolescent that, first of all, I am not interested in "changing" a sexual identity I have every reason to believe deserves to be treated seriously. Second, I need to reassure the adolescent that I will not interpret other behavior as "caused" by homosexuality, as in, "Ah, ha! No *wonder* you're having trouble in school/with your parents/with your peers" or any variations on that theme. The gay adolescent may indeed be having trouble in some or all of those areas: if so, however, the issue is apt to be less a consequence of the homosexuality than the result of the person's being treated as a homosexual by people who do not understand homosexuality. As one researcher puts it, "The issue is not whether lesbianism is a sickness, but what pressures create sickness or stress in some lesbians. Indeed, a possible cause of problems among lesbians is the tendency of misguided professionals to attach the label of sickness to their clients' preferred sexual practices" (Chafetz 1974, 715). In a broader sense, we need to look at who is "causing" what: "The charge by the Moral Majority that gays are destroying the family unit is ironic considering the fact that it is the Moral Majority's charges against gays which are contributing to the alienation of many parents of gays from their children" (Becker 1981, 107).

PRACTICE ISSUES

In this section I will discuss aspects of consulting practice, including some initial reservations I have encountered. There are three major techniques I will describe: consciousness-raising, projective techniques, and role playing. I will also provide examples of the materials I have developed.[1]

In practice, I have found that it is difficult to get started in consulting about gay behavior among adolescents. The first line of defense is, "Gay kids? What gay kids? We don't have any gay kids." Since responsible estimates of the gay population in the United States range from 4 percent to 10 percent or higher, such a response is ignorant at best, disingenuous at worst. There is also a double bind on who one is oneself. If one is straight, gay people, particularly gay adolescents, are apt to be justifiably suspicious of one's agenda. Gay adolescents usually have not had resounding success in getting much help from straight adults. If one is gay, there is suspicion from the other side, perhaps an assumption that one will be "biased" in some way, or that one's research or credentials are suspect. Indeed, straight researchers and consultants are often viewed with suspicion, too, as "fellow-travelers" of some sort whose motives or personalities are questionable ("Why would you want to work with *those* people?") I have no answer to this dilemma except to keep being readily available and unfailingly willing to handle problems when they arise and can't be ignored. This willingness to be there to use the fire extinguisher may have to go on for years, but it is what eventually seems to build trust and confidence. No one will stick *forever* if she is honestly trying to do anything other than be helpful and effective.

The Environment

I try to stress macro-level responsibility for the problems that people, both gay and straight, have in dealing with homosexuality. We are all raised in an environment that seems to make homosexuals either invisible or all too visible. We all see the lurid newspaper accounts of the discovery of the mass graves of young men sexually molested and killed by some "pervert." How many of us have access to garden-variety, adult, job-holding, tax-paying, home-owning homosexuals who are "just plain folks?" If we do, how many of us go out of our way to introduce them *as homosexuals* to our teenage sons or daughters?

Goldberg and Schoenberg (1981, 79) make the point that "most heterosexuals still are acquainted *knowingly* [their emphasis] with very few homosexuals. Many observers have noted, however, that it is this factor precisely—the conscious acquaintance of a gay person—that is the single greatest influence on an individual's attitudes toward homosexuals in general." This also points up the difference between bringing in outsiders who are "queens for a day" on a college campus or at a workshop, and assiduously seeking out and cultivating qualified indigenous gay staff as an on-going presence and resource within an organization. I ask camp directors, for instance, to consider how their gay staff (of whom there are bound to be *some*, as I hasten to assure them) can serve as a resource to them in dealing with difficulties that might arise as gay campers come to terms with who they are and are desperately in need of a friend, someone in whom to confide, of whom to ask questions.

This presents gay staff in a different light: a resource, not a potential problem or source of embarrassment. What camp director really wants to face the question from a parent: " "You mean you knew she was dealing with wondering if she might be gay, and you didn't provide any help for her? You didn't tell her to talk to that counselor who's been through all this, and could have relieved her worries?" The presence of responsible, functioning, productive gay people is an unremarkable but effective answer to the question, "But what did you *do*?"

The presence of gay people as an accepted part of an environment is not the same thing as promoting homosexuality, allowing "recruitment," or advocating inappropriate behavior in a particular setting. Camps with gay staff who are known to be gay can also have very strict rules about appropriate limits on sexual interaction between campers, campers and staff, or staff members. But these rules concern *sexual* behavior, not homosexual or heterosexual behavior. If smooching behind the canoe house is out of line, then it is out of line for everyone. Behavior, not identity, is the appropriate issue. This is one of the points I try to make in my consulting. What rules do you have? Do they apply to everyone equally? If not, why not? Can you explain the *reasons* for differences if you have them? Are those reasons upheld by what we know to be true about gay people and gay behavior? It is certainly appropriate to have different rules for camper-staff interaction than for staff-staff interaction, but for gay staff and straight staff? For gay campers and straight campers?

Major Techniques

The major techniques that I use involve a combination of consciousness-raising, projective techniques, and role playing, along with the bibliotherapy previously noted. None of these techniques is either new or unique. I owe considerable debt to Values Clarification work, to qualitative sociological methodology, and to the Women's Liberation and Gay Liberation movements. Information is the first step. Again, this is a macro-level issue. I try to begin by reassuring people that there is no reason they should be well-informed about a behavior or type of lifestyle systematically excluded from the formal training they have received, which was designed to help them be able to do their jobs effectively. My role is initially educative, as befits an academic by background, predilection, and current profession. I begin this way partly because I'm comfortable with it, partly because it is necessary, and partly because it works. As people realize they cannot be expected to understand that which they have not been taught, they begin to relax, and questions begin to seem less threatening and less apt to expose them as ignorant in front of others.

Consciousness-Raising and Projectives

Consciousness-raising involves letting people talk about what "society" says or "what you were taught when you were little" about homosexuality, without hanging the albatross of contemporary adherence to these ideas around reluctant necks. I think that this is important; we all share many stereotypes and prejudices of which we may remain unaware until and unless we are given an opportunity to confront them directly but without risk of exposure. As has been demonstrated in many examples of behavior modification, awareness of current levels of behavior targeted for reduction often, all by itself, seems to result in at least some diminution of the target behaviors.

This approach also leads into the use of projective types of techniques. I have created a set of situations or stories, written as descriptions of the goings-on at "Camp Tent-in-the-Woods" (TITW), involving a cast of characters: counselors, campers, a unit head, a camp director (see Figure 17.1). I ask the participants in a workshop to complete a story, or describe what they think a character will "do next" in a given situation. Then I ask participants to share their fictional "solutions" in small groups, and eventually with the whole group. This allows them to see how others might resolve a situation, gives us comparative illustrations of reactions for discussion, and, again, takes the onus off of the individual in terms of the "characters'" actions or solutions. It is not uncommon for my fictitious situations to parallel closely enough real-life situations that an individual may have confronted to allow the individual to compare what was actually done with what might have been done, again, without publicly identifying either the situation, the specific participants, or the individual's role and solution at the time.

Figure 17.1
Examples of Characters

AMY: An archery counselor and Senior Unit counselor, AMY is 21, a Psychology major at the state university, and has been at Camp Tent-in-the-Woods since she was a six-year-old camper. She is described as STEADY and LOVELY.

BRENDA: Also an "old camper" at Tent-in-the-Woods, BRENDA is a tennis counselor and has a junior unit cabin. She's 20, an English major at a women's college. ATHLETIC and ATTRACTIVE.

CAROL: New to Camp Tent-in-the-Woods this year, CAROL is a canoeing counselor who came highly recommended from a private camp that closed last year; the director there was a close friend of HELEN (director of TITW). CAROL is 25, and has been a waterfront counselor for eight years. RESPONSIBLE, QUIET.

The set of situations I have developed involves a set of characters whom I hope become "real" over time, in that I use the same characters over and over, and have endowed them with talents, backgrounds, styles of responding, and, not incidentally, sexual orientations. I ask the participants to select various characters to help them solve problems, take on added responsibilities, handle campers with questions about identity, and, in general, to become fictional extensions of the participant's own camp "family." I also switch characters' sexual orientations, and then ask participants if that makes any difference in the stories or their resolutions to problems in the stories. Do they ask for the same help from a fictional staff member if that staffer is gay as they would if that staffer were straight? Does a female camper with a "girlfriend" issue get the same response as a female camper with a "boyfriend" issue? Again, always, underlying the method is not merely the establishment of difference when and if it exists, especially not in an accusative fashion, but the question of *why* a difference exists. I do not assume that differences are always inappropriate, but I think the reasons why differences in handling gay or straight campers or staff may be appropriate are crucial.

It is important to note that none of the characters has an assigned sexual orientation in this initial description. I have purposely retained that as a variable that can be changed, for any of the characters, as indicated above, to allow participants to assess what difference an individual's sexual preference makes in how she is regarded or treated. In dealing with stereotypes, one of the mechanisms I use is a "Staff Assessment Form" that I distribute to participants. I ask them to think

Figure 17.2
Examples of Situations

---

1. EMILY (the Junior Unit head) thinks that two of BRENDA'S campers are spending too much time together. EMILY....

2. AMY comes to talk with FRAN, her unit head. She tells FRAN that Jennifer, one of her campers, seems to have a crush on her. FRAN....

3. GINGER (the program director) sees FRAN and AMY walking, late at night, on the path from the Main House to the Senior Unit. They stop for a moment. GINGER can't tell exactly what's going on, but she thinks they're embracing. GINGER....

4. AMY tells BRENDA that she thinks CAROL is a lesbian. BRENDA....

5. Try that one again. AMY tells BRENDA (who is gay, but no one knows that) that she thinks CAROL is a lesbian. BRENDA....

---

about the following questions, among others, in assessments of the "characters" just described: Which of the staff members do you think is/are gay? Why? What are the "cues" you are using to make that assessment? If you needed to talk about a problem relating to a camper you thought might be gay, which of the staff would you approach as a resource? Why? What else do you think you could tell me about each of these staff members? Describe each person, physically, emotionally, professionally, and so on. (It's true that you don't "know" enough to do this, but try.) List three additional adjectives you feel would be likely to describe each of the individuals. Which staff member would you identify as most likely to be inappropriately involved with another staff member? With a camper? In each case, why? Was your choice the same in both cases? Why or why not? These questions are designed to get people thinking about stereotypes and assessments (see Figure 17.2).

After each situation has been presented, and each participant has had a chance to write down thoughts on what would happen next, I ask them to answer, to themselves, the following questions: In which of the situations above do you think the incident or behavior is "gay?" Why? What are your "cues?" What does BRENDA do differently in #4 and #5, if anything? Why? If you were GINGER, which incidents, assuming you knew about them, if any, would you mention in your daily conference with HELEN? Why? Which of the incidents do you regard most "serious"? Why? These questions are asked after a more complete set of items than the examples presented above have been used. Again, the purpose is to allow participants to think about and share both their own initial responses and the alternatives developed by others.

Figure 17.3
Situations for Counselor Training

SANDY is a 20-year-old who is going to be a Junior in the fall. She's a third-year counselor at Tent-in-the-Woods, and spent a counselor-in-training (CIT) year there as well. She's counseled archery and athletics, and is counseling canoeing this year. She has a Senior Unit cabin of eight 14-year-olds, with no junior counselor to assist her. Her unit head, SARAH, views SANDY as mature and dependable, and tends to encourage a fair amount of autonomy in her staff. Above SARAH in the camp hierarchy are GINGER, the program director, and HELEN, the director of the camp. SANDY views GINGER as judicious and fair, sees HELEN as pretty remote, and feels she can rely on SARAH for good advice and help. In the following situations, what do you think SANDY would do?

1. SANDY knows that two of the Senior campers who seem to be particularly good friends take a canoe out every afternoon during Free Swim, which is allowed under camp rules; she thinks they beach the canoe on an island which is out of view, and spend an hour or so there. She's not sure what they're doing....

2. SANDY has been spending some of her free time in camp with JEN, a Junior Unit counselor who likes to go canoeing in her spare time. One day, when SANDY and JEN are talking as they put equipment away in the canoe house, JEN tells SANDY that she's gay, and that she's becoming attracted to SANDY. SANDY'S not gay. SANDY....

3. This sitution is the same as #2; SANDY's gay. SANDY....

4. SANDY is in her cabin one afternoon after rest hour. Karen, one of SANDY'S campers, seems to be waiting to talk with her. "What's up, Karen?" "Sandy, I...I'm scared...I think I'm falling in love with you...." Sandy....

The situations in Figure 17.2 were developed for use with supervisory staff and camp directors; for staff training with counselors, there is a slightly different emphasis to some of the story-completion items. Those designed for use with staff who will become counselors are shown in Figure 17.3.

Some examples from an additional set of items, designed to elicit reactions to situations involving campers, again from individuals who are undergoing staff training in order to become counselors, are shown in Figure 17.4.

I have presented a number of examples of situations in order to indicate the relatively fine degree of difference that may be present in some very tricky real-life situations. I have some reason to believe, based on research that a student and I conducted a number of years ago, that

Figure 17.4
Situations Involving Campers

SANDY, our Senior Unit counselor, has agreed to switch to a Junior Unit cabin at midseason. The situation is similar to the Senior Unit, eight campers to a cabin, but these kids are ten-year-old 5th graders. In these situations, what will SANDY do?

1. Two of SANDY'S campers seem to be spending all their time together, to the exclusion of other kids in the cabin. SANDY....

2. SANDY hears PAULA, one of her campers, tell MARCIA, a camper in another cabin, that one of the Senior Unit counselors is "a lezzie." SANDY....

3. SANDY is gay. She really enjoys the company of LEIGH, a counselor in the Senior Unit. SANDY doesn't know whether LEIGH is gay or not, and she's not interested in a relationship with her anyway. PEGGY, one of SANDY'S campers, says, "How come you spend so much time with Leigh?" SANDY....

4. SANDY and LEIGH are involved in a relationship off-camp, during the year. They are roommates at the same college. Their on-camp behavior has been impeccable, in that they are very careful of boundaries, don't spend time with each other that isn't appropriate, and definitely have not engaged in sexual behavior with each other on-camp. Still, everyone knows that they're best friends and roommates, and their interaction is warm and caring, which makes everyone around them feel warm and cared-for, too. One day, down at the canoe docks, a Senior Unit camper and a CIT are sitting around with SANDY discussing friendship. Finally the Senior Unit camper, who SANDY thinks may be gay, says, "Um, Sandy, I don't want to pry or anything, but I wonder... how close is your relationship with Leigh?" SANDY....

dealing with the issue of homosexuality has some of the properties of a U-curve. That is, if the responses of people to homosexuality and gay people are graphed, there is a high level of acceptance when the issue is remote from them, a much lowered tolerance/acceptance rating when the issue touches them, but not too directly or intimately, and a return to a high level of acceptance when the issue is very close to them. In the abstract, at a considerable "social distance," it is easy to be accepting of the idea of gay, and some people treat the existence of gay behavior and gay people essentially as a matter of civil rights on that level. Conversely, when the social distance is very close, involving a family member or good friend of "primary" standing, acceptance is also likely; one does not give up a close friend lightly. If my friend is "for" a behavior, would I easily be "against" it, and therefore perhaps against her? Balance theory suggests not. In the "middle distance," however, where the behavior involves people about whom one is not so sure, or if the situation might lead to guilt by association in the eyes of others, perhaps those who are not close friends, merely work colleagues or casual acquaintances, the issue becomes more complex and less easily resolvable. Labels are *not* fun to handle; there are, almost inevitably, consequences to being thought to be a lesbian, whether one is or not. These examples of story-completion items for use in staff training purposely run a precisely calibrated gamut from rather distant, or as distant as one can get in a residential camp setting, to very close, very immediate, very intimate and personal. The interesting thing for participants to notice involves the points at which their thoughts, feelings, and reactions shift from tolerance, nonchalance, or understanding to suspicion, from empathy to fear, or even revulsion, from wanting to work at a situation to looking for a way to avoid either the situation or the individuals involved.

Role Playing

An additional aspect of staff training involves role playing. This, too, in a sense, removes direct responsibility from the participants, as the "characters" have delineated and delimited personae, but it adds to the projectives the dimensions of reacting to others, and doing so on the spot, and in front of an audience that may itself react to what the participant does. Four role-plays I have designed are shown in Figure 17.5.

All of the techniques illustrated in the situations and role plays can be adapted to specific situations, and they are certainly neither exhaustive nor perfect. Other situations might be preferable, for instance, in working with staff development for a boys' camp. Similar changes would allow for use in the context of college athletic teams, dormitories, or other settings.

DISCUSSION AND A FINAL CAUTION

As a consultant, acting as a sociologist with an orientation toward clinical sociology, I find that my major ethical and practice considerations lead me to the following priorities:

1. reduction of ignorance, thereby
2. reducing fear, in order to
3. extend the parameters of "OK" behavior, because of
4. the need to respect the emerging identities of individual adolescents

"Stopping" behavior is not, from this perspective, an ethical, or even probably a possible, activity, because the behavior is most likely not a

Figure 17.5
Role Plays

One evening, after taps, GINGER is walking behind FRAN and AMY as they return from counselors' free time to their respective cabins in the Senior Unit. They don't know she's behind them. She overhears FRAN say, "Sweetheart, I love you so much," and hears AMY respond softly, "I love you, too, you know." Everything about both FRAN'S and AMY'S job performance has been excellent all summer. The next day, HELEN asks GINGER to fill her in on how all the staff are doing, as she's beginning to decide whom to invite back for the following summer. Person #1 is GINGER, Person #2 is HELEN.

BRENDA has been spending a great deal of her free time with JAN, her tennis CIT. GINGER decides that this is causing notice, and unfavorable comment, so she decides to talk with BRENDA about it. (A) Assume BRENDA and JAN are involved in a lesbian relationship; assume GINGER is straight. (B) Assume BRENDA and JAN are not involved in a lesbian relationship; assume GINGER is gay. Person #1 is GINGER, Person #2 is BRENDA.

A parent arrives on Visiting Day, and is being introduced to some of the senior staff. Late in the day, the parent asks to speak privately to HELEN. Almost immediately, the parent says, "I'm surprised that EMILY is on your staff; she teaches Phys Ed in my community, and there are many rumors that she's a lesbian. What do you have to say about that?" Person #1 is the parent, Person #2 is HELEN.

HELEN has decided that AMY is having a lesbian relationship with one of her campers (she's right). She calls AMY in, with the intention of dismissing her immediately. Person #1 is HELEN, Person #2 is AMY. Replay the scene as you would if HELEN is *not* right.

"symptom" of a "problem." The behavior, conversely, is most likely viable learning conducted within the context of an emerging identity at an appropriate age.

A final caution: getting trapped in the idea of "accepting" the person, conditional on the individual's changing, modifying, or ceasing the behavior, that is, rejecting the behavior while seeming to accept the identity, is not a solution. It is *not* okay to love the homosexual or lesbian so long as he or she does not "behave" homosexually. Identity is integral; it can be neither bargained nor negotiated in a conditional context. That is analogous to telling a person that needing nutrients is part of being human, but that eating is immoral. Being homosexual is human, and "doing gay" is OK.

NOTE

1. These examples are only part of an overall set of materials. A full set may be obtained from Jean H. Thoreson, Associate Professor, Department of Sociology and Applied Social Relations, Eastern Connecticut State University, Willimantic, Connecticut, 06226. Any questions or discussion about the materials will also be cheerfully entertained.

REFERENCES

Alyson, Sasha, ed. 1980. *Young, Gay, and Proud*. Boston: Alyson Publications.

Becker, B. 1981. "Gays Have Parents, Too." *Catalyst* 3 (4): 105–9.

Bell, Alan P., and Martin S. Weinberg. 1978. *Homosexualities: A Study of Diversity Among Men and Women*. New York: Simon & Schuster.

Bell, Alan P., Martin S. Weinberg, and Sue Keifer Hammersmith. 1981. *Sexual Preference: Its Development in Men and Women*. Bloomington, Ind.: Indiana University Press, An official publication of the C. Kinsey Institute for Sex Research at Indiana University.

Berzon, Betty, and Robert Leighton, eds. 1979. *Positively Gay*. Milbrae, Calif.: Celestial Arts.

Chafetz, Janet. 1974. "A Study of Homosexual Women." *Social Work* 19: 714–23.

Clark, Don. 1977. *Loving Someone Gay*. New York: New American Library.

Garden, Nancy. 1982. *Annie On My Mind*. New York: Farrar, Straus & Giroux.

Goldberg, R. S., and R. Schoenberg. 1981. "Defining Gay Social Work: Beginning with Beginnings." *Catalyst* 3 (4): 77–81.

Silverstein, Charles. 1977. *A Family Matter*. New York: McGraw-Hill.

Vida, Ginny, ed. 1978. *Our Right to Love*. Englewood Cliffs, N.J.: Prentice-Hall.

Bibliography

Ablen, J. 1964. "Relocated Indians in the San Francisco Bay Area: Social Interaction and Indian Identity." *Human Organization* 23: 296–304.

Alexander, Kenneth O. 1981. "Scientists, Engineers and the Organization of Work." *American Journal of Economics and Sociology*, January: 51–66.

Alyson, Sasha, ed. 1980. *Young, Gay, and Proud.* Boston: Alyson Publications.

Applebaum, William. 1968. "The Analog Method for Estimating Potential Store Sales." In *Guide to Store Location Research*, edited by C. Kornblau, pp. 232–43. Reading, Mass.: Addison-Wesley.

Armour, Audrey. 1984. "Teaching SIA in Times of Transition." *Impact Assessment Bulletin*, Special Issue: Teaching and Learning Impact Assessment, edited by Sally Lerner, 3 (2):219–26.

Arnstein, Sherry R. 1969. "A Ladder of Citizen Participation." *American Institute Planners Journal*, July:216–24.

Babbie, Earl R. 1979. *The Practice of Social Research*, 2d ed. Belmont, Calif.: Wadsworth.

Bailyn, Lottie, and John T. Lynch. 1983. "Engineering as a Life-Long Career: Its Meaning, Its Satisfactions, Its Difficulties." *Journal of Occupational Behavior* 4:263–83.

Balswick, Jack. 1979. "The Psychological Captivity of Evangelicalism." Paper presented at the combined annual meeting of the Society for the Scientific Study of Religion and the Religious Research Association, San Antonio. Photocopied.

Barnes, Harry Elmer. 1929. *The Twilight of Christianity.* New York: Vanguard.

Bart, Pauline, and Linda Brankel. 1981. *The Student Sociologist's Handbook.* Glenview, Ill.: Scott, Foresman.

Bartholomew, John Niles. 1969. "A Study of Planning Techniques for Local Congregations." *Review of Religious Research* 11:61–65.

Beardsley, Jefferson F. 1985. "Quality Circles." In *Human Resources and Devel-*

opment Handbook, edited by William R. Tracey, pp. 326–40. New York: Amacom.

Beaudry, James A., and Steve Wray. 1982. "Consulting in the Public Sector: From Research to Legislative Action." *Wisconsin Sociologist* 19 (Fall): 87–95.

Becker, B. 1981. "Gays Have Parents, Too." *Catalyst* 3 (4): 105–9.

Becker, H. 1967. "Whose Side Are We On?" *Social Problems* 14:239–47.

Bell, Alan P., and Martin S. Weinberg. 1978. *Homosexualities: A Study of Diversity Among Men and Women*. New York: Simon & Schuster.

Bell, Alan P., Martin S. Weinberg, and Sue Keifer Hammersmith. 1981. *Sexual Preference: Its Development in Men and Women*. Bloomington, Ind.: Indiana University Press. An official publication of the Alfred C. Kinsey Institute for Sex Research at Indiana University.

Benny, Mark, and Everett C. Hughes. 1956. "Of Sociology and the Interview." *American Journal of Sociology* 62 (July): 137–42.

Berger, Peter L. 1961a. *The Noise of Solemn Assemblies*. Garden City, N.Y.: Doubleday.

———. 1961b. *The Precarious Vision*. Garden City, N.Y.: Doubleday.

Bermont, Hubert I. 1982. *The Complete Consultant: Roadmap to Success*. Washington, D.C.: Consultant's Library.

Bernard, Luther L. 1934. *The Fields and Methods of Sociology*. New York: Long & Smith.

Berzon, Betty, and Robert Leighton, eds. 1979. *Positively Gay*. Milbrae, Calif.: Celestial Arts.

Biddle, W., and L. J. Biddle. 1965. *The Community Development Process: The Rediscovery of Local Initiative*. New York: Holt, Rinehart and Winston.

Bierstedt, Robert. 1965. "Social Science and Public Service." In *Applied Sociology*, edited by Alvin W. Gouldner and S. M. Miller, pp. 412–20. New York: The Free Press.

Blake, Robert R., and James Moulton. 1983. *Consultation: A Handbook for Individual and Organizational Development*. Reading, Mass.: Addison-Wesley.

Blau, Theodore H. 1977. "Quality of Life, Social Indicators, and Criteria of Change." *Professional Psychology*, November:464–73.

Bonacich, Edna. 1982. "Task Force To Study Employment and Other Issues." *ASA Footnotes* 10 (August): 3.

———, ed. 1974. *Demonstrations in Indigenous Deaf Development*. Kent, Ohio: Kent State University.

Boros, A. 1979. "Deaf Leaders Inspire Cleveland." *The Broadcaster* 1:10–14.

———. 1981. "Alcoholism Intervention for the Deaf." *Alcohol Health and Research World* 5:26–30.

———. 1984. "Sociology: The Workable Myth." Founders address, Second Annual Conference of the Society for Applied Sociology, Covington, Kentucky, October 13.

Boros, A., and R. J. Adamek. 1984. "The Applied Sociology Internship." *Journal of Applied Sociology* 1:71–81.

Boros, A., and D. Boyd. 1976. "Serendipity and the Deaf Expo." In *VII World Congress of the World Federation of the Deaf*, edited by F. and E. Crammatee, pp. 61–63. Silver Spring, Md.: National Association of the Deaf.

Boros, A., and J. Hawkes, ed. 1974. *The Deaf Create an Expo*. Cleveland: Northeast Ohio Deaf Development Organization.

Boros, A., and B. Lavin, eds. 1973. *Encounters in Deaf Development*. Cleveland: Northeast Ohio Deaf Development Organization.

Boros, A., and E. Sanders, eds. 1977. *Dimensions in the Treatment of Deaf Alcoholics*. Kent, Ohio: Kent State University.

Bowen, William. 1981. *Graduate Education in the Arts and Sciences: Prospects for the Future (Report of the President)*. Princeton, N.J.: Princeton University Press.

Boyd, D., and A. Boros. 1975. "Bridging the Gap with Deaf Paraprofessionals." *Journal of Rehabilitation of the Deaf* 8:9–14.

Bradley, V. J. et al., eds. 1984. *Citizen Evaluation in Practice: A Casebook on Citizen Evaluation of Mental Health and Other Services*, Rockville, Md.: National Institute of Mental Health.

Brewer, Earl D. C., and Douglas W. Johnson. 1970. *An Inventory of the Harlan Paul Douglass Collection of Religious Research Reports*. New York: Department of Research, Office of Planning and Program, National Council of The Churches of Christ in the U.S.A.

Brown, William. 1984. "Identification of Specific Non-Research Competencies to Prepare Sociology Majors for Non-Academic Careers." Orlando: University of Central Florida. Mimeographed.

Brown, William R., John T. Washington, and Allyn M. Stearman. 1983. "Perceptions of Central Florida Employers Regarding the Competencies that Need Greater Emphasis." Paper presented at the 1983 Annual Meeting of the Southern Sociological Society.

Business Week. 1981. "Consulting Springboard." August 17, pp. 101–2.

Byrne, John A. 1983. "Are All These Consultants Really Necessary?" *Forbes* October 10:136–44.

Campbell, Angus, Philip E. Converse, and Willard L. Rodgers. 1976. *The Quality of American Life*. New York: Russell Sage Foundation.

Carey, J. T. 1975. *Sociology and Public Affairs: The Chicago School*. Beverly Hills, Calif.: Sage.

Catton, W. R. Jr., and R. E. Dunlap. 1978. "Environmental Sociology: A New Paradigm." *American Sociologist* 13:41–49.

Chafetz, Janet. 1974. "A Study of Homosexual Women." *Social Work* 19:714–23.

Chakiris, B. J. 1982. *The Human Resource Audit Facilitation Manual*. Chicago: BJ Chakiris Corporation. Offset.

―――. 1984. "Organizational Climate Survey." Chicago: BJ Chakiris Corporation. Offset (Copyrighted).

Chinoy, Ely. 1970. *Knowledge and Action: The Role of Sociology*. Northampton, Mass.: Smith College.

City and County of Honolulu. 1973. *Revised Charter of the City and County of Honolulu*.

Clark, Don. 1977. *Loving Someone Gay*. New York: New American Library.

Colamosca, A. 1981. "White Man's Burdens: American Consultants Selling Services to the Third World." *New Republic*, April 4, pp. 12–15.

Considine, Ray. 1977. *The Great Brain Robbery*. 521 South Madison Avenue, Pasadena, CA 91101.

Converse, P. D. 1949. "New Laws of Retail Gravitation." *Journal of Marketing* 14:379–84.

Cottrell, F. 1955. *Energy and Society: The Relation Between Energy, Social Change and Economic Development.* New York: McGraw-Hill.

Cox, F., J. L. Erlich, J. Rothman, and J. E. Tropman. 1970. *Strategies of Community Organizations.* Itasca, Ill.: F. E. Peacock.

Crammette, A. B., and L. E. Schreiber, eds. 1961. *Proceedings of the Workshop on Community Development Through Organizations of and for the Deaf.* Washington, D.C.: Gallaudet College.

Craven, P., and B. Wellman. 1973. "Informal Interpersonal Relations and Social Networks." *Sociological Inquiry* 43:57–88.

D'Antonio, William V. 1982. Correspondence to ASA Members, December 30. Washington, D.C.: American Sociological Association.

Davies, R. L. 1984. "Introduction." In *Store Location and Store Assessment Research,* edited by R. L. Davies and D. S. Rogers. Chichester, England: John Wiley.

Davis, F. J. 1965. "The Effect of Freeway Displacement on Racial Housing Segregation in a Northern City." *Phylon* 26:209–15.

Decision Analysts Hawaii. 1983. *A Proposed Social Impact Management System for the City & County of Honolulu.* Honolulu.

Delgado, G. 1986. *Organizing the Movement.* Philadelphia: Temple University Press.

Deutscher, Irwin. 1983. "Sociological Work: The Mystique of Applied Sociology as Dirty Work." Addison Locke Roache Lecture, Indiana University-Purdue University, Indianapolis, April 15, 1983. Akron: The University of Akron. Mimeographed.

Duncan, O. D. 1959. "Human Ecology and Population Studies." In *The Study of Population,* edited by P. M. Hauser and O. D. Duncan, pp. 678–716. Chicago: University of Chicago Press.

Dunlap, R. E., and W. R. Catton, Jr. 1979. "Environmental Sociology." *Annual Review of Sociology* 5:243–73.

Etzioni, A. 1983. *An Immodest Agenda.* New York: McGraw-Hill.

Feinberg, Lawrence. 1982. "American U. Faces Financial Squeeze as Enrollment Declines 5% This Fall." Washington *Post,* September 4, p. B1.

Fellman, G. 1968. "Planning Implications of Neighborhoods' Resistance to Proposed Housing and Highways." *Digest of Urban and Regional Research* 15:61–69.

Fichter, Joseph H. 1951. *Southern Parish: Dynamics of a City Church.* Chicago: University of Chicago.

———. 1980. *Religion and Pain.* New York: Crossroads.

———. 1982. *The Rehabilitation of Clergy Alcoholics.* New York: Human Sciences.

———. 1984. "The Myth of Clergy Burnout." *Sociological Analysis* 45:373–82.

Finsterbusch, Kurt. 1981. "The Use of Mini Surveys for Social Impact Assessment." In Kurt Finsterbusch and Charles Wolf, *The Methodology of Social Impact Assessment,* 2nd ed., pp. 261–66. New York: Hutchinson, Ross.

Forester, J. 1982. "Planning in the Face of Power." *APA Journal,* Winter:68–80.

Fornaciari, Gilbert M., and Mary Coeli Meyer. 1982. "Generating Consulting Contracts in the Socio-Technical Field." Paper presented at the 1982 Illinois Sociological Association Annual Meeting, Bloomington, Illinois.

Fowler, Elizabeth M. 1985. "For Engineers: The M.B.A. vs. the M.S." *New York Times*, Sec. 12, March 24, p. 63.

Freeman, H. E., R. R. Dynes, P. H. Rossi, and W. F. Whyte, eds. 1983. *Applied Sociology*. San Francisco: Jossey-Bass.

Freeman, Howard E., and Peter H. Rossi. 1984. "Furthering the Applied Side of Sociology." *American Sociological Review* 49 (August): 571–80.

Freidson, Eliot. 1970. *Profession of Medicine: A Study of the Sociology of Applied Knowledge*. New York: Dodd, Mead.

Gale, Richard P. 1984. "The Evolution of Social Impact Assessment: Post-Functionalist View." *Impact Assessment Bulletin*, Special Issue: Teaching and Learning Impact Assessment, edited by Sally Lerner, 3 (2): 27–36.

Gallessich, J. 1982. *The Profession and Practice of Consultation*. San Francisco: Jossey-Bass.

Garden, Nancy. 1982. *Annie on My Mind*. New York: Farrar, Straus & Giroux.

Gardner, Burleigh B. 1965. "The Consultant to Business—His Role and His Problems." In *Applied Sociology*, edited by Alvin W. Gouldner and S. M. Miller, pp. 79–85. New York: The Free Press.

Gardner, J. W. 1981. *Self-Renewal: The Individual and the Innovative Society*. New York: Norton.

Gechwender, J. A. 1968. "Civil Rights Protest and Riots: A Disappearing Distinction." *Social Science Quarterly* 49:474–84.

Gelfand, Donald E. 1975. "The Challenge of Applied Sociology." *The American Sociologist* 10 (February): 13–18.

———. 1976. "Sociological Education and Sociological Practice." *Teaching Sociology* 3:148–59.

Gibb, Jack. 1978. "Current Theory and Practice in Organization Development." Speech given at OD Network Annual Conference, March 16–17, 1978, San Francisco, California.

Giles-Sims, Jean, and Barry Tuchfeld. 1983. "Role of Theory in Applied Sociology." In *Applied Sociology*, edited by Howard E. Freeman, Russell R. Dynes, Peter H. Rossi, and William Foote Whyte, pp. 32–50. San Francisco: Jossey-Bass.

Glazer, Nathan. 1978. "Graduate Training Needs Professional Perspective." *Footnotes* 6 (October): 1 and 12.

Glock, Charles Y., Benjamin B. Ringer, and Earl R. Babbie. 1967. *To Comfort and to Challenge*. Berkeley: University of California Press.

Goldberg, R. S., and R. Schoenberg. 1981. "Defining Gay Social Work: Beginning with Beginnings." *Catalyst* 3 (4): 77–81.

Gouldner, Alvin W., and S. M. Miller, eds. 1965. *Applied Sociology*. New York: The Free Press.

Green, Howard Whipple. 1954. "Serving the Urban Community." In *Methodism Looks at the City*, edited by Robert A. McKibben, pp. 43–50. New York: Division of Missions, Board of Missions—The Methodist Church.

Green, Kenneth C. 1984. "Talent Migration and Major Field Preference Among Entering College Freshmen." Paper presented at the Council of Graduate Schools Conference in Washington, D.C.

Greenwald, Howard P. 1978. "Politics and the New Insecurity: Ideological

Changes of Professionals in a Recession." *Social Forces*, September:103–18.

Greenwood, Ernest. 1972. "Attributes of a Profession." In *Sociological Perspectives on Occupations*, edited by Ronald M. Pavalko, pp. 3–16. Itasca, Ill.: F. E. Peacock.

Grusky, O. 1983. "Graduate and Postdoctoral Education." In *Applied Sociology*, edited by H. E. Freeman, R. R. Dynes, P. H. Rossi, and W. F. Whyte, pp. 348–76. San Francisco: Jossey-Bass.

Guba, Egon G., and Yvonne S. Lincoln. 1981. *Effective Evaluation: Improving Responsive and Naturalistic Approaches*. San Francisco: Jossey-Bass.

Guterbock, Thomas. 1980. "Sociology and the Land-Use Problem." *Urban Affairs Quarterly* 5 (March): 243–67.

Guttentag, Marcia, ed. 1977. *Evaluation Studies: Review Annual*. Beverly Hills, Calif.: Sage.

Gutteridge, Thomas G. 1978. "Labor Market Adaptation of Displaced Technical Professionals." *Industrial and Labor Relations Review*, July:460–73.

Hadden, Jeffrey K. 1969. *The Gathering Storm in the Churches*. Garden City, N.Y.: Doubleday.

———. 1974. "A Brief Social History of the Religious Research Association." *Review of Religious Research* 15:128–36.

———. 1980. "H. Paul Douglass: His Perspective and His Work." *Review of Religious Research* 22:66–88.

Hakel, Milton D., Melvin Sorcher, Michael Beer, and Joseph L. Moses. 1982. *Making It Happen: Designing Research With Implementation In Mind*. Beverly Hills, Calif.: Sage.

Heberlein, Thomas. 1976. "Some Observations on Alternative Mechanisms for Public Involvement: The Hearing, Public Opinion Poll, The Workshop and the Quasi-Experiment." *Natural Resources Journal* 16 (January): 197–212.

Heller, Scott. 1984. "Bad Market for Sociologists Prompts Efforts to Train Them for Posts Outside Academe." *The Chronicle of Higher Education*, May 23:21–23.

Heumann, L. F. 1983. "The Grassroots Response to Government Housing Intervention." In *Handbook of Social Intervention*, edited by Edward Seidman. Beverly Hills, Calif.: Sage.

Higgins, P. C. 1980. *Outsiders in a Hearing World*. Beverly Hills, Calif.: Sage.

Hoge, Dean R., and David A. Roozen, eds. 1979. *Understanding Church Growth and Decline*. New York: Pilgrim.

Holland, John L. 1973. *Making Vocational Choices: A Theory of Careers*. Englewood Cliffs, N.J.: Prentice-Hall.

Holtz, Herman. 1983. *How to Succeed as an Independent Consultant*. New York: John Wiley.

Howrey, Carla B. 1983. *Teaching Applied Sociology: A Resource Book*. Washington, D.C.: American Sociological Association.

Huber, Bettina J. 1985. *Employment Patterns in Sociology: Recent Trends and Future Prospects*. Washington, D.C.: American Sociological Association.

Hunt, Jennifer. 1984. "The Development of Rapport Through Negotiation of

Gender in Field Work Among Police." *Human Organization* 43 (Winter): 283–96.

Hutslar, John L. 1975. "Social Factors Influencing Superior Male Bowling." Ph.D. dissertation, The Ohio State University.

———. 1984. "Using Organizational Development Techniques to Improve Teaching." In *Ideas II*, edited by Ronald P. Carlson, pp. 30–34. Reston Va.: NASPE.

———. 1985. *Beyond X's and O's: What Generic Parents, Volunteer Coaches and Teachers Can Learn About Generic Kids and All of the Sports They Play.* Welcome N.C.: Wooten Printing Company.

Institute of Medicine. 1985. *Personnel Needs and Training for Biomedical and Behavioral Research.* Washington, D.C.: National Academy Press.

Janowitz, Morris. 1971. *Sociological Models and Social Policy.* New York: General Learning Systems.

———. 1978. *The Last Half Century.* Chicago: University of Chicago Press.

Johnson, Paul L. 1983. "Human Services Planning." In *Applied Sociology*, edited by Howard E. Freeman, Russell R. Dynes, Peter H. Rossi, William Foote Whyte, pp. 106–17. San Francisco: Jossey-Bass.

Jones, Earl. 1976. *An Instrumentation Study of the Purdue Social Attitude Scales for Primary Children (English and Spanish Versions).* San Antonio, Tex.: Development Associates.

———. 1982. "Process Evaluation: Documenting Project Management." In *Guide to Bilingual Program Evaluation*. Washington, D.C.: Evaluation, Dissemination and Assessment Center - Dallas. pp. 123–50.

Jones, Earl, Sarah Berkowitz, and Robert Roussel. 1981. *Evaluation of Title II Food for Peace in Ghana.* San Francisco: Development Associates.

Jones, Earl et al. 1980. *Evaluation of California's Educational Services to Limited and Non-English Speaking Students* San Francisco: Development Associates.

———. 1984. *Baseline Survey of the Honduran Small Farmer Titling Project: Descriptive Analysis of the 1983 Sample.* San Francisco: Development Associates.

Keller, A. G. ed. 1913. *Earth-Hunger and Other Essays.* New Haven, Conn.: Yale University Press.

Kelley, Dean M. 1972. *Why Conservative Churches are Growing.* New York: Harper and Row.

Kelley, Robert E. 1981. *Consulting: The Complete Guide to a Profitable Career.* New York: Scribner.

Kidder, Louise H. 1981. *Research Methods in Social Relations*, 4th ed. New York: Holt, Rinehart and Winston.

Kincheloe, Samuel C. 1929. "The Behavioral Sequence of a Dying Church." *Religious Education* 24:329–45.

Kinloch, Graham C. 1982. "Undergraduate Sociology Majors and the Job Market: A Case Study." *The Southern Sociologist* 14 (Winter): 20–21.

Knepler, Henry. 1977. "The New Engineers." *Change*, June: 30–35.

Kolack, Shirley, and McDougall, John. 1982. "Teaching with Engineers and Scientists: What Role for Sociology?" *Humanity and Society* May:162–75.

Komarovsky, M., ed. 1975. *Sociology and Public Policy: The Case of the Presidential Commissions.* New York: Elsevier.

Kopelman, Richard E. 1977. "Psychological Stages of Careers in Engineering." *Journal of Vocational Behavior*, June:270–86.

Kramer, Marlene. 1974. *Reality Shock: Why Nurses Leave Nursing*. St. Louis: C. V. Mosby.

Lageman, August G. 1984. "Marketing Pastoral Counseling." *Journal of Pastoral Care* 38:274–80.

Landis, P. H. 1949. *Man in Environment: An Introduction to Sociology*. New York: Crowell.

Lant, Jeffrey L. 1981. *The Consultant's Kit*. Cambridge, Mass.: JLA.

Lazarsfeld, P. F., and J. G. Reitz. 1975. *An Introduction to Applied Sociology*. New York: Elsevier.

Lazarsfeld, P. F., W. Sewell, and H. L. Wilensky, eds. 1967. *The Uses of Sociology*. New York: Basic Books.

Lees-Haley, Paul R., and Cheryl E. Lees-Haley. 1985. "Attitude and Opinion Surveys." *In Human Resources Management and Development Handbook*, edited by William R. Tracey, pp. 715–27. New York, Amacom.

Lewin, Kurt. 1947. "Feedback Problems of Social Diagnosis and Action." In *Frontiers in Group Dynamics*, edited by Kurt Lewin, pp. 441–44. London: Tavistock Publications.

———. 1948. *Resolving Social Conflicts*. New York: Harper.

Lippit, Gordon L. 1982. *Organization Renewal: A Holistic Approach to Organization Development*. Englewood Cliffs, N.J.: Prentice-Hall.

Lippit, Gordon L., and Ronald Lippitt. 1978. *The Consulting Process In Action*. LaJolla, Calif.: University Associates.

Litwak, E. 1970. "An Approach to Linkage in 'Grass Roots' Community Organization." *In Strategies of Community Organizations—A Book of Readings*, edited by F. Cox et al. Itasca, Ill.: F. E. Peacock.

Longmire, Dennis R. 1983. "Ethical Dilemmas in the Research Setting." *Criminology* 21 (August): 333–48.

Lyson, Thomas A., and Gregory D. Squires. 1982a. "The Promise and Perils of Applied Sociology: A Survey of Non-Academic Employers." Clemson, S.C.: Department of Agricultural Economics and Rural Sociology, Clemson University. Mimeographed.

———. 1982b. "Sociologists in Non-Academic Settings: A Survey of Employers." *Society for the Study of Social Problems Newsletter*, Spring:16–18.

Marsh, Lawrence C., Kenneth P. Jameson, and Joseph M. Phillips. 1983. "Production Conditions in Guatemala's Key Agricultural Product: Corn." *Land Economics* 59 (1): 93–106.

Melton, Willie. 1982. "Equality and Freedom: Exploring Social Values and Social Issues Among Engineering Students." *Michigan Academician*, Winter:273–83.

Mink, Oscar G., James M. Schultz, Barbara P. Mink. 1979. *Developing and Managing Open Organizations*. Austin, Tex.: Learning Concepts.

Molotch, Harvey. 1976. "The City as Growth Machine: Towards a Political Economy of Place." *American Journal of Sociology* 82 (2): 309–22.

Moore, B. 1972. *The Causes of Human Misery*. Boston: Beacon Press.

Morison, Elting. 1980. "The Uncertain Relation." *Daedalus*, Winter:179–84.

McKenzie, Bill. 1983. Presentation at Recreation-Management '83. April 17, 1983, Philadelphia, Pennsylvania.

Morris, William, ed. 1976. *The American Heritage Dictionary of the English Language.* Boston: Houghton Mifflin.

Morrissey, Joseph P., and Henry J. Steadman. 1977. "Practice and Perish?: Some Overlooked Career Contingencies for Sociologists in Nonacademic Settings." *The American Sociologist* 12 (November): 154–62.

Mott, B. J. F. 1970. "Coordination and Inter-Organizational Relations in Health." In *Inter-Organizational Research in Health: Conference Proceedings*, edited by P. E. White and G. J. Vlasak, pp. 55–69. Washington, D.C.: National Center for Health Services Research and Development.

Mukerjee, R. 1930. "The Regional Balance of Man." *American Journal of Sociology* 36:455–60.

———. 1932. "The Ecological Outlook in Sociology." *American Journal of Sociology* 38:349–55.

Munoz, Adolfo H., Earl Jones, and Barry Wardlaw. 1978. *Self Evaluation Guide for Health Projects.* San Francisco: Development Associates and Region IX Office of Public Health.

Nadler, David A. 1977. *Feedback and Organization Development: Using Data-Based Methods.* Reading, Mass.: Addison-Wesley.

Naisbitt, John. 1982. *Megatrends: Ten New Directions Transforming Our Lives.* New York: Warner Books.

Nash, J. E., and A. Nash. 1981. *Deafness in Society.* Lexington, Mass.: Lexington Books.

National Institute of Justice. 1980. *How Well Does It Work?: Review of Criminal Justice Evaluation, 1978.* Washington, D.C.: U.S. Government Printing Office.

National Institute of Mental Health. 1977. *Needs Assessment Approaches: Concepts and Methods.* Washington, D.C.: U.S. Department of Health, Education and Welfare (Public Health Services—Alcohol, Drug Abuse, and Mental Health Administration).

National Science Foundation. 1984. *Characteristics of Recent Science/ Engineering Graduates: 1982.* Washington, D.C.: U.S. Government Printing Office.

Olsen, Marvin E. 1981. "Epilogue: The Future of Applied Sociology." In *Handbook of Applied Sociology*, edited by Marvin E. Olsen and Michael Micklin, pp. 561–81. New York: Praeger.

Olsen, Marvin E., Penelope Canan, and Michael Hennessy. 1985. "A Value Based Community Assessment Process: Integrating Quality of Life and Social Impact Studies." *Sociological Methods & Research* 13 (February): 325–61.

Olsen, Marvin E., and Michael Micklin, eds. 1981. *Handbook of Applied Sociology.* New York: Praeger.

O'Neill, Patrick I. 1982. *Community Consultation.* San Francisco: Jossey-Bass.

O'Riordan, T. 1976. "Policy Making and Environmental Management: Some Thoughts on Processes and Research Issues." In *Natural Resources for a Democratic Society: Public Participation in Decision-Making*, edited by A. E. Utton, W. R. D. Sewell, and T. O'Riordon, pp. 55–72. Boulder, Colo.: Westview Press.

O'Toole, Richard. 1982. "Sociology: A Consulting Profession." *The Applied Sociologist Bulletin* 3 (Summer): 3–6.

O'Toole, Anita W., and O'Toole, Richard. 1983. "Negotiating Cooperative Agreements Between Health Organizations." *Journal of Nursing Administration*, December:33–38.

O'Toole, Richard, and Anita Werner O'Toole. 1981. "Negotiating Interorganizational Orders." *The Sociological Quarterly* 22 (Winter): 29–42.

Parsons, R. D., and J. Meyers. 1984. *Developing Consulting Skills*. San Francisco: Jossey-Bass.

Passmore, William S. 1982. "Socio-Technical System Interventions." *In Organization Development: Managing Transitions*, edited by Ernest J. Parlock, pp. 73–80. Alexandria, Va.: American Society of Training and Development.

Pavalko, Ronald M., ed. 1972. *Sociological Perspectives on Occupations*. Itasca, Ill.: F. E. Peacock.

Perrucci, Robert, and Marc Pilisuk. 1970. "Leaders and Ruling Elites: The Interorganizational Relations Among Public Agencies." *American Sociological Review* 35 (December): 1040–57.

Peters, Thomas J., and Robert H. Waterman, Jr. 1982. *In Search of Excellence*. New York: Harper and Row.

Pettigrew, Andrew M. 1982. "Towards a Political Theory of Organizational Intervention." *In Making It Happen*, edited by Milton D. Hakel, Melvin Sorcher, Michael Beer, and Joseph L. Moses, pp. 41–60. Beverly Hills, Calif.: Sage.

Piven, F. F., and R. A. Cloward. 1979. *Poor People's Movements: Why They Succeed: How They Fail*. New York: Vintage.

Reed, Myer S., Jr. 1981. "An Alliance for Progress." *Sociological Analysis* 42:27–46.

———. 1982. "After the Alliance." *Sociological Analysis* 43:189–204.

Reilly, W. J. 1931. *The Law of Retail Gravitation*. New York: Knickerbocker Press.

Riesman, David. 1950. *The Lonely Crowd: A Study of Changing American Character*. New Haven, Conn.: Yale University Press.

Rock, Vincent P. 1965. "The Policy-Maker and the Social Sciences." In *Applied Sociology*, edited by Alvin W. Gouldner and S. M. Miller, pp. 358–66. New York: The Free Press.

Rodman, Hyman, and Ralph L. Kolodny. 1965. "Organizational Strains in the Researcher-Practitioner Relationship." In *Applied Sociology*, edited by Alvin W. Gouldner and S. M. Miller, pp. 93–113. New York: The Free Press.

Rogers, Everet E. 1962. *Diffusion of Innovations*. New York: The Free Press.

Rogers, Everet E., and Floyd Schumaker. 1971. *Communication of Innovations: A Cross Cultural Approach*. New York: The Free Press.

Roof, Wade Clark. 1976. "Traditional Religion in Contemporary Society." *American Sociological Review* 41:195–208.

Ross, Edward A. 1936. *Seventy Years of It*. New York: Appleton-Century.

Rothauge, Arlin J. 1983. *Sizing Up a Congregation for New Member Ministry*. New York: Education for Mission and Ministry Office, Episcopal Church Center.

Ruckelshaus, William D. 1985. "Risk, Science, and Democracy." *Issues in Science and Technology*, Spring:19–38.

Rumley, Jacqueline, and Gordon Lippitt. 1982. *Organization Renewal* (workbook). Washington, D.C.: Organization Renewal, Inc.

Russell, T. 1981. "Undergraduate Education in Applied Sociology and Anthropology: Some Issues in Programming." Presented at the North Central Sociological Association Meeting, Cleveland.

Satariano, W. A., and S. J. Rogers. 1979. "Undergraduate Internships: Problems and Prospects." *Teaching Sociology* 6:355–72.

Schein, Edgar H. 1969. *Process Consultation: Its Role in Organization Development.* Reading, Mass.: Addison-Wesley.

Schein, J. D. 1968. *The Deaf Community: Studies in the Social Psychology of Deafness.* Washington, D.C.: Gallaudet College Press.

Schnaiberg, A. 1972. "Environmental Sociology and the Division of Labor." Unpublished manuscript, Department of Sociology, Northwestern University, Evanston, Illinois.

Serrin, William. 1985. "Engineering: Outlook is Rewarding in Most Specialities." New York *Times*, Sec. 12, March 24, pp. 21, 24.

Silva, E. T., and S. A. Slaughter. 1984. *Serving Power: The Making of the Academic Social Science Expert.* Westport, Conn.: Greenwood Press.

Silverstein, Charles. 1977. *A Family Matter.* New York: McGraw-Hill.

Smith, Nick L. 1982. *Communication Strategies in Evaluation.* Beverly Hills, Calif.: Sage.

Sorokin, P. A. 1942. *Man and Society in Calamity.* New York: Dutton.

Steadham, Stephen V. and Maria A. E. Clay. 1985. "Needs Assessment." In *Human Resources Management and Development Handbook*, edited by William R. Tracey, pp. 1338–52. New York: Amacom.

Strauss, Anselm. 1978. *Negotiations: Varieties, Contexts, Processes, and Social Order.* San Francisco: Jossey-Bass.

Street, David P., and Eugene A. Weinstein. 1975. "Problems and Prospects of Applied Sociology." *The American Sociologist* 10 (May): 66.

Struening, Elmer L., and Marcia Guttentag, eds. 1975. *Handbook of Evaluation Research.* Beverly Hills, Calif.: Sage.

Successful Farming. 1982. "Hired 'Gun' Pulls the Sell Triggers." November:21.

Survey of Buying Power. 1985. New York: Sales and Marketing Management.

Swatos, William H., Jr. 1980. "Liturgy and Lebensform: The Personal God as a Social Being." *Perspectives in Religious Studies* 8:38–49.

———. 1981. "Beyond Denominationalism?: Community and Culture in American Religion." *Journal for the Scientific Study of Religion* 20:217–27.

———. 1982. "The Power of Prayer." *Review of Religious Research* 24:153–63.

———. 1984. *Faith of the Fathers.* Bristol, Ind.: Wyndham-Hall.

Swift, D. F. 1965. "Educational Psychology, Sociology and the Environment: A Controversy at Cross Purposes." *British Journal of Sociology* 16:334–50.

Takooshian, Harold. 1983. "Entering Nonacademic Social Psychology." *SASP Newsletter* 9 (February): 6–9.

Teevan, R. C. et al. 1983. "Conflicts and Defenses in Engineering and Psychology Undergraduates." *Psychological Reports*, 53:554.

Terry, Geraldine B. 1983. "Developing a Program of Study for Sociology Majors

Who Anticipate Government Careers." *The Southern Sociologist* 14 (Winter): 20–21.

Thorne, Charles. 1974. Reaction to Hadden (1974). *Review of Religious Research* 15:155–56.

Thursz, D. 1969. *Consumer Involvement in Rehabilitation*. Washington, D.C.: HEW Social and Rehabilitation.

Townsend, Robert. 1970. *Up the Organization*. New York: Alfred A. Knopf.

Trela, James E., and Richard O'Toole. 1974. *Roles for Sociologists in Service Organizations*. Kent, Ohio: Kent State University Press.

Twain, David. 1975. "Developing and Implementing a Research Strategy." In *Handbook of Evaluation Research*, edited by Elmer L. Struening and Marcia Guttentag, pp. 27–52. Beverly Hills, Calif.: Sage.

United States Department of Education (formerly Office of Education), National Center for Educational Statistics. 1948–82. *Degrees and Other Formal Awards Conferred (HEGIS)*. A computational data file. Washington, D.C.

University of Hawaii, Department of Geography. 1973. *Atlas of Hawaii*. Honolulu: University of Hawaii Press.

U.S. Census of Retail Trade Market Guide. 1982. Washington, D.C.: U.S. Department of Commerce, Bureau of Census.

Van Horne, W. 1976. "The Sociologist as Organizational Newcomer: Problems of Role Emergence." *Sociological Practice* 1:10–26.

Van Wagner, Charles A. 1983. "The AAPC: The Beginning Years, 1963–1965." *Journal of Pastoral Care* 37:163–79.

Vaughn, Jack, Parke Massey, and Donovan Rudishule. 1983. *An Administrative Analysis of the National Agrarian Institute: Honduras*. Arlington, Va.: Development Associates.

Vernon, M. 1971. "Crises of the Deaf." *Journal of Rehabilitation of the Deaf* 5:31–33.

Vida, Ginny, ed. 1978. *Our Right to Love*. Englewood Cliffs, N.J.: Prentice-Hall.

Vlachos, Evan. 1981. "The Use of Scenarios for Social Impact Assessment." In Kurt Finsterbusch and Charles Wolf, *The Methodology of Social Impact Assessment*, 2nd ed. pp. 162–74. New York: Hutchinson, Ross.

Warren, D. I. 1975. *Black Neighborhoods: The Dynamics of Community Power*. Ann Arbor: University of Michigan Press.

Warren, R. B., and D. I. Warren. 1977. *The Neighborhood Organizer's Handbook*. Notre Dame, Ind.: University of Notre Dame Press.

Warrick, D. D. 1985. "Organization Development." In *Human Resources Management and Development Handbook*, edited by William R. Tracey, pp. 915–925. New York: Amacom.

Watkins, Beverly T. 1981. "The Sociology of Sociology: Fewer Positions on College Faculties, Falling Enrollments, and Budget Cuts." *The Chronicle of Higher Education*, September 9:6.

Webb, E. J., D. T. Campbell, R. D. Schwartz, and L. Sechrest. 1966. *Unobtrusive Measures: Nonreactive Research in the Social Sciences*. Chicago: Rand McNally.

Weber, Max. 1958. "Science as a Vocation." In *Essays from Max Weber*, edited by Hans Gerth and C. Wright Mills, pp. 129–156. New York: Oxford University Press.

Wendell, Walter I. 1972. "A Marginal Professional Role: The Chiropractor." In *Sociological Perspectives on Occupations*, edited by Ronald M. Pavalko, pp. 40–55. Itasca, Ill.: F. E. Peacock.

Wyckoff, H. 1980. *Solving Problems Together*. New York: Grove Press.

Young, Malcolm, Tania Romashko, and Earl Jones. 1982. *Evaluating Cooperative Development Projects: A System for Planners, Project Staff, and Evaluators*. Arlington, Va.: Development Associates.

Zager, Robert, and Michael Rosow, eds. 1982. *The Innovative Organization*. New York: Pergamon.

Zetterberg, Hans L. 1962. *Social Theory and Social Practice*. New York: Bedminister Press.

Subject Index

Name Index

About the Editors and Contributors

JOYCE MILLER IUTCOVICH is an Associate Professor of Sociology at Villa Maria College and President of Keystone University Research Corporation, both in Erie, Pennsylvania. She received a B.A. in Sociology from Edinboro State College (1971), an M.A. and Ph.D. in Sociology from Kent State University (1973 and 1982, respectively). Her major area of interest is applied sociology, specifically evaluation research. She has done consulting work on the national, state, and local levels on projects concerning the desegregation of schools, alcohol abuse, vocational education, and aging. As well, in applying her research skills, she works in the area of political polling and marketing research. She is currently a member of the Board of Directors of the Society for Applied Sociology and the Co-editor of the *Journal of Applied Sociology*. She has several publications in books and professional journals concerning the application of sociological knowledge in a variety of topic areas.

MARK IUTCOVICH is full Professor of Sociology at Edinboro University of Pennsylvania. He is Director of Research for Keystone University Research Corporation and Northwest Institute of Research, Erie, Pennsylvania. He received a Licentiate degree in sociology from University of Bucharest (1951), an M.A. in Anthropology from University of Manitoba (1962), and a Ph.D. in Sociology from Case Western Reserve University (1970). He was awarded the Certificate for Exceptional Academic Service by the Department of Education, Commonwealth of Pennsylvania (1977) and received Citation for Distinguished Teaching and Academic Service, House of Representatives, Commonwealth of Pennsylvania (1977). He is president of the Society for Applied Sociology. He has published many articles in such journals as *Sociological Focus*, *The American Sociologist*, and *Evaluation and Program Planning*. His consulting and applied work has been in such areas as criminology, medical sociology and psychiatry, alcoholism, marketing, evaluation research, education, and political research.

RAYMOND J. ADAMEK is Professor of Sociology at Kent State University, Kent, Ohio.

ALEXANDER BOROS is Professor of Sociology at Kent State University, Kent, Ohio.

PENELOPE CANAN is an Assistant Professor of Sociology at the University of Denver, where she is Director of the Center for Community Change Studies.

BETTY JUNE CHAKIRIS is President of BJ Chakiris Corporation, Chicago.

GILBERT M. FORNACIARI is President of Fornaciari Consulting, Chicago.

HOWARD H. GARRISON is a Senior Staff Associate at Applied Management Sciences in Silver Spring, Maryland.

JACK HUTSLAR, Ph.D., is a sport management consultant, the founder and director of the North American Youth Sport Institute, as well as the editor and publisher of *Sport Scene*, Kernersville, North Carolina.

BERNIE JONES is Associate Professor of Planning and Community Development, as well as Associate Director for Research for the Center for Community Development and Design, at the University of Colorado at Denver.

DONALD E. JONES is the Law Enforcement Specialist for the Governor's Crime Commission, North Carolina Department of Crime Control and Public Safety.

EARL JONES is Senior Associate with Development Associates, Inc., in its San Francisco office and Professor of Sociology and Education at Pacific Oaks College.

BRUCE KOPPEL is a Research Associate at the East-West Center Resource Systems Institute, Honolulu.

JEFFREY K. LANGE is a market research analyst for The Cleveland Electric Illuminating Company.

MARY EVANS MELICK is a Principal Research Scientist with the New York State Office of Mental Health, Albany.

JOSEPH W. MERCURIO is Manager of Real Estate Research in Walgreen Co.'s Planning and Research Department, Deerfield, Illinois.

ANITA W. O'TOOLE is a Professor of Nursing and Director of the Graduate Program in Psychiatric Mental Health Nursing at Kent State University, Kent, Ohio.

RICHARD O'TOOLE is a Professor of Sociology at Kent State University, Kent, Ohio.

KEITH L. SMITH is currently Senior Associate and Chief Engineer with Science, Engineering and Analysis, Incorporated, in Arlington, Virginia.

WILLIAM H. SWATOS, JR., is Vicar of St. Mark's Episcopal Church, Silvis, Illinois, and Lecturer in the Department of Sociology of Northern Illinois University.

JEAN H. THORESEN is an Associate Professor of Sociology and Applied Social Relations at Eastern Connecticut State University, Willimantic.

J. PATRICK TURBETT is an Associate Professor and Chairman of the Department of Sociology at the College of Arts and Sciences, State University of New York at Potsdam.

JAY R. WILLIAMS is currently a consultant to the North Carolina Governor's Crime Commission and an Adjunct Lecturer at Duke University, Durham, North Carolina.